THE ONE, OTHER, AND ONLY DICKENS

THE ONE, OTHER, AND ONLY DICKENS

GARRETT STEWART

CORNELL UNIVERSITY PRESS
Ithaca and London

First published 2018 by Cornell University Press

Printed in the United States of America

Library of Congress Cataloging-in-Publication Data

Names: Stewart, Garrett, author.
Title: The one, other, and only Dickens / Garrett Stewart.
Description: Ithaca : Cornell University Press, 2018. | Includes bibliographical references and index.
Identifiers: LCCN 2018023449 (print) | LCCN 2018025995 (ebook) |
    ISBN 9781501730115 (pdf) | ISBN 9781501730122 (ret) |
    ISBN 9781501730108 | ISBN 9781501730108 (cloth ; alk. paper) |
    ISBN 9781501730139 (pbk. ; alk. paper)
Subjects: LCSH: Dickens, Charles, 1812–1870—Literary style. | Dickens, Charles,
    1812–1870—Criticism and interpretation.
Classification: LCC PR4594 (ebook) | LCC PR4594 .S84 2018 (print) |
    DDC 823/.8—dc23
LC record available at https://lccn.loc.gov/2018023449

For Ian and Renata—
who first took their books by ear

CONTENTS

FOREWORD: PREPARING THE WAY

You are reading along, hooked, until snagged by some aggressively arresting phrase. You hold your breath over twisted mysteries and psychologies until that breath is taken away by a sideswipe of language far outstripping the needs of narrative. You get in the swing between cliff-hangers until the whole lifeline of plot momentarily unravels in a daft excess of craft. You are left hanging on word forms alone. You are, after all, reading not just any Victorian fiction, but a novel by one Charles Dickens. Or, more exactly, reading the Prose of one such fiction, which can be Another Thing Altogether.

Words make their own ebullient way in Dickens, rather than just giving way to story. But they've paid their dues to begin with. This foreword charts the path ahead, of course, but only because it traces Dickens's way forward as well—on his own industrious behalf. The double training ground of his linguistic intensity involves back-to-back chapters in a well-documented biographical epic that have never been brought together for the extra origin story they tacitly narrate about the gestation of an incomparable prose. Indeed, like many a later Dickens novel, the formative tension of such an inaugural subplot involves one bad parent, one good—an unyielding shorthand taskmaster, on the one hand, and a looming literary inspiration, on the other: namely, the rigors of vowel-scoured stenographic reporting in the Thomas Gurney method versus the contrary aural invigorations of William Shakespeare, devoured by the young Dickens from page as well as stage. As with the vulnerable characters of many a Dickens novel, from such fostering tension something of a dual personality results—but in this case textual rather than psychological: what I am dubbing the One and his Other as internal rather than fraternal twins, secret sharers, inbred shadow collaborators in the rotary vocalic motion of Dickensian narrative prose. This will emerge, as it did for Dickens, in good time—and under, I trust, demonstrable pressure from these two divergent sources. This foreword is only a brief effort to look ahead from early shaping influences, and from the inevitable vantage point of retrospect, at the first stirrings of a world-historical career in letters. Letters and their sounds.

Charles John Huffam Dickens, early pen name Boz—in being published unbridled from 1836 till his death in 1870, and of course beyond—brought to the prose of prose fiction the contours it had been waiting for, listening for, ever since the genre's inception in the preceding century. With Shakespeare and the Romantic poets behind him, Dickens delivered—by delving into unstintingly—what was for literary fiction a new and self-propelling harmonics of the syllable within the rolling, and often roller-coaster, grammar of his unprecedented sentences. Somehow, continuously, a mass audience attuned itself to the seemingly effortless exertions of his phonetic as well as semantic wordplay, to the whole tireless ferocity of his verbal invention. Whatever labor there was could not have been entirely on his side. Coming to all this, as a modern reader, with an ear to its often raucous complexity in the variable strata and staminas of attention it elicits, and with turns of prose so often "other" than one has any way to foresee, can only make clearer the lineaments of such prose's rhetorical demands, not so much on comprehension as on linguistic attention itself.

Dickens's way with words, his sway over them: way overwrought, or say, fiercely worked over—if rarely what we would call overwritten. As a phenomenon of verbal energy rather than a style, there has never been anything quite like it—including itself from moment to moment, whose own immediate patternings it can veer from deliriously. Despite its characteristically flamboyant and familiar moves, the most telling maneuvers of Dickensian prose are perpetually restless—and hard to remember precisely, even from passages otherwise filed lovingly in mind. This book will remember some of them for you by direct quotation. Its premise concerns the delights of such Dickensian writing at their least predicable; its gist: that one can *give in* to them without giving up on accounting for them, though never thinking to tabulate their profusion, let alone explain it away. And *in* is where you do get as a result: deep into the very possibilities of English wording beneath the irrepressible byplay of one Victorian author's fictional words. This is what I will be referring to as an immersive reading. And by "one," of course, I mean the One and Only.

But where to begin, if only again—over and over again, in ever-renewed awe at such linguistic ingenuity? How is it that one always seems to keep coming with fresh attention to Dickens's prose? Why, in other words, in a book like this, does it make perfect sense for an "Introduction" to come second, with no prefatory matter likely to steal its thunder or exhaust its avenues of approach? How, in short, can Dickens's prose harbor such residual surprise across a multitude of readings—so that each time we pick up one of the novels, we feel initiated yet again into the word-by-word wonder of Dickensian phrasal intensity? In this light, is there perhaps a conceptual space to be imagined, in his own pages, between just those modifiers: Dickens's and Dickensian? My best answer lies in the deliberately offered paradox of the book's shuffled title, where Boz, the fabled One and Only, is at one with its own Other in the always startling departures from expectation. The Victorian Inimitable, master of plot and social panorama—and, of course, rhetoric too—brings his linguistic alter ego in continuous tow. Between them, the One and the Other, distinction isn't an issue in the attentions ahead—but, rather, synergy. Simply put, my topic is the stylistic Other within. So intimate is the latter with the comings and goings of Dickens's narrative through-lines, their multiplex doings and the frequent rhetorical perorations that punctuate them, that what comes forth—as *inherently* Other (let the paradox stand)—is the very agency and spirit of their own *over*doing.

What I wish to stress again (as late Victorian critic G. K. Chesterton did in pinpointing this quality, and quantity, of inflation as the essence of Dickensian fiction) is the intrinsic and quite radical "exaggeration,"[1] not just of the storytelling, but of the Writing in particular—in every-thing from the flashiest strokes of caricature to the quickest flecks of lexi-cal double-take in the onward flow of prose. This is the othering thrust of phrases that appear rebellious toward any simple telling, yet that are braided in with narrative's every move: so inextricable in reception from those "signature" effects of Boz the popular novelist that traditional criti-cism seldom lends the insurgent energies of such prose even the least, and never more than passing, consideration. This book attempts a fuller hear-ing of phrases that are, indeed, ear-opening in their phonetic rigor and often revelatory wit.

Inimitable entirely, yes, is Boz the One and Only, the breakthrough Victorian bestseller—even while his influence changed the *sound* (in the broadest sense) of the English novel for at least half a century. This is the sound that the Victorianist work of teaching and writing about his novels tends, alas, to play down, even tune out. One loses thereby an important aspect of precisely the author's historical impact. His wasn't just a no-holds-barred style, but a prose that kept holding itself to its own higher bar all the time—and dragging competitors with it, everyone from Wilkie Collins and William Makepeace Thackeray through George Eliot and George Gissing down through Joseph Conrad to the later modernist moment. Dickensian Writing: always a shameless intensity and distension of phrase, checked only by an uncanny grammatical tact. His storytelling powers were sustained upon just such phrasing, however little beyond implicit recognition is given to this aspect of his fiction in the received Dickens of more familiar scholarly discussion: narrative innovator, cari-caturist, social commentator, Victorian cultural weathervane, even "styl-ist" in the more canonical sense. The Other Dickens: phrasemaking in process—or, more to the point yet, wording in action. And when focusing in this sense on the unique "sound of" such prose, one must in fact listen as well as look. In an etymological nutshell of cross-purposed idiomatic metaphors, the idea of sound in Dickens is to be understood *literally*, a matter of lettering in process—spoken under one's breath into the ear of uptake.

The topic here is thus very different from the Other Dickens of John Bowen's important study from 2000: his title indicating the early, the less read and taught, the sometimes underestimated "minor" Dickens down through *Martin Chuzzlewit*—those books that made popular waves well before the later symbolic masterworks hit the literary scene (and cemented their place in the canon and the academy).[2] In contrast, the Other Dickens in these pages is everywhere in Dickens's own pages, from first to last. To use an apt nineteenth-century term (Wordsworth's, from the 1805 Prelude, line 71), this Otherness is an "under-presence" in any and every novel, though more richly entwined in the sentences of the later works, from *Dombey and Son* on. As distinct from the second-tier Dickens of Bowen's treatment, that no semester course tends to have space for, this stylistic Other Dickens is what few classes have time for even in featuring the "biggies"—with that honorific slang bespeaking, all by itself, the standards of textual scale by which tiny verbal turns can get relegated to oblivion.

This book is one attempt at a retrieval action. Though inextricably coordinated in the moment of reading, the two manifestations of Dickens I have in mind remain, therefore, rather sadly estranged in critical discussion. The distractions of the Other get instrumentally—if unconsciously—tabled in service to the One and Only as standard-bearer of genre and Victorian zeitgeist alike. When *David Copperfield* is assigned alongside *Jane Eyre* in a course on the bildungsroman, it is the mainstream thematic Dickens that is typically being studied. So with *Hard Times* read alongside *North and South* in a course on industrial fiction. Or *Bleak House* next to *New Grub Street* in a survey of class critique in Victorian narrative. Dramatic passages are frequently quoted, to be sure, and the general drift of their rhetoric perhaps noted—but mostly investigated in the name of structural irony, polemic, elegy, what have you. Teachers can all recognize the motive. Effects need to be made functional for ready discussion. I don't therefore wish to minimize how part of the impetus for this book came when teaching a course designed to attract not just literature majors in my home department but students in a new creative-writing track. With Dickensian sentences unfurled before us, the creativity of the Writing itself took center stage, rather than its merely serviceable rhetoric. Our focus was less on the Dickens of record in this regard—paragon of thematically motivated Style with a capital S—than on the often tricky cadence of the sentences themselves. It is at this level of response that the Other Dickens names the way prose *sounds* from passage to passage—including what it *plumbs* in the depth of verbal process across even the tiniest blindsiding moves of sheer phrasal virtuosity.

Come upon amid the most obvious charms and powers of the fiction, then, there is nothing outré in this Other. It is, instead, the very fiber of Dickensian storytelling and its author's Victorian fame. But its warp and woof get minimized in the ordinary cast of analysis. Setting and plot in the novels, to be sure, call up extraordinary reserves of descriptive vocabulary and syntax so as to place an action and activate a scene. Setting, plot—and of course character(s). No doubt about it, Dickens is incomparable at both broad strokes of characterization and the least quirks or neurotic festerings of psychology. But the strokes are verbal to begin with, manners and gestures caught in the matter of a turned phrase, one after and upon another, countless. That magnificent proliferation is both the topic and the challenge of this treatment. Even if the judgment call could be made from amid some impossibly thorough culling, there would be no attempt in these chapters to anthologize the "best of." Spread across the widest possible range of effect, my examples don't comprise anything like the "most memorable moments." Often quite the opposite. Even leaving aside the personal favorites it's still hard to get right in mental rerun, the general workings of the Other Dickens involve things that—in rereading—I realize I hadn't remembered at all. They illustrate in this way not "high points" but undertones: the consistent surprise of the Other Dickens in the very working (up) of the prose, for which a previous encounter (or two) with a given novel is no true preparation. Even the "crispest" litany of description can harbor a little startle in wrap-up. In *Bleak House*, for instance, after his wife has been said in passing, and in a rare intransitive form, to "rouge a little," Mr. Badger is discovered to be "himself a pink, fresh-faced, crisp-looking gentleman with a weak voice, white teeth, light hair, and *surprised eyes*." Rounding out a sixfold adjectival pileup is a kind of extra lexical pictogram: putting the widened "eyes" back in the bulging center of "surprised." Similar effects can sneak up on us at any turn. In this sense, I trust that nothing will smack here of selective delectation in the dated mode of a belletristic homage, which, even in its heyday, was never lip-smacking enough in the sounding out of Dickens's syllabic magic, to say nothing (as seldom it did) of his syntactic panache. And citation alone won't do. Quotation will be attended, at every (phrasal) turn, by actual reading: less a stylistic appreciation in passing than language's apprehension in action.

But that said, there remains something perhaps too sweeping and global, however deliberately ingrown, about *The One, Other, and Only Dickens* as a title, something that makes me uneasy enough to mention. I do so by way of a caveat meant to defuse, once and for all, any lingering aura of false advertisement. If this were in fact "greatest bits from greatest hits," what readers wouldn't be happy to have their instincts refreshed and confirmed? It isn't, though, and the problem isn't just one of space. Not only are the examples here selected to favor the quick and dirty brilliance of a single turn of phrase, rather than the more extended and often indelible, but space-devouring, passages of studied rhetorical elaboration (such passages, at quite a different scale from that Badger snapshot, as the foggy launch of *Bleak House* itself, the "best of times" and its antithesis at the start of *A Tale of Two Cities,* and the iterated and grammatically fragmentary—as if already shattered—"Reflects" of the Veneering mirror near the start of *Our Mutual Friend*). And not only is this principle of selection due partly to the fact that I find the most distinctive genius of Dickens, or at least the most incomparable, in such alternative minor turns. It's also because some of the illustrative choices, not only just short and sweet, are unavoidably rather private fascinations. This privacy is also the point. The Other Dickens is differently Other to Boz in the ear of any and every reader. It isn't simply that we each have our preferred touches. It's that our cognitive equipment, our linguistic register, differs from reader to reader. As with other thrills, each of us is poised to be differently smitten.

Almost arbitrarily chosen here at the start, from a welter of examples easily summoned, the following instance, also from the middle novel *Bleak House,* is the kind of Dickensian effect that strikes me time and again, "me personally," as playing between lexicon and grammatical momentum in the style of descriptive irony. Characterization, yes: one forefront of the Dickensian genius. But, above all, *word* portraits. Take, then, a double one: that of the Snagsby rather than the Badger couple in *Bleak House,* scoring its ironies, straight off, in a highly compressed linguistic form. The suspicious and needling wife of the effaced Mr. Snagsby was originally, we learn on introduction to her, his partner Peffer's "short, shrewd niece, something too violently compressed about the waist, and with a sharp nose like a sharp autumn evening, inclining to be frosty towards the end"[3]—and thereby, before the pun on "end," giving, after two thrusts of "sharp" across that incremental simile, a further turn to the implied but unsaid *shrew* of "shrewd." Note as well the dizzy switch from a day declining to a nose angled—or, more abstractly, "inclining"—as if personified in its willful descent. And if that's not enough symbolic physiognomy, there is a "rumor" in the neighborhood that, when being cinched too tight about the waist as a girl in order to perfect her figure, "she exhibited internally pints of vinegar and lemon-juice, which acids . . . had mounted to the nose and temper of the patient"—as if, given her general irritability and intemperate marital suspicions, she were the lifelong victim of an abused spleen.

And the portraiture here is indeed part of a satiric diptych, the beleaguered spouse getting equal time. Picking up next on that anatomical-versus-affective divide of "nose and temper," a second grammatical forking—staple of Dickensian phrasal instability—attends the move to her husband's description. For, after this disposition of her portrait, as the very portrait of her disposition, we now encounter a parallel syntactic split (this being, as it were, the couple's one compatibility) in the attributes of Mr. Snagsby. In precise contrast to his partner, he "tends to m*ee*kness and ob*esi*ty"—while tending, all the while, to the importunities of his wife. It is as if he is emptied of spirit from within his own bodily inflation. The long *e* sounds of "meekness and obesity," along with the mounting syllable count, only exaggerate a shift from mental to bodily constitution whose overt disjuncture—as in the previous reverse variant of "nose and temper"—is an alternate vector of the same comic paradigm. If a reader, so inclined, wants to add that the phrasal inspiration of "t*en*ding to m*ee*kn*ess* and ob*esity*" benefits from designation as a version of syllepsis cross-hatched with two modes of assonance, one chiastic (*en/ne* as well as *ee/ee*), plus a dollop of sibilant alliteration, then by all means let such technical terms come to the aid of notice and fascination. In the spirit of this book's venture in immersive reading, however, with a premium on first reactions rather than seasoned scrutiny, the populous family of such descriptors from technical stylistics won't regularly be solicited. Keeping response "fresher" is truer to the moment of midstream syntactic recognitions—and amazements. Such amazements are what this book means to log.

We'll meet many variants of the lexical and syllabic diversions just noted—including, as in the sketch of Snagby's better half, the likes of such a seemingly redundant but quietly studied repetition ("sharp") that actually shifts senses (from something like *pointed* to "frosty") in a single distended simile. We'll come again upon the frequent habit of a slightly stuffy subordinator like "*which* acids had mounted," operating here in rich assonant astringency to distill (rather than dispel) this gossip concerning the wife's splenetic nature—and then lathered up further with the next sentence's clarification: "*With whichsoever* of the many tongues of Rumour this frothy report originated, it either never reached or never influenced the ears of young Snagsby." Only the Other Dickens would think to make "either never" funny. More often yet, we'll follow the vault within a single phrasal pairing—or more like somersault—from physical to emotional register in the circuit of the same compound syntax ("nose and temper," or, in reverse, "meekness and obesity"). Then, too, in the description of Mrs. Snagsby, there's even a miniscule stunner in that sudden upsurge, comma-less, of the adverb "internally" from within a predicate whose verb it should rightly (and more rhythmically) have preceded—as if displaced by the pressure of its own regurgitation: "exhibited *internally* pints of vinegar and lemon-juice" In phrasal terms, one begins meditating on what's internal to what. In any case, with her sourness on "exhibit" in this strangely clinical phrasing, the manifested symptom needs no further diagnosis.

Permeating the entire double portrait of the Snagsbys as well, the very comedy of naming is at odds across the ill-matched pair, where a semantic othering of the surname seems rigged by sheer alphabetic contingency. Under nominal pressure from the Other Dickens, that is, and never quite spelled out, Mr. Snagsby embodies, straightforwardly enough, the tacit *snag* of any and all private freedom under the tyrant eye of his acerbic mate. In contrast, Mrs. Snagsby (first name never given) releases her essence a split second later in the married name's elided syllabic sequence—isolating by the sibilant hook of "Missus" the persistent and punning *nag* she is. From one novel to the next, examples of all such colloquial linguistic densities, cross-word puns sometimes included, are to be found again and again—when we are really listening. Let me put it this way for now: phrasing like this, at once taut and logically unspun, can sneak up on us from the Other side of narrative sense like prose taking dictation from its own phonetic unconscious. Or this way: let the snags be—and thus your guide in reading.

This, and more, is what comes to be involved in an immersive response to Dickensian prose, as opposed to merely "reading Dickens." Indeed, by an almost-forgotten personification, that very idiom usually identifies one level of widely imagined encounter with the novelist's pages. The Author is an extrapolation from his own words, in Dickens's case from the due renown of his intricate contrapuntal story-lines and the fluent verbiage that conducts and peoples them. This literary lion, Boz Himself, is easy to meet anywhere in his chapters. Initiation to the Other Dickens is a simultaneous rite of passage, of passages—one after the other in their turns of word. But this is only because reading Dickens is always like reading the very possibility in language that such invention could exist. And this is what the Other Dickens never lets us forget. Beneath the burnished and sculpted surfaces of descriptive periods or satiric perorations, behind even the outright and knockout jokes, there is a further (and fundamental) level of writing—Writing as such—never wholly subsumed to purpose. In moments of incorrigible showiness and concerted delicacy alike, the confident roll of Dickensian prose may in this way entertain a strange subterranean frolic or a clenched, disruptive intensity. This is where the Other Dickens comes in—as another kind of back-formation (though not a personification this time) from the flexed contours of sheer wording. The effects exceed anything ordinarily circumscribed as rhetoric. In both rhetorical understanding and common parlance, irony, for instance, is the saying of one thing while meaning another. In Dickensian style, irony—saturating the excess at every turn—is a saying of more things than meaning requires or can readily motivate. Writing lives a sly life of its own. This is the Other Dickens operating in the happy shadow of the namesake Master, and sometimes under the radar of any manageable narrative intent: a style keeping us nerved and alert across the sweep of event and theme.

It is this aspect of the Writing that seems tapping into some kind of pure verbal intuition in a thickened, unfiltered form—drafting it out: in the etymological sense, "drawing" it into the open, letting (and lettering) it through. Crowned in his day "the Immortal Dickens" (by fellow novelist George Gissing) as well as the Inimitable, the canonized Writer has, I'm suggesting, an equally indomitable twin in the Writing itself. The One and Only Dickens is a celebrated and driven novelist; the Other, an impersonal function of prose's own drive, incalculable in advance. If Style is the Man Himself (as French writer Buffon famously quipped in the century before Dickens)—and thus offers some fantasy of a stabilized creative subjectivity issued in words—the Other locates a Writing dehumanized by language's own prior claims. The Other Dickens stems from the place where wording takes the lead over meaning, the depth of verbal potential over specific intent.

So it is that Dickens the spellbinding narrative author gives way at times to an unbound spelling-out of word forms—forms, and deformations, from which the most elusive and curious patterns well up. Here is a Writing, rather than a Writer, whose syllables seem to have, if not a will of their own exactly, at least a playful willingness for mutation on the fly: a restless surging that can overflow word borders in crosscurrents of sometimes weird pertinence, sometimes sheer jubilance. At any moment, this might be ruinously distracting for storytelling; that it isn't can stand as a testament, of course, to Dickens the Master Stylist, with all his supervening orchestration of managed continuity. For it is he who secures the arcs of description and episode across those shifting granulations of phrase unleashed by an Other whose writing plies its indulgent trade (its, not his; again, no personification of design intended here) by multiplying its cellular sound bites beyond all economies of sense. Not between the lines of a novel by Charles Dickens, then, but often between its functional words, uprears this Other—surfacing a unique version of the aesthetic in a variant of Kant's defining formulation: a purposiveness without purpose, here at the level of wording's inner, rather than story's outer, form. This is the verbal drivenness underlying (without directly undergirding) the recognized track of story. And there would be no reason for a book like this if the Other Dickens weren't, in just this way, at least as timeless as the Immortal Himself.

In tallying such energized tensions between Writer and Writing, no crude distinctions need apply. There is no pitched battle between the

bluntly serviceable and the subtle, between the obvious and the subversive. No reader is asked, or allowed, simply to choose between function-
ality and festive burst, still less between the lucidly relaxed and the perversely exacting, the facile and the fractious, finesse and blatant excess.
Boz is always confidently at the helm, steering story with his overall even
keel. We're not dealing with Dickens the reliable master craftsman getting
dealt the odd wild card by his crafty, parasitic Other, with some unwieldy
counterforce suddenly overheating the prose and thus undermining the
narrative drive. Across the twin Dickenses I find in reading, there is no
clear division of literary labor. Their formative powers operate in tandem,
neither's prose being in the least deaf to phonetic and semantic surcharge,
neither's bent exclusively on narrative suspense. In this way they emerge
together—if only into felt divergence—whenever Writing, in process, puts
the drift of the written at even minor risk. At such times prose itself seems
threatening to disorder with its wild license, if only instantaneously to
recoup, story's own vested interests.

But, safe to say, in reading Dickens, we never actually lose the thread
amid the verbal filigrees, loops, or occasional knottiness. So there is certainly no strict division intended here between the propulsive and the imp-
ish, between narrative trajectory and unscheduled jolts to its coherence.
The Other Dickens claims no premium on dormant sonorities, even while
given to their overdraft. Strategically, Dickens Himself, the mass-marketed
Boz, certainly sees to the sound of his sentences with determination and
aplomb, stage-managing their syllabic microdramas at every turn of tone.
But that sovereign ingenuity only opens the back door to interloping and
errant phrasing, sometimes to incautious trespass upon the very premises of the story. Often perverse and truant, the Other Dickens can seem
at times almost deranged by the stray hearing (or sounding) of things,
orphan wordlings—especially when folding them back on themselves in
redoubled undertone: involute, oddly voluble, both evanescent and even
"catchy" in more senses than one, incurring snags (think the Snagsby
passage) or snarls in their own aggregation. Whether timed to, or out of
sync with, the splendid dexterity of dilated syntax in those recognizable
Dickenisan "periods" (that rhetorical term for suspended grammatical
arcs)—with all their lift and levitation, their giddy pivots and sardonic
comedowns—the Other Dickens offers both a further gunning of language's generative engines and the chanciness of sudden slipped gears. So
it is that the Other can stand to the One and Only strictly as inmixed and
inextricable—and in a zone of response to which reading is initiated anew
with each curious wrinkle.

And so a few further prefatory words about Dickens's own initiation.
As suggested at the start, it was a twin birth, this origin of One and the
Other, conceived and brought to term in ways never quite attended to

in strictly biographical commentary. No one knows where a genius like Dickens's comes from, certainly, but we do know where—the very young man had been in incubating it—in the precincts of which books, play texts, and primers, that is. Early reading and early writing, of course, are always partly determinate, but in Dickens's case some of the "writing" that needs to be highlighted deserves scare quotes around it—what with the nearly half decade that young Charles spent in the grips of stenographic constriction. Given the onerous, unyielding handbook by Gurney from whose exercises he worked to master the craft, one can only imagine the contrast he must have felt when relieving the strain and tedium of his parliamentary stenography by plunging into his favorite author in his free hours. So my stress on a divided verbal influence in Dickens's formative years is thus to be focused less on Smollett and Scott, say, than on shorthand and Shakespeare: Shakespeare, whose plays—whose syllables—Dickens was imbibing on an equally programmatic basis with his stenography practice in just these years.

In the third paragraph above, I wrote "with Shakespeare . . . behind him." Not as far behind, however, as that might have suggested. At least for the first half of Dickens's career in fiction, Shakespeare was a continually replenished and proximate cause. In Dickens's apprentice years, the impact of hard-won stenographic mastery and, quite separately, of ongoing Shakespearean tutelage is well known. The scholarship on each facet of his early self-improvement campaign is as exhaustive as one might wish—without actually bringing the two poles of linguistic engagement into alignment and cross-reference.[4] Or, more to the point, without attempting their triangulation with the coming prose of Dickensian fiction. It is more than just a matter of reported versus imported rhetoric: the shorthand transcription of political oratory versus the long and devoted saturation in Shakespearean tonality and its organizing resonance. It is the unpredictable miracle of their convergence. A script depleted, for speed, of all syllabic richness had its best antidote at hand.

As fuel for any sense of some deeper transfusion between early influences, positive and negative, the record, to begin with, shows clearly how Dickens—who spent years, on and off, steeping himself in Shakespearean idioms and syntactic tropes as well as character types, turns of phrase as well as turns of plot—began this regimen and this relish as early as he did his shorthand labors. He was later to become a frequent extemporaneous quoter of Shakespearean lines, a friend of Shakespearean actors, a member of Shakespeare clubs and societies, an actor in Shakespearean burlesque, a backer of serious stage productions, and, not least, a deft raider of the plays for character archetypes and plot patterns. So attached was he to the Bard that his friend and biographer John Forster made sure that Dickens wouldn't be too much divorced from this source of inspiration by gifting him with a portable edition of the plays to accompany him on his 1842 American tour, from which *Martin Chuzzlewit* emerged a year later. Such was the handy companion volume meant to complement his publisher's gift of a complete set of Shakespeare after the success of *Pickwick Papers* in 1837, as followed by Dickens's own purchase of a twenty-four-volume variorum set of the *Plays and Poems* in 1841, the year before his departure for America. And we see the manifest effect of all this, as fermented during the writing of *Chuzzlewit*, not just fulfilled in the entanglement of the Lear, Iago, and Cleopatra prototypes in *Dombey and Son* (1848), the last with her burlesque Ant(h)ony (Bagstock), but in the newly powerful language — syntactic, lexical, and phonetic — by which these debts are paid back in kind.[5]

Besides these shaping influences surfacing in *Dombey*, detectable as impinging and indeed structuring "intertexts," what else do we imagine Dickens drawn to in the reading, the actual reading, of Shakespeare? And later drawing on? One knows well what T. S. Eliot meant by the punning "Shakespeherian Rag" in *The Waste Land*, but it can't hurt to illustrate it briefly — in ways that should help evoke Dickensian vocalic strategies well beyond his own fondness for the "fatal Cleopatra" (Samuel Johnson's term for Shakespeare's easy seduction by the pun). For the homophony of punning is only the special case of a radiant polyphony that Dickensian prose, if not self-consciously extracting from Shakespeare, had certainly contracted by addiction. And with no "contraction" of phrase, in the other sense, whatsoever. Quite the opposite. Pruned back, compressed, elliptical, is just what the Shakespearean rhythm isn't, in its continuous appeal to Dickens — in contrast to the shorthand discipline that weighed so heavily on his mind when first studying the Bard.

What, then, was the sound in Shakespeare, by later internal evidence from Dickens's own prose, that he must have cottoned to? Examples leap to earshot (and will be scooped up further near the start of chapter 2). We needn't resort to the hard evidence of his juvenilia, where the Moor Othello was refigured as the implicitly drunken Irish-like bully O'Thello, his nemesis as the eager ogre (no full Christian name given) E Argo: one name thus wedged open, the other fused by cross-word homophony.[6] Soft evidence, in the subtler malleability of phonemes, is ultimately more suggestive. The imperative in *Twelfth Night*, for instance, "Be not a*fraid* of *great*ness," approaches its advice in a bonding harmony seemingly as natural as the phrase's own assonance across the negative admonishment. Yet it is, rather, *The Tempest*'s later variant in Caliban's mouth, "Be not afeard," that is delegated to the semiliterate, rather than archaic, argot of Captain Cuttle in *Dombey and Son* when expressing his continued hopes for Walter Gay's seagoing ambition in the face of any and all tempests — or at least putting a good face on it for the worried Florence — with a repeated

"I am not afeard, my Heart's-delight." In Shakespeare, this variant of "afraid" has a more immediate motivation, since it is meant to assuage an anxiety that is as if half rectified in advance by a music that links "afeard" to "ears" in bracketing Caliban's famous admonition "Be not af*eard*; the isle is full of noises, / Sounds, and sweet airs," so that "Sometimes a thousand twangling instruments / Will hum about mine *ears*." Enjambment, of either line or letter, isn't enough to secure the barely plausible distinction (and sibilant elision) of the all but redundant pairing at "noise*s*, / sound*s*," even as followed by their rarefaction into the almost punning atmospherics of the ear: those musical "airs" floated (in conveyance from "afeard" to "ears") in the very medium of this island world. Before the bookending echo of "ear" with "afeard"—the latter evoking that very discomfort from which the ear needs extricating—the "instruments" are not just "twangling" rather than "twanging" but plucked as well by the legato-like *d/t* "hold" of the phonetical "thousan*d t*wang—." Further, these airborne murmurs do what instruments, the voice included, sound like they should do: release such echoes as "um" (from "will hum") into the thrum of the subsequent trisyllable ("instruments"). Suffice it to say that many a Dickensian passage to come—in his writing at large, as well as exemplified in this book—will boast the scintillant phonetic intricacy of such verse. And let it be further mentioned that not only was *The Tempest* a play Dickens saw, at least twice, with his friend William Macready, leading Shakespearean actor of his day, in the role of Prospero—but a play by which the just-published novelist was inspired in 1838 to write a poem called "To Ariel" about his eagerness to answer such a spirit's breath-borne and musical call.[7]

The kind of woven vocalism that inflects Caliban's verse lines, when transmuted into Dickensian prose, may be harder to assert, let alone prove, as Shakespearean per se than is an overt punning like Scrooge's to the ghost in *A Christmas Carol* (1843), written in the same year that Dickens had probably seen Macready in *Hamlet* before arranging a subsequent benefit performance of the same ghost-haunted play. Confronting the first of his own ghostly avatars, Scrooge is trying to write off his apparition as indigestion, with an uncharacteristic bit of wordplay that seems handed off directly to him from his author, or say, his own Other Dickens: "there's more of gravy than of grave about you." Aside from such a pointed motif of ghostly visitation, the broader feel in Dickens for theatricalized phonetic recurrence is not difficult to pinpoint there, just hard to warrant as directly Shakespearean—so endemic had it become by the time the novelist hit his stride. Indeed, such wordplay often "reads" as a case of the intrinsic Other Dickens at work, injecting a (neo-Bardic) festive excess into the prose lexicon of comedy or melodrama alike. This has happened already, long before *A Christmas Carol*, in the mock-lugubrious assonance at play in the first sentence of Dickens's first novel: "The first ray of light which illumines the gloom, and converts into a dazzling brilliancy that obscurity in which the earlier history of the public career of the immortal Pickwick would appear to be involved, is derived from the perusal of the following entry in the Transactions of the Pickwick Club," where it is nothing less than a long-pursued (and long-*u*'d) "assid*u*ous" research that rises to the enlightening occasion and "il*lum*ines the g*loom*" of the Pickwickian archives for the pending readers. It is in the inveterate phonic tradition of such tongue-in-cheek euphonies propelling Dickens forward from book to book that we come upon that sounding rhythmic dichotomy in the first "stave" of Boz's Christmas "caroling." Even at the peak of his independent fame, the One and Only still seems famished for the cadences, comic or otherwise, of the Shakespe*hear*ian jive—varying Eliot's riff, or rag, here in order to *spell out* the internal syllabic pun. Such jiving would certainly include the split ends of phrasing on offer in Scrooge's splayed objects of the preposition ("more of gravy than of grave"), a wording that has its own extra ring of indebtedness to the loose-limbed grammatical skids, or lateral accretions, of the playwright (to be discussed ahead under the category of phrasal "straddling").

But that's only the half of it—or one pole, again, of the double and contrary influence on Dickensian wording that needs acknowledging at the start, his start and ours. Once more, I'm quick to appreciate that biographical scholarship has scarcely ignored any of this—just its implications for prose style. Well known: that Dickens doted on and dipped into Shakespeare repeatedly for inspiration. And just as widely acknowledged: that he made the most of the very different churn of words, in the form of contemporary ponderosities, that he heard on a daily basis in the House of Commons as a legendary reporter, mired continuously, for several formative years, in such political speechifying. Much scholarship is on record testifying to the ambition and linguistic facility of the stenographer Dickens, including the leaden rhetoric of the parliamentary drone he recorded, imbibed, and then either parodied or purified later. But commentary has been slow to mark any contrast in this with the Shakespeare he was reading for relief and instruction at the same time: the same phase of what we might call his verbal education. Nor, therefore, has criticism gone so far as to speculate on how his day job—beset, and at first bested, by shorthand's butcheries of vocalic excision—must have rubbed exactly against the grain of his luxuriant immersion in the plays and poems.

There's exactly the convergence, amid the contrast, I have in mind. It only takes reading around in his coming prose, after the briefest acquaintance with his biography, to make the early endeavors seem proleptic. Dickens had, with considerable difficulty, learned shorthand from a tortuous instruction manual called *Brachygraphy* in order to become a freelance reporter, working as such for a year, 1828–29, before beginning a three-year stint as a parliamentary reporter in 1831. In between, at age eighteen, as soon as he was eligible, he got a pass at the British Library and began a three-year reading program of literary acculturation devoted in part to the two different editions of Shakespeare's complete works that he immediately checked out, before being able to afford his own. Between the denaturing of English into compressed stenographic code in the long hours of the parliamentary sessions and, in contrast, the expansiveness of Shakespearean intonation when the young Dickens was at leisure to pursue it arose the quite literal difference of day from night, professional labor versus avocation. A keen awareness of this rift, unabated by time, could only have helped form his style and lift it slowly toward the aural sparkle and syntactic command of his major fiction, as marked especially in his breakthrough with *Dombey and Son*. From the British Library to his own study and on to his portable readings of Shakespeare in overseas travel, the result of Dickens's abiding apprenticeship in the power of invented speech reads, nonetheless, as if his prose instincts never forgot those antithetical constraints in the counterfluency of stenographic gridlock, where consonants were crushed bumper to bumper with no breathing room for the sounded breath of animating vowels.

As the first chapter will examine in detail, the stenographic compaction in which Dickens was schooled—eliding medial vowels between foreign-looking consonant brackets in reductive graphic code—would, for instance, indicate no difference, or a minimal and cryptic one, in Shakespeare's alternation between "afraid" and "afeard," each shrunk to the swifter clip of their nonalphabetic equivalent for *afrd*. One needn't specifically imagine Dickens pondering these alternate spellings in his move from reading *Twelfth Night* to reading *The Tempest*, nor dwelling on the variously patterned assonance that embeds the adjective in each case, in order to note how the most convulsively timorous character in his fiction, prominent in *Little Dorrit*, is named, in a variant of Aphra, none other than Affery: pronounced with a soft or nearly silent *e* (as in "affry")—as if only timidly beginning to assert how affrighted she is. Whether or not Shakespeare or shorthand, either of them, is on call in this christening, my main point is that the Other Dickens can certainly be heard in attendance at the baptismal font, nudging the name toward wordplay. This obstreperous Other, then, is my own shorthand for the manifold repercussions of what chapter 1 will spell out when it turns, by contrast, to the "brachygraphic" coding of Gurney's daunting manual and the straitjacketing of vowel forms: sounds denatured from word to word rather than rendered lavish in any sort of Shakespearean resonance or recurrence.

The last thing at stake here is any effort at proving some explicit verbal allusion in choices like "afeard" and "Aff(e)ry[aid]." Shakespeare is brought forward, rather, to stake out a broader proving-ground for the modeling of Dickens's general syllabic dexterity. For such is the very timing of wording that allows him to describe the intermittence of street noise, as it penetrates to Affery in the isolated Clennam house, with a pulsional echoic rhythm all its own, "mak*ing* the *listen*ing M*istress A*ff*ery feel* as if she were d*eaf*, and recovered the sense *of* hearing by *instanta-neous* flash*es*"—a paranoia indistinguishable, in cross-word effect, from her other tremors "*of hearing.*" To the ambidextrous but overstressed young writer, veering between literary absorption and the stenographic squeezing out of vowel forms in shorthand's stringent economy of signi-fication, Gurney must have seemed the burial urn of all Shakespearean vocal grandeur and echoic comedy alike. Hence, I suspect, the unchecked festivity of resurrection from there out. Then, too, and quite apart from the patiently invested reading, banked debts, and increasingly midcareer withdrawals from the fund of Shakespearean syllabic richness on Dick-ens's part, the world's typical reaction to Shakespeare himself can in fact offer a parallel to what may at first seem odd in my posited relation of Dickens to his Other on one and the same page. For this distinction is, roughly speaking, akin to the one anyone readily makes—readers, listen-ers, critics, everyone—in the audition of Shakespearean theater. We can always distinguish between (if never separate) the dramatist and the poet, his plot-embroiled Characters and his daredevil Figures of speech. The novels of Dickens operate in a similar "poetic" fashion when guided—in a two-channeled, stereophonic vein—along the very tracks of plot. My more particular emphasis on the shorthand regimen as a negative impetus to the vocalic momentum of Dickensian prose is offered to complement this intuition rather directly: to speculate, that is, on how Dickens's adopted shorthand code, given his always preternaturally alert ear, could have stood forth only in an exacerbated contrast, in its parade of shriv-eled lexemes, not just to parliamentary oratory but to the Shakespearean glories the young writer was simultaneously reveling in—and trying to incorporate into his own craft.

So it is, for Dickens, that twin force fields may be sensed to converge in those preparatory years upon the absent core of vowel-free script. What seems to have resulted for the incipient writer, in these conflicting cur-rents, is, as we'll be charting, the eye of a too-perfect storm. His workaday jots could only vacuum out the sounds, not just of any *Shakespehear-ian* elocution, but of all the words the would-be literary writer in Dick-ens scrambled to take down in Parliament—and would wish to improve upon in his own snappier eloquence or parody. The low-pressure eye of that storm, in its suppressed aurality, therefore marks by negation the potential storming of the ear by a sonority, however dubious in most of its stentorian political cases, that has suddenly gone mute. Certainly, for the verbally impressionable Dickens, there would have been something like a continuous three-way interference across political oratory, poetic theater, and the stenographic antithesis of each: a potentially blunting shunt among rhetorical bombast, suave aural drama, and radical vocalic constriction. Instead of Dickens being numbed by all this, what developed was, it would certainly appear, a stockpiled instinct for prose adaptation and amplification waiting to break out. The next step is clear, and was to make the name Dickens famous almost overnight.

Escaping from a labored public prose not his own and a language not even English, from Parliament and Gurney alike, the journalistically observant Boz published *The Sketches* and *Pickwick Papers* in rapid succession, with the poetically gestated Other Dickens fully on board—in a vehement mode of liberation and phonic reparation that provides an apparent blueprint for much to follow, then and also here. With the budding writer having prepared his own way forward from this fraught interplay between the vocal gag orders of stenography and the contagious intonations of Shakespearean diction, the passages waiting to take the stand—next in a further preliminary sampling, as well as in the subsequent quartet of separately focused chapters—will regularly meet our reading, halfway and head-on, with the striking freshness of the unexpected. Theirs is the power to captivate even long-standing lovers of Dickens with a sense of newfound energies in the very workings of phrase. This is the verbal charge to which an immersive attention always feels newly, innocently, initiated—through reading's own version of "surprised eyes" and, yes, un-"afeard" ears. So let quotation now, at fuller scope, begin just such work of responsive witness, often against the drift of more predictably "academic" considerations.

THE ONE, OTHER, AND ONLY DICKENS

INTRODUCTION

SOME "REAGIONS" FOR READING

n biographical terms: preparations laid, ways paved. Yet in going forward, as noted, we are involved with only a depersonified sense of "reading Dickens." Even so, the vernacular way of putting this yields an extra advantage, an unexpected leverage. It pries from idiom an oblique insight into what it might mean to read the Other Dickens as well: that wholly impersonal prose one finds fitfully legible—and only *legible* at that, as Writing itself, dependent of course on its phonological basis—across the print-busy page of the novels. This isn't just another Dickens, therefore: any other Dickens, yours or hers or mine, one among the many coming down to us—the blockbuster mass entertainer at the dawn of a media epoch, the quintessentially insecure Victorian male, the residual Christian, the scrupulous urban ethnographer, the female idealizer and misogynist alike, the much-biographized rags-to-riches careerist, the aspirant middle class personified, the complacent imperialist, nor even the studied rhetorician. This is *the* Other Dickens, the one there always, if only in abeyance, never entirely withdrawn or at rest: an otherness latent in the slant of narrative's every phrasing, waiting to break out in unexpected coruscations of syllables and syntax.

Such is the Dickens destined to puncture whatever "Dickensian" signature effects, even those of the Master Stylist, that a given reader, academic or avocational, already tends to recognize and feast on. Regarding this introduction's anomalous title, such are the "reagions" for reading to be isolated by example (borrowing from *Martin Chuzzlewit*, quite out of context, Mrs. Gamp's tipsy pronunciation—and accidental portmanteau term): namely, loci and motives alike. By this "reagioning," our sensing *where* to look can help us in knowing how to listen—and ultimately why. And in doing so, the backstory continued here from the foreword, and pursued in detail via the first chapter's turn to *David Copperfield* and its texture of "internal evidence," is not biographical either, but linguistic. It concerns the comically elaborated traumas of shorthand code as they may, more seriously, have warped the formative phonetic unconscious of the writerly imagination, springing a hypersensitized Other from the pressure cooker of a mercilessly crimped inscription.

One may say that this Other Dickens is simply the prose one reads at a certain pitch of response—where Writing speaks up, and for, itself from within the pockets of ideology, the energy of polemic, the blind spots of gender or race, even the confident machinations of Style itself. Gone public as Boz, Charles the tireless verbal and narrative craftsman was a phenomenon, a troubled man, a moody superstar, a working journalist, a resourceful magazine editor, an inspired caricaturist, and a seasoned if unschooled maestro of plot and descriptive art alike. The Other Dickens isolates itself (not Himself) as the intransigent genius of verbalism per se, the agitated underside of just such art. This coterminous rather than alternate Dickens has no personality traits to speak of, to read of. Emptied into the flow of its own ink, such an Other Dickens maneuvers the straits and rapids of a fluent, coursing aurality of prose thus Other to narrative's own purport at times: not actively counter to it, but syncopated, impulsive, and only implicitly bidden.

This Other Dickens isn't an author at all, then. "Dickens" is in this sense the effect, not the cause, of anything associated with this verbal percolation beneath the lid of semantic and narrative sense. When "reading Dickens" in the everyday sense, you are likely to be reading one of his novelistic products. In a rather dated Victorianism still casually flourished in journalistic (and student) prose, he *penned* fourteen of them, with one left unfinished at his death. Yet it is not enough just to say that he left his stories in writing. When taken up for reading, we may still sense their *being* written, rather than simply having been. The inventive pen is still evident in prose action. For if only in the right mode of attention, not mood of response, one reads in a way that deciphers something at the springs not so much of the writer's narrative oeuvre as of his immanent linguistic verve. The Other Dickens is simply a way of christening this disposition. One responds, when prompted, to exactly the upsurge and onrush, the catch and drag, the bends and rents, of a language not quite gelled (yet, ever) into the print that transmits it. Or say, prose in the process of its own getting done and setting down, a Writing often still sounded on the inner ear before being entirely penned in by the rectangular page. And thus it is that the Other Dickens has little or no critical bibliography for consultation. I honor this fact by writing for once with a bare minimum of notes—and with uncited quotations from passages now most easily searched in the Project Gutenberg e-texts (with the two provisos that all italics are my own unless otherwise specified, and that any very rare errors in the e-text are noted alongside the verified quotation). As to the thin critical trail brought to light in the notes, I'm not out to tabulate all the incisive things said here and there in the scholarly backlog about Dickens's style, by way of either generalization or local perception. The purpose, instead, is to gather up for consideration some limited but convincing evidence of all that has regularly gone uncommented on.

Dickens the Eminent Victorian Author portrays, narrates, pontificates, raises hackles, wrings tears. Beneath all possible mastery or authority or suspect ameliorative politics, wholly given over to language in motion, the Other Dickens scribes. In reading this Dickens, we audit along imprinted lines the formative waver and vibration of words in emergence, sometimes half out of sync with sense, veering slantwise on the ear. This Other Dickens, as we will see, and hear, isn't exactly a secret Dickens, though such a localizable effect — derived from the introversions of a somehow occulted style — has been proposed in admiration, as we'll explore, by the novelist Graham Greene. Rather than esoteric or encrypted, this Other Dickens is more steadily *scriptive,* writerly: his prose creased and pleated in a way that never permits us to ignore the phonetic alphabet and its clustering syllables out of which all the novels' lustrous as well as sardonic phrases are made.

Concerning the dual but coordinated aspect of such prose, can we say that Dickens is alone among great novelists in this dimension — or stratum — of his style, at least before Joyce, even as it might seem to articulate the deep fact of all writing? Maybe. Where else do we find so clear a case of sheer lingual impulse coming now under, now out from under, the imposed continuities of discursive control? Language on the loose and the run: that is the Other Dickens. From moment to moment, Boz the nicknamed superhero of serial fiction, as of Victorian three-decker publication, reins in this Other manifestation, rallies it to the narrative call, trades its drastic liberties for a stabilized if still volatile phrasing. But sometimes, in the intermittent counterpoint set in play by the irrepressible Other, reading may seem to audit a barter and compromise still at work in an unstable fillip of phrase. With meaning only provisionally setting in, settling down, these word-sounds are caught just a bit reluctantly succumbing to syntax — and thus taxing its logic with a momentary ludic back draft.

I've more than once, in print, called Dickens the great "syntactician" of English fiction. True enough, when need arises. But such praise can seem too narrowing, too much an emphasis on strategy rather than spontaneous acrobatics. Reason not the need. Analysis can easily betray the energetics of the sentence in Dickens when thinking too much, too soon, or too exclusively of its instrumentality, without giving full slippery weight to those mellifluous or quizzical ripples hedging a given phrasing from within — or edging it from without. One certainly understands, however, why Dickensian style in scholarly discussions tends to be subordinated to the themes it manifests and coordinates. To be sure, the commanding embrace of his syntactic frameworks and lexical arsenals serves quite directly a satirist's broad canvas in a panoptic urban vision, as elsewhere the roving details of a flaneur's avid gaze. But in all this and more, a flexed capaciousness of report comes through, because *only* through, the theatrically maximized capacities of just that syntax itself and the diction it marshals — which thus come first, foremost, and even at times in the absence of plotted utility. Even when all else fails, or when little else seems at stake or in play, the show of verbal bravura is in its own right the motive force, the vital drive, the very trajectory, of the Dickens experience. In this way Writing alone, primed for action even in its absence, charged and indefatigable, can seem the true hero of page after page.

The centrality of the writtenness is incontestable — and at the syllabic center of one word after another. To spot this in what follows, the "shutter speed" of attention is slowed, not at the acceptable risk, but for the very *purpose*, of extra exposure — more light let in — on the shifting focal points of wording's own advancing plane of inscription. I am, of course, speaking metaphorically. Discussion will be coming back, however, to the sense in which I find Dickensian writing at least as "filmic" as it is (more famously) cinematic: a matter of verbal frame-advance as well as framed vista or panoramic sweep. At this point, however, the trope of photographic exposure-time is simply meant to position the reader, rather than the writer, in the place of a close-up still camera — for sequential spotlit snapshots of effects as incomparable as they are ephemeral. The result is to isolate and preserve certain salient "moments" of a sustained prose duration. If the result seems more an album than a monograph, so be it.

Phrasal Montage

But to fend off any misplaced expectation at this early turn, a cleaner cutting of the above distinction is no doubt in order — even before examples come across our path. The "filmic," as material category, concerns the discontinuous celluloid basis of the moving image strip, thousands of little transparent frames (called photograms) accruing to screen image over projection time: the very *imageering* of the so-called motion picture (now of course replaced by digitization). At the scale of display, instead, the "cinematic" has to do with the whole ocular apparatus in action, with vistas and events materialized and animated on screen. That latter aspect of the seventh art is what Dickensians usually have in mind, by analogy, when celebrating various features of the novels as techniques of visual spectacle and scenic "montage." The former or "filmic" dimension is evoked in these pages, instead, to close in on the serial plasticity of the prose itself, where the nearest equivalent of molecular "photograms" would be the "phonemes": the smallest units of speech sounds, alphabetically imprinted.[1] These are the cellular components that, when fused into syllables and then bunched into words, constitute the very motor of style—quite apart from (or at least at the base of) any visual proclivities of description or plot.[2]

Under certain narrative pressures, of course, photograms may be evoked on-screen in their own microprocesses by slowed motion or freeze frames, for instance, just as phonemes may tip their hand in skids—and puns—like *Mrs. Nagsby*. Instead of 24fps—as in French director Jean-Luc Godard's famous quip about indexical cinema as "truth 24 times [frames, photograms] per second"—one underlying truth of Dickenisan stylistic deviance rests with the irregularities, if I may, of *ppi* (phonemes per inch). The unique double sense that the term "frame" has in cinema (first as module on the filmic strip, then as the window-like screen itself in its sustained rectangular image) finds its nearest equivalent, on the page, in the coordination—meshed more evidently in Dickens than in most narrative prose—between the saying and the said, between alphabetic sequence and scenic consequence. Where a much earlier French artist than Godard, the *philosophe* Voltaire, could famously compare the act of writing to a "painting of the voice," the same spirit of paradox should allow the present book to stress instead Dickens's time-based medium as a virtual filming of enunciation.[3] It is by these lights that any notice of the "flickering glints" of syllabic irony, say, would have at least a distant media-historical overtone.

I come to such metaphors, even such deeper analogies, honestly enough, I'd like to suppose. Apart from three books concerned in part with the evolution from filmic to digital cinema, where photograms are replaced by pixel array, my own literary work has for years been drawn to diction and syntax as not just inherent to narrative writing but as generating, and in Dickens preeminently, almost a subplot of their own. In this spirit, I have repeatedly directed attention to the way not just the telling phrase but the very dynamic of wording is part of the narrative told. Yet I want here to stress not so much the *way* things are brought about in prose fiction, the ways and means of story, but rather the *things* themselves: the word objects rather than their tool use, phrasal linkage rather than tactical grammar. This entails no recantation in the least. What I have come to call "narratography" has offered one specifying name for the close-grained and intensive reading moment by which the microstructures of style are assimilated to narrative drive by responsive notice, whatever interpretive impetus may then follow. This seems to me still manifestly—or at least demonstrably—true. But there are more funny phrasings in Dickens than are dreamt of in anyone's narratology—or its scalar variant in narratography. This includes both senses of funny: involving either risibility or odd uprush, inducing laughter or just bursting obstreperously to recognition when intruding upon the norms of fictional discourse. I wish in this book to concentrate on just these funny moments in particular, separated to varying degrees (however artificial this detachment may be) from their plot imperatives or thematic instrumentality.

And if I may retain the filmic as much as cinematic analogy long enough to attach it specifically to the self-conscious "editing" of prose, and its split-second montage shifts, the effort may shed light on one unique moment in that notable Dickens novel about the making of a novelist, *David Copperfield* by name. Here the filmic leverage, turned metatextual, is exerted in cutting away abruptly from plot to its own discourse—all from the estranging distance of a not-yet born, let alone apprenticed, writer. In David's reconstruction of a prenatal scene between his aunt and mother, with the former's imminent disappointment over his emergence in male gender, there is the following perverse lexical equivalent of a jarring cinematic match-cut (the classic on-screen shift between parallel graphic elements in discrepant spaces). In this prose version, a single word is passed as a baton from character to narrator in an anomalously self-conscious relay race of plot development. I can think of no other blatant finesse quite like it in Dickens, so blunt as to be unrecuperable by Style—but offering, instead, a laying bare of the author's own verbal free-association, usually more tactfully masked. The aunt has wanted to satisfy herself that her nephew's will has taken due care of his surviving child bride, and has heard that he left everything to her. Prose becomes, at this point, as bluff and peremptory as Aunt Betsey herself: " 'He might have done worse,' said my aunt," in her typically stingy approbation. And immediately, in a new paragraph: "The word was appropriate to the moment. My mother was so much worse that Peggotty, coming in with the teaboard and candles, and seeing at a glance how ill she was . . . conveyed her upstairs to her own room with all speed." Not just "appropriate to the moment"—in the general goal of all Dickensian writing—but here appropriated for that moment by the Other Dickens, articulating a transition on behalf of the plot from within a passing snatch (and fragile latch) of dialogue as its own kind of strained vocabular hook. It is a segue so forced as to be covertly paradigmatic: of transitional labors typically kept at least fractionally more discreet.

One might sense a further shift from plot to discourse, though more fully disguised as a comic phrasing, in the first description of Biddy in *Great Expectations*, through the patronizing eyes of Pip the narrator. The frowsy girl seems worth only passing comment: "She was an orphan like myself; like me, too, had been brought up by hand." Selective and dismissive, what follows are some sheer physical attributes about her everyday (in every sense) person, with an attached exception concerning the Sabbath. Cast in the tones of Pip's incipient prissiness, the latter is lodged in the language not of the girl's lived body but of an explicit word picture, alluded to but excluded from the prose itself. For after her usual lacka-daisical appearance is detailed: "This description must be received with a week-day limitation. On Sundays, she went to church elaborated." Or would have done, if the prose had seen fit to elaborate. In this ingrown metatextual wrinkle, we find mentioned only a style of address rather than of dress. In the category slippage of this wit, Dickens might as well have said that during the week she was idiom itself, but on Sunday got all troped up.

Either with a given word lifted from a character and recycled by dis-course through the ensuing scene, as in *Copperfield*, or with a character treated here as if she were only the discursive function of a phrased ef-fect, wording has taken over the world. As so often in Dickens, the more extreme the departure, the clearer the norm. Verbal self-consciousness can be semantic and phonetic by turns, or both at once. The invested act of Writing, rather than transparent narration, seems to be tipping its hand in that last rather high-handed but low-impact example. Or say that the Writing is giving a strictly lexical rather than logical nudge to Story. In such discursive reflexes, we may sense the Other Dickens delving more closely (and openly) than usual into the all but mechanical main-springs rather than wellsprings—the linguistic gearbox rather than native fluency—of narrative momentum.

In any case, the verbal invention and dexterity are unrelenting, in what-ever facet of Dickensian representation. Phrased ironies are drawn taut around their satiric targets in a mordant stranglehold. With no less con-trol, melodrama can proceed at fever pitch without losing syntactic aim. So, too, a rarer lyricism can be relaxed in its music without turning limp or vaporous. Every mode has its own decisive measure and tread. Despite impatience in certain quarters—about Dickens composing his works as if he were, as in fact he once was, being paid by the word—even his cir-cumlocutions can be luminous, as well as frequently hilarious. The issue isn't wordiness, but *wordness* per se: a deep verbal libido, a lust for enun-ciation itself. In isolating and honoring all this, the hardest thing about writing the present (for me) little book, given the profusion of its topic, was keeping it little and not too hard. Every seasoned, not to say calci-fied, instinct in my scholarly anatomy urged me at first to pin down the mercurial wording of Dickensian prose in its full linguistic specification, all relevant terminology brought to bear. But I kept realizing that this would sabotage the message by overmassaging it. For the intended point was just this from the start: that the palpable demiurge of Dickens's intri-cate Writing lies in the fact, against all odds, that it does come easy, even if from unsaid depths—the tapped reserves of language in continuously renewed vitality.

The ease would have to be respected here above all, I came to realize: the almost spooky fluency felt as such, not always easy to read at first pass, but unthrottled in its forward thrust. Hopeless as well as supererogatory would be this task, this labor of love, I had set myself—if, that is, I were somehow intent on "explicating" the comic brio of Everybody's Dickens by killjoy quotations under clinical vivisection: that well-known autopsy of all comedic panache that results from poking a joke to death. Not so here, if only because the net is cast more widely than it would be in any concentration on "one-liners" or their extended equivalents. For what I find in the Other Dickens is, again, funny in the other sense as well, whether in passages of brutal revolutionary riot or those we would tend to call laugh riots, as much in *A Tale of Two Cities* as in *Martin Chuzzlewit*: a phrasing often odd, aberrant, perplexed, uncanny—and strangest most of all when it seems to be operating on automatic pilot from some inwardly fueled energy more sheerly linguistic than descriptive. Say for now that the Other Dickens is the funny feeling we have, with a Dickens novel, that more is going on verbally than meets either the needs of narrative or the immediate reading eye. Which is why this book can afford to be short. Since what it seeks to remind readers of is to be found everywhere, they may then choose to notice it in their further reading—woven in with the Big Dickens two or three times per page, or more, as what we might call narrative's own base of operations.

It is there that the funny encompasses the whole range of the unexpected—and the unchecked—in the barreling onward of an often untoward prose. To put the actual jokes together with these other odd yokings of syntax and phonetic flare-ups is to find a common denominator that invites some nonlethal probing. And it may well be that one of the most influential theories of comedy in the twentieth century, that of French philosopher Henri Bergson in his 1907 essay, "Laughter," can suggest, indirectly, the funny business of Dickensian writing in and beyond the knee-slappers.[4] Indeed, with slapstick being a quintessential example in the Bergsonian model, we laugh when, according to his account, the natural, the human, is made mechanical. So with the repeated gags of a character's inveterate verbal as well as facial tics in Dickens. But so, too, with the verbalism of narrative discourse itself when, rather than appearing like the enunciation of an expressive authorial intent, it seems not manic but machinated, gone into overdrive on its own speeding wheels—making fun of (as well as with) the very momentum of its own inertial verbiage. As Bergson theorizes such moments, they are a default in referential signification itself, so that "the play upon words makes us think somehow of a negligence on the part of language, which, for the time being, seems to have forgotten its real function and now claims to

accommodate things to itself instead of accommodating itself to things."
A negligence—or a hidden agenda? For the Other Dickens, indeed, the
word is often the *very thing*, its byplay gleefully out ahead of all service to
the world under representation.

Certainly this is the case with the first sentence of Dickens's first novel,
where logorrhea (involving the larded assonance mentioned in the foreword) is unleashed to celebrate a supposed rigor of "discrimination":

> The first ray of light which illumines the gloom, and converts into a
> dazzling brilliancy that obscurity in which the earlier history of the
> public career of the immortal Pickwick would appear to be involved,
> is derived from the perusal of the following entry in the Transactions
> of the Pickwick Club, which the editor of these papers feels the high-
> est pleasure in laying before his readers, as a proof of the careful
> attention, indefatigable assiduity, and nice discrimination, with
> which his search among the multifarious documents confided to him
> has been conducted.

One is actually buttonholed, in this single subordination-heavy sentence,
with eight doled-out *u* sounds: *illu/gloo/obsu/peru/pleasu/proo/assidu/
docu*, tailing off into the mere vocalic eye rhyme at the otherwise alltera-
tive resting place (and soft-*u* comedown) of "conducted." Nor does "brilliancy" rather than "brilliance" (in sibilant shimmer with "dazzling")
seem chosen just for the rhythmic contrast with "obscurity," but for a
silly extra syllable of word(i)ness to boot.

From there out, in this novel and beyond, the style can at any moment mutate, bulge, spread to the very brink of nonsense—while
tethered always to some lucidly ironic intent in a manner as easy to
recognize as it is hard to characterize, let alone to pin down (in its
continuous process of overtopping itself). To say the least, the Dickens
style is "hyper" in the contemporary sense—for all its rooted syntactic confidence and cool.[5] Its paraded aplomb in the matter of grammatical embedding and embellishment is incomparable. Hyper, yes,
but *hyperbolic* isn't exactly the best word for it, at least in the etymological sense. It doesn't go too far, shooting beyond the mark. It is
just "too much"—also in contemporary idiom's honorific colloquial
sense. The opposite of hyperbole (a throwing beyond) is understate-
ment: Austen territory. Dickens seldom goes there. If all things understated help delimit, by polarization, the tenor of the hyperbolic, it's
again useful to suggest (after Chesterton) that, in Dickens, the almost
unremitting opposite of the straightforward is the *exaggerated*: not the
over-thrown but the piled-up: amplified, magnified, heightened. *Ex* +
aggerare = thoroughly + heap up, accumulate—as related indirectly

to aggregation. Encountering Dickens's finest comic moments in this vein—hundreds of them per novel—we laugh both at and with this additive expansiveness (rather than overkill): in the matter, say, of relentless character detail and its phrasal presentation alike. As distinct from what grammarians call paratactic construction (a and b and c, etc.), Dickens doesn't just add on and stack up, one thing after another. In the so-called periodic rhythm of his characteristic syntax (with details stretching out a suspension bridge between subject and object, and sometimes via more than one subclause), his inordinate subordinations can be said to *pile inward*, thickening from the center, swelling at times to the bursting point of cognitive retention.

Leaving behind the satire of editorial rhetoric in *Pickwick*'s first sentence, and as soon as an actual scene is set, the prose continues indeed to aggregate, accrue, and exaggerate in the already established way. In introducing the first of Pickwick's minions, prose gives us the still amorous (if tubby) clubman as "the too susceptible Tupman, who to the wisdom and experience of maturer years superadded the enthusiasm and ardour of a boy in the most interesting and pardonable of human weaknesses—love." The syntactic suspension of that relative clause ("who to") aside, "super-addition" is indeed the name of the verbal game: manifest in the ricochet of yet more long and short *u* sounds serving to "illumine" any feared prose "gloom" across the almost goofy echoism of *too/sus/Tup/who to/ture/supe/thus/ove*—and prolonged further by the play of "*ardour*" first against "*pard*onable," then ("*ardour*") against "int*er*esting." In the very next sentence, we find that the man's person is in fact swollen to match this overplus of his passionate urges: "Time and feeding had expanded that once romantic form." There, in one of the most noticeably recurrent of all Dickensian effects, as explored in the third chapter, a splaying between abstract and concrete descriptors (time consumed as well as food) spreads out its contrast from within a given phrasing in a facetious disjunctive linkage. Under less romantic circumstances yet, we recognize the syndrome (as with the "Time and feeding" doublet) in the echoic "meekness and obesity" of Mr. Snagsby nine novels later, with prose still battening on such comedic effects, indulging in both sudden disjunctions and their subliminal bonds at once. But even just two pages into Boz's mock-epic first novel, we have found the Other Dickens in full swing, executing effects too fast for assimilation to whatever plot may be building. Such are the embedded minor extravagances within the steady exaggeration of Dickensian wording.

And Bergson, by his own lights, might well be dubious—or at least on alert. Unlike a serious and "illuminating" metaphor in the work of rhetoric (one of Dickens's general strengths elsewhere, of course), reminding us that "language and nature" are "two parallel forms of life," the comic "play upon words" does indeed ignore momentarily the more specific debt language owes to nature in the former's referential function. In the case of the Other Dickens, this "negligence," this intermittent divorce of wording from its immediate narrative work, represents not a "lapse of attention," as Bergson has it (in French, "une *distraction* momentanée du langage"), but a collapse into the linguistic itself: less as a "form of life" than in the sheer liveliness of its form. Induced at times is almost a double-tracked reading in the momentum of storytelling. We encounter the Other not diluting the fuel of plot so much as oiling language's own syntactic and syllabic loquacity—and thus matching the greased wheels of story with a strange phrasal viscosity in progress, "mechanistic" only in regard to the linguistic engine itself.

The Roominess of Prose

Right at the novelistic starting-gate of Dickens's career, then, delivered up full-blown from the word mill of the sketch-master Boz, that opening sentence of *Pickwick* remains perhaps the most obvious and unmitigated stretch of pay-as-you-go word-mongering anywhere in the repletion of Dickensian syntax. But it can nonetheless be recognized as a litmus test of such syllabic, lexical, and syntactic elaboration (in tempered form) ever after—beginning, not least, with many a sentence to come in that same opening chapter, and for years to come. Take his next great comic master-piece of characterization after Mr. Pickwick and company, his conjuring of Mrs. Gamp the inebriate nurse. In *Martin Chuzzlewit*, the floor space of Mrs. Gamp's cramped lodging has barely room in it for her bedstead—but the passage about it eventually waxes unduly spacious in its lampoon of common sense. The rhetorical effects start small, as befits her square foot-age. Readers are addressed at first as if we were fussy visitors. But why stand on ceremony, wherever you decide to stand? "For only keep the bedstead always in your mind; and you were safe. That was the grand se-cret. Remembering the bedstead, you might even stoop to look under the little round table for anything you had dropped, without hurting your-self much against the chest of drawers." Only a jaded mansion-dweller or a spoiled punctilious ingrate would find anything inhospitable about these reduced quarters. Thus does the descriptive tongue go straight to the cheek for an expatiation upon just such a lesson in moral, social, and aesthetic tolerance. Certainly the equivalent of an opera quiz for literary readers would find the resulting circumambulation (of prose and spatial radius alike) easily recognizable as by Dickens: "Visitors were much as-sisted in their cautious efforts to preserve an unflagging recollection of this piece of furniture, by its size; which was great." Where, before the semicolon, that bulking first clause takes the long way around the described object in quintessential Dickensian prolixity, the straightforward economy of "which was great" contrasts with the nearby circumlocutions that seem meant to compensate, by inflation, for the smallness of Mrs. Gamp's abode.

To sustain the tone of hyperbole, another aspect of the "grand secret" here is the space opened by circumlocution for an extraneous sound play ("Visitors"/"assisted") that achieves more *syllabic* scope or latitude than this cramped lodging can boast in its own air space. Typical, as well, is that rooting of scenic detail through an imagined perception of it somewhere halfway between reading about it and an embodied on-site inspection. The way in which the reader is summoned to the very lair of character as well as characterization, getting a fix on Mrs. Gamp by negotiating the space from which her description emerges, returns in a different form in the imputed public chorus of wonder at Miss Tox in *Dombey and Son*. The gossamer superfluity of that lady's wardrobe is mated, via the animism of its mismatched fabrics, to a rather diaphanous stretch of circumlocution in saying that, recalling Mrs. Gamp's visitors (as reader stand-ins), "it was observed by the curious" — raise your hands! — "of all her collars, frills, tuckers," and the like, "indeed of everything she wore which had *two ends to it intended* to unite" — yes, not just "*ends intended*" but a further and extraneous *two/to/to* chime — "that the two ends were never [via contentious personification] on good terms, and wouldn't quite meet without a struggle." From one angle, it may seem as if every verbal detail of Miss Tox's dithering shabby-genteel presentation avoids — even while exfoliating — anything so predictable or succinct as the cliché of a woman *at loose ends*. The Other Dickens, in other words, is manifest there in a pulled punch, or call it a swallowed truism. But the notion of Miss Tox's "mincing" manner is next and quite directly *literalized* as a kind of desperate "chopping up" of life's meager provisions, all in a final flourish of rhetoric at its most verbally spendthrift and circumlocutionary: "These and other appearances of a similar nature, had served to propagate the opinion" — again among the "curious," no doubt — "that Miss Tox was a lady of what is called a limited independence," as further propagated in inflationary prose, in a more explicit twist of idiom, by the splendid mention of the fact that "her mincing gait encouraged the belief, and suggested that her clipping a step of ordinary compass into two or three, originated in her habit of making the most of everything." As does the prose here — but by no means through economizing its own store of words.

Beyond figuring the budgeted frugalities of demeanor itself in Miss Tox's description, there is the broader distinction this economic analogy may call to our on-the-scene notice: Dickens tells stories, draws characters; the Other Dickens contributes to wording them—even in excess of strict representation. The impulses can intersect at the strangest of angles. As seen just now in the nonconjuncture, not only of ribbons and gauzy strands, but of metaphor (the unsaid "loose ends") and its exfoliation, there is a figural economy in its own right that is often found calling the shots in such loquacious portraiture. And, as with Miss Tox's fashion missteps, some of the best comedy in the novels bubbles up from unspoken counterparts to scripted figuration, where such alternative formulations may seem the surest manifestation of the Other in the very biting of a lexical tongue. If Miss Tox's stinginess of dress is there in part to trope her vulnerability to the lure of wealth in the Dombey circle she enjoys orbiting, in *Our Mutual Friend,* by a reverse logic, an entire economic saga, strictly metaphoric, sprawls out in one almost ungainly sentence from an awkwardness of person and wardrobe in the first description of one Sloppy. The very formality of the inverted kernel clause that begins the sentence is part of the irony in this picture of gawkiness, even before prose breaks out into half a dozen monetary metaphors: "A considerable capital of knee and elbow and wrist and ankle, had Sloppy, and he didn't know how to dispose of it to the best advantage, but was always investing it in wrong securities" (read: curtailing garments), "and so getting himself into embarrassed circumstances." The subliminal, and rather sublime, Otherness inflecting this passage rests with the almost unmissable hint that prose is cashing in—as if by second thought, at the head of that anatomical list—on the suppression of the vernacular "knee cap," inverted to "capital of knee" instead. For all the garrulous aggregations of the Other Dickens, the unspoken is equally the stomping ground of such a prose dynamic, its slyly fallow turf.

In pursuing such deflections of the unsaid by the wordiest of figuration, the "curious" among us may wish also to return to Mrs. Gamp's economic management of stores and their storage in the crowded space of what might otherwise have been termed her bed-sitting room—including certain hidden-away sources of warmth, ranging from everyday fuel to the teapot that houses her booze. We learn of this latter convenience in an extended metaphor punning on spirituous liquor: "Mrs Gamp stored all her household matters in a little cupboard by the fire-place; beginning below the surface (as in nature) with the coals, and mounting gradually upwards to the spirits, which, from motives of delicacy, she kept in a teapot." Delicacy—and deception. Dickens is even funnier, and almost uncharacteristically oblique—or is this the Other Dickens on understated overdrive?—about a less persuasive camouflage of storage space for an alliteratively bulking array of "various miscellaneous valuables" introduced just before. Their containers have no bottoms, only covers—like porcelain-topped cake plates, one might say, with only decorative lids, no plates. The novel says it better. For, "though every bandbox had a carefully closed lid, not one among them had a bottom; owing to which cause"—again the love affair of such prose with the fastidious "which," in all its stretched permutations—"owing to which cause the property within was merely, as it were, *extinguished*." These protective coverings are thus the equivalent of unsaid but implicit *candle-snuffers*. Not like Boz at all in his more obvious metaphoric flare, this may well seem like some whimsical off-kilter wit of the Other Dickens: a diffident metaphor hiding its own light under a barrel, tamped down, but by no means extinguished, in the flickering glimmers of phonetic similitude across "o*wing* to *which/within/w*ere/ext*inguish*ed." Then, too, the whole joke is all the more potent, as well as thematic, for the quasi euphemism of its indirection: the very picture in diction of Mrs. Gamp's own deceptive, faux-genteel housekeeping.

The sublexical nuance of extruded phonetic recurrence aside, it is certainly the case that a linguistic principle is to be recognized here in the very instances that might seem to outstrip its logic. Whether through pun ("spirits") or figurative as-if ("extinguished"), such wordplay—however much elaborated in syntax and sound—is an act of conceptual economy and compression in its own right. As such, it prepares for an even more extraordinary sentence that again releases a contrapuntal sound play from its own hyperbole. In avoiding the aggressive bedstead in Mrs. Gamp's tight quarters, we bump up against a typical Dickensian circumlocution (and then some!) in the form of a highly aerated tautology. For all we know, Mrs. Gamp thinks of her cramped pad as a "stately pile." Authorial commentary wouldn't bother to puncture this fantasy without ballooning itself in the process: "If it were not exactly that, to restless intellects, it at least comprised as much accommodation as any person, not sanguine to insanity, could have looked for in a room of its dimensions." Given the square footage, who can deny—so goes this circular wordiness—that Sairey's "accommodation" is fully and responsibly accommodating: offering everything one might have reason to anticipate unless blindly, indeed madly, expectant about low-rent roominess.

Only the wording itself has the room for maneuver it needs to dwarf the quarters of its own representation. The whole effect is less claustrophobic than vertiginous in its wit. What reader, attending closely enough to follow, wouldn't at least feel deliciously tripped up by this? Amid such a perverse and tautological circumlocution, as if pushing in its own swollen right against the spatial constraints of Mrs. Gamp's hole-in-the-wall, we have landed momentarily, squeezed between commas, on that chiasmus-enforced syllabic compaction of "*sanguine* to [the point of] *ins*anity" (chiastic grammar, *abba*, as in *Great Expectations*: "with a smile that was like a frown, and a frown that was like a smile"; chiastic phonetics here: *an/in/in/an*). In the midst of a sentence everything about which is unnecessary, the Other Dickens gives a further verbal turn to the screw. The closest thing to it in sheer ingrown syllabification, and this by a radical antithesis of description that nonetheless taps something of the same *a/i* phonetic matrix, comes at the zenith of Boz's maturity in describing the blasé Lady Dedlock in *Bleak House*, a lady of tedious leisure characterized — in three appositional dead ends of affect — as suffering blandly enough from "exhausted composure, a worn-out placidity," and, in the most languid gargoyle of restatements, "an *equanimity of fatigue* not to be ruffled by interest or satisfaction." Yet again prose leads with the ear.

Then, too, with that negative touchstone of mad expectation concerning Mrs. Gamp's quarters in *Chuzzlewit*, compaction is only the half of it. With the impetus of diction operating as if to bloat the unsaid substantive form, *sanguinity*, into the strained phrasing "sanguine to insanity," such phrasal dilation may almost seem to insert itself as the Victorian lexical equivalent of the modern-day brand of wide-angle lens used in real-estate photos to annex an untold breadth to the limited footprint of a given rental. One may well think that, in a phrasing like this, verbal elbow room is made to overcompensate for a described constriction of domestic space. In its lateral syllabic ex-aggregation, call it an anamorphic hyperbole. No local proof needed of a Shakespeare-inspired ear-play; just an inkling here will do. And certainly no intertext required in the several passages where Shakespeare uses the word "sanguine." With prose like that of the Other Dickens — once Boz has come under a general influence and influx from the Bard — the inspired vocabular blood is already at full flow in the veins of euphonic exaggeration.

Fluent, wily, sometimes all but loony, but never alone for long, such verbal effects are thus hard to "single out." That's the trouble, the double trouble, faced by a book like this, quite apart from the occasional risk (seriously resisted) of sacrificing comedy on the altar of its dissection. Celebration, even weighted down with some further cerebration, is nothing without the highlighted excerpt. But to lift even the typical phrase from context is to deny its place as never better than first-among-equals in an immediate prose surround. Even the stand-out moments, as suggested, are never stand-alone. You can't call them out without breaking stride with their own native rhetorical medium in more of the same. At varying wavelengths of relaxation and zap, one never waits long for the zinger, which is always funnier when flanked by kindred ingenuities jostling each other at different scales of emphasis, compression, and protraction.

These are effects, of course, unlike those temporarily "extinguished" valuables of Mrs. Gamp's masked by their bottomless cylindrical snuffers, that are seldom left to speak so coyly for themselves. Discourse stands watch, sometimes closely vigilant, over its own performance, ready to pump it up at every turn—as well as to intercede in invented dialogue in order to gloss its own secondary "funniness." Later in this same chapter, it is Sairey Gamp's own thick-tongued, drunken idiolect (much of it baffling to historical philology in its not strictly Cockney sources) that centers the comedy, as when she tries explaining her sudden distrust and excommunication of her previous associate, Mrs. Prig, pretending to have exposed her as a hypocrite. " 'Now that the marks,' by which Mrs Gamp is supposed to have meant mask, 'is off that creetur's face, I do not think it ever would have done. There are reagions in families for keeping things a secret . . . and havin' only them about you as you knows you can repoge in." In the narrator's own transliteration of such cockeyed speech, we shunt between script and enunciation, first guided by the partial graphic (or alphabetic) anagram in "marks" (for "mask"). A similar visual aid, rather than audial cue, is given with "reagions" (for "reasons")—as if barely to distinguish it from its unslurred cousin "regions." Indeed, it is just this same *graphonic* interplay (to apply a portmanteau term of my own[6]) that the Other Dickens has elicited from us—in the previous manner of hyper- rather than subliteracy—for that crisscrossed syllabification of "sanguine to insanity." Any effort to diagnose the "regionally" unreal aberrations of Sairey Gamp's metropolitan idiolect is thus to begin probing the alphabetic tension of letters and sound forms in the narrative writing more extensively spread before us, and thus to do the Other Dickens the honor that the Writer bestows on Mrs. Gamp in the very act of singling out her own oddball linguistic transgressions.

Added to which: the matter, again, of scale. The fact is that any anomalous expansion of phrase at the syllabic level (as in a tacit "sanguinity" become "sanguine to insanity") has its parallel distension of sense in Dickens's comic grammar as well. There is, for instance, the moment when, in order to denounce Mrs. Prig, "Mrs Gamp rose—morally and physically rose"—as if from her chair and her alcoholic stupor at once, or, in other words, to both her feet and the occasion. The paradigm regularly implied by analogy in such turns of phrase: "literally *and* figuratively *alike*," in this case mounting up in bodily and spiritual (as well as spirituous) terms at once. Such is the two-for-one hinge point of so much comedy in the Other Dickens, its divisiveness only superficially "masked" by grammatical "marks" of conjuncture in which attention is allowed to "repoge" momentarily. In looking at such dis/junctural phrasing's most abrupt and arresting moments in chapter 3, I will sometimes be calling these discrepant pairings (beyond their technical designation as "syllepsis") a matter of "handcuff grammar"—of the sort we've seen already in the cross-coupled subject of "time" and "feeding" as twin causes for Tupman's paunch. Or say, an enforced bridging of alternatives, otherwise splayed or forked into discrepancy. Even in the mild form of "rose" and its explicit reiterated afterthought, "morally and physically rose," the phrasing itself seems to be thinking on its feet—even if not always landing squarely on them (hence the notion of "phrasing astraddle" in the third chapter). It's part of the Dickensian legacy of prose stepping out on its own with an idea it chooses to shuffle, if not exactly to run, with. Dickens's most famous forked phrasing from *Pickwick Papers* concerns not Tupman the clubman, or even Pickwick himself, laid low by too much punch when he "fell into the barrow and fast asleep, simultaneously," but one Miss Bolo, who, in-furiated by Pickwick, "went home in a flood of tears and a sedan-chair." Here is the direct precedent for Groucho Marx's snippy send-off to the bothersome Mrs. Teasdale, an idiomatic soup of its own from *Duck Soup*, ladled out at the end with a sound pun on "half": "You can leave in a taxi. If you can't get a taxi, you can leave in a huff. If that's too soon, you can leave in a minute and a huff."

The wry (always slightly awry) impact of such fanned-out—but still cross-bound—wording comes down even to the toolkit of contempo-rary journalism. Like Dickens reporting on Parliament in his own day, the front-page *New York Times* coverage of the 2016 Republican Na-tional Convention, anticipating the subsequent campaign trail, rang three changes on one phrasal verb in a single sentence, looking ahead to chal-lenges after not just "the lights go down in Cleveland" but "the balloons go limp and the delegates go home." And by way of influence *on* rather than *from* Dickens, who had sported such phrasal frolics from early in his career, there is, beyond the eighteenth-century comic novelists he cut his teeth on, a certain relaxed Shakespearean complexity to such forked phrasings, as we'll see later by example amid other cadences from the plays. Such impact can be anticipated by two instances about similar "go-ings" and comings, besides the exit of Miss Bolo, in the first of the novels to capitalize fully on Boz's rereading of the Bard. In *Dombey and Son*: "Then into the quiet room came Susan Nipper and the candles; shortly af-terwards, the tea, the Captain, and the excursive Toots." And later in this same novel, on exit from another room, the ego-swollen Major Bagstock "took his lobster eyes and his apoplexy to the club."

A category-straddling prose thinking on its feet, yes—and keeping us on our toes. But a question remains. When one "gets into" Dickens in this way, where is one going exactly? What latitudes and horizons of response are engaged by the Other Dickens in the process? To what conceptual spaces are we transported? Where, in short, does such reading get us? Not just further into the urban bustle and crush of his cityscapes, hovels, pubs, prisons, workhouses, and incommodious flats. Nor, to round out the narrative demography, are we just ushered as well into the cushioned deadly splendor of his penumbral townhouse interiors, haunted by the walking dead of wealth and idle privilege. The reader is conducted first of all into the rustle and plush, the shove and hover, of wording itself. Such wording may be thought to detonate one image after another in the virtually filmic track—and sometimes jump cuts—of reading. But even so, the resulting mental screen of event, while resolving into a pictured world elsewhere, is never cleared completely of that phrasal scrim—there's no good name for this—that overlays even while releasing such ignited word pictures. For such is the opaque skein of phrasing itself, whose aura ghosts the people and places it conjures. To put it succinctly: the Other of sheer enunciation is palpably coextensive with depicted event.

As a means to Dickensian meaning, then, words never get in the way, they *are* it. More than making way for story, paving our routes of access to it, they pervade its actualization. There's no murky Thames misadventure in Dickens without the churning flux of phrase, as turbid as anything it might render, all its telltale details floated past in a restless turning of the syntactic tide. There's no mob violence without the shouldering crowd of words. No alleviating fade into death without the decelerated pace and levitation of grammar. No violent murder without the hammer blow of verbal force. No fog-bound vista without a blanket of agglomerating phrases and their occluded delineations. And, of course, no tight squeeze of living quarters to which language fails to annex some extra room for maneuver. What is true for any fiction writer, the steady dependence of world on words, is *writ large* for Dickens, not just unmistakable but everywhere at stake in the very texture of the writing. One doesn't read for the plot in his fiction. One reads for reading—its delights but also its lesson, internalized as one goes: namely, the lesson that out of words other than expected, and more than necessary, is the Dickens world spun—and sometimes unraveled.

In contrast to Boz the artificer of a virtual London and its invented, eccentric people, this is one definitive reason why the Other Dickens is not "Dickensian"—in the sloppy sense of screen adaptations, for instance. We'll return, as mentioned, to the way his writing is more "filmic" than, in the marketing sense, cinematic. That aside, nothing is further from his manner than the 2015–16 BBC series actually titled *Dickensian*, with a mash-up of characters lifted from separate novels and herded together without even his own narrative tethers, let alone the prose that gives shape to such fictional people. Certainly the Other Dickens is among the casualties of such commercial "translations." Beyond the hawking of brand consciousness by media publicity machines, the fact that screen reviewers seldom notice or regret this discrepancy between writing and its derivative fictions is another way of positing a Dickens truly Other to the cult of Victoriana and its storytelling. With any such ersatz screen vignettes in mind, the least quotation from one of the novels exposes the gap at once: the chasm between articulation and depiction, prose and episode.

We are speaking, then, when present, of a Writing that speaks, I repeat, for itself. Dickens comes easy enough in the reading, yes, without any crying need for explanatory linguistic apparatus, whether for his syntactic balancing acts or, within the spectrum of word choice, for his choicest of words. Yet Dickens's prose, for all this, is not a language in which one seeks to rest easy, accompanied as it often is by a heady buzz of phonic as well as lexical and grammatical associations. We feel the force of excluded sounds or sentence formats taking their leave from the phrasing, as given, without their having to give in altogether to the selections that constrain its present form. The Other Dickens has a way of keeping options open even in dismissal, as if many of his greatest turns seem to surface like the droll revision, in process, of a near miss. Dickens's own actual revisions, as we'll see, can sometimes confirm this. Outside of the archives, however, the Other is more immediately at work upon us in our very "reagions" for attuned response: again, zones of attention as well as motives for it. Hence the energy of this bustling Otherworld in regard to syllables as well as incidents: sounds playing across syntax in loops and slipknots of sheer phonetic suspense; the crowd scenes of aurality as well as of urban congestion; the etymological mellow-dramas of phrasal contestation and harmonic resolution; in short, then, the syllable *as* incident. These regions of subnarrative flow can thus be felt as localizing that ambient linguistic environment within which the inner ecology of Dickensian phrasal resource works its wonders.

So an obvious-enough disclaimer is in order going in. I'm scarcely bringing to light anything that doesn't otherwise scintillate on its own. What I'm broaching isn't the archaeological exposure—and exposition—of a Dickens otherwise lost to notice in the sedimentations of time or critical fashion. The Other Dickens is in fact the one everyone knows, at least in one's bones, but that few go to by way of academic citation. The more convinced of this I've become, the more I see why. To stall over such flickering or even refractory word forms for comment is never the same as to be caught up by them in passing, caught off guard by their own breath-catching turns on the run. No matter how lightly noted and gingerly estimated in their effect, investigation of the sort attempted here can't help but do some minor damage, I admit again, in lifting them out of context. My consolation, hence defense, is that no matter how much an analytic probing may seem suddenly to have spoiled the salient (or reclusive) turn of phrase by diverting it, further yet, from its narrative habitat to the zoo of species display, any subsequent degree of newly encouraged reading will return from the separate study of such a caged prize back to the broad topography of Dickensian prose with, at the very least, no dimming of interest or numbing of uptake. It remains a tricky business, though, such detailed appreciation. I don't exactly *like* reading Dickens more for having isolated so steadily, rather than just noticed in progress, certain insurgencies of the Other Dickens, nor do I expect any such enhanced enthusiasm (or not much) on the part of my readers. But I know a little bit more about the captivating nature of those phrasings that grab me. And since to know them is still to love them, they remain both open and ultimately invulnerable to the very scrutiny they deserve and invite.

And another mitigation. Even where my wrench of such language into an isolating spotlight does some mischief to the wit and rhythm of wording in the onrush of its native element, what I can at least promise *not to do* is subordinate such phrasing wholly to bigger and more "important" things. This can, of course, easily happen — and usually does. On display here, then, isn't everyone's Dickens after all, at least not in scholarly study — and to judge from recent articles and monographs, hardly anyone's these days (with exceptions to be happily noted as we go). Now in championship, now in effigy, scholarship has gravitated lately to Dickens the muckraking reformer, the sexual stereotyper, the colonial apologist, the class satirist, the flashpoint of Victorian homosociality, the eco-polemicist, the Orientalist, the intermittent antisemite, the allegorical pedophile, the battler for the poor and the prostituted. From perspectives materialist, historical, and theoretical by turns, we have seen the advertising-supplemented serialist, the political economist, the gadfly of bureaucracy, the textual deconstructor, the consolidator of the bourgeois subject, the marriage plotter, the thanatologist as well as the intuitive narratologist, the casual theorist of mass media and technological innovation, the hardly disinterested spokesman for international copyright, the crossover playwright, and the stage star to boot in his lectern performances. And even from a linguistic perspective, criticism has brought out Dickens the historian of dialect, the distorter of prose by lyric meter, and, above all, the reciprocal ironist of human-object relations, metaphorizing furniture and machines into life while depersonifying human agents in a counteranimist figuration.

All true, to one extent or another. But not true enough, so to say, to form. From one unexpectedly inflected phrasing to another, the Dickens of these pages (and often, I'm proposing, of his own) is Other to all of these, though pervading each with sometimes no more than a feather-light cleverness of verbal diversion—though elsewhere, of course, from within many a bravura set piece. Diversion, that is, from any vernacular norm, whether of word or phrase: othered in this intrinsic sense, charged with the burden of excess energy and its ironic reinvestments—and exaggerated at times in its very phrasing (rather than its mere perception) almost, but never quite, beyond control. One might identify that "never quite" as our truest topic.

Pending

The kaleidoscopic facets of this inexhaustible verbal drive are parceled out across the chapters ahead in an inevitably somewhat arbitrary—but nonetheless incremental—division of attentive focus. Chapter 1 ("Shorthand Speech/Longhand Sounds") sets forth from my own initial (and stamping) encounter with *David Copperfield*, hearing it read to me as a boy—and thus having it imprinted on my verbal imagination. Launched in this way from the full flush and gusto of Dickens's middle period, beginning with this personal favorite (his own, and for a long time mine) of the novels, we proceed to the barely veiled autobiographical account in that same novel of Dickens's own former "initiation" into the cramped nonprose of phonetic shorthand during his time as a parliamentary stenographer. Invited by much varied evidence, the chapter speculates on the traces such a regimen would have left, and the lingual energies it may later have helped release, in the unique phonetic density of the Other Dickens.

The level of attention in the remaining chapters derives in good part from this intuitive gambit. Though delving into verbal effects less specifically earmarked by certain devices of syllabic or grammatical play, as, for instance, in the ping-pongings of assonance or the forkings of syntax, chapter 2 ("Secret Prose/Sequestered Poetics") is directed at what the novelist Graham Greene quite vaguely, if famously, called Dickens's "secret prose," in *Great Expectations* specifically. This notion involves a temper and timbre of wording that we can also trace back to *David Copperfield* in the effort to identify more precisely its effects—in a way Greene chose not to do. We move next, in "Phrasing Astraddle" (chapter 3), to those more tightly localized and ironic verbal cleavings that split open—and oddly rejoin—certain grammatical (as well as frequently syllabic) constructs, and do so with both a productive doubleness of association and a recurrent comic double-take. In returning to a fuller manifold of stylistic effects in *Dombey and Son*, the first masterwork among Dickens's midcareer triumphs, chapter 4 ("Reading Lessens") finds the Other Dickens very much at work when—beneath the considerable strain of its frail plot motivation—we enter upon an internal parable of prose's own piecemeal reading, one letter at a time, thereby lessening immediate narrative coherence on behalf of the recognized means of its normative production. Throughout, what our immersive reading is on the listen (as much as on the lookout) for is the almost continuous interlace between incidents of story and the generative episodes of prose: as two dovetailed modes of event.

Whatever critical commentary of a more conventional or periodically dominant sort may leave you with, ideological or otherwise, there is something else you may well come back for—if not explicitly back to—in a Dickens always slightly estranged from routine novelistic expectations. The rhythms of harmonic counterpoint in the prose kinetics of just this Other Dickens—whether in the lilt of hilarity, the hum of reflection, or the frenetic densities of suspense—are, at least on any nonacademic basis, a good part of what draws an audience again and again to the novels: in an elicited keenness of "audition" that may often call to mind Victorian habits of family recitation and reception. My book wishes simply to keep open the invitation held out in this way, doing so by revisiting some of its most irresistible lures to the ear—as Mrs. Gamp might have it, those multiple "reagions" for response (again, both sites and incitations): dispatched as they are in a sometimes madcap vehemence of phrasing that can seem, in its own right, *sanguine* almost to insanity. With that adjectival dead metaphor (for full-blooded) ratcheted into hyperbole, the instance occasions generalization—since such exaggerated surges of sound and sense together are the very lifeblood of Writing in the microcircuits of Dickens's celebrated phrasal "flow."

Moreover, these are rhythms of aural intensity that can perhaps best be recognized—in a context larger than their own—from the perspective of literary-historical inheritance as well. So that what is pending here, beyond the waiting evidence of my itemized chapters, is the prose afterlife of a genre Dickens helped to mold and solidify—and stylistically reshape. Attending to the Other Dickens, then, is partly a way of hearing with the ears of prose fiction's own future as prose. For many of the effects to come in these pages will come again in later writers, dispersed but rhetorically pertinent. Writers often lesser, of course, but no less ambitious to have their words sing. I am referring to the broader stylistic legacy of Boz's novels across the uptake of Dickensian prose rhythms—and their vocalic undersong—not just among the Victorians but from Conrad to Faulkner and beyond. When Don DeLillo, in a 1993 interview in the *Paris Review,* says that to be a "writer" means "to construct sentences" first and foremost, with special attention to the "look and sound" of words, can there be any doubt that he is speaking up for narrative speech at large across a longer tradition in British as well as American fiction?[7] He admits that he "likes to match word endings," and that if he uses the word "rapture," he is likely to put "danger" nearby, more for the sake of cadence than dichotomy. He is scarcely alone.

In Dickens, just for example, two separate pairings of the disyllables "rapture" and "danger" with cousin lexical rhythms, each linkage thick on the ground with further phonetic webwork, can briefly attest to one benchmark (and progenitor) for such a linguistic lineage—if not necessarily any conscious line of inheritance. In this further spirit of things "pending" across literary history as well as in the pages ahead, let this circumscribed mode of internal echo represent, for starters, the welter—and wealth—of such lexical undulations in the nervous phonetic energy of the Other Dickens. In a heightened satiric vein for *Dombey and Son*, a run of plosive sounds traces out Mrs. Skewton's "bewitching vivacity" of purpose (even syllable buildup can be hyperbolic in Dickens!) as she "*p*ushed Florence behind her couch, and dro*pp*ed a shawl over her, *p*re*p*aratory to giving Mr Dombey"—and giving the reader as well, in a chiastic internal version of the DeLillo lexical lilt that draws in part on the inner lining of "pre*parat*ory"— nothing less than "a ra*pture* of sur*p*rise." A few years later, Esther Summerson, half-time narrator of *Bleak House*, is usually forced to keep her "inner Dickens" credibly under wraps, or say, her Other Dickens at bay. Yet the words themselves don't always obey. And here the "danger"/"finger" echo is almost the least of it when Esther's "atten*tion* was distracted"—hers by physical risks at the Jellyby household, ours by the material ridges of wording even the first time through— "distracted by the constant appari*tion* of noses and fin*ger*s in situa*tions* of d*anger* between the h*inges* of the doors." In this syntax of many-hinged echoes, the tripled *tion* pattern is interlaced with the hard *ger* of "fingers" even while releasing the slant rhyme between "d*anger*" and "h*inges*" (with its gentle anticipation in the *ch*/*g*-like soft *t* of "si*t*uation").

All this is rolled out in the immediate wake of the pronounced (and DeLillo-like) *er* iteration—and all, we might add again, with its own muted "rapture of surprise." We encounter under focused audition at such points, rather than just by in-spection, that same Other Dickens for whom—half a decade further on from *Bleak House*—a sparse and dim pair of "mirrors," in a bleaker house yet, the Clennam quarters of *Little Dorrit*, could find no more fitting epithet than in the phrase "meagre mirrors." By contrast, it is in this same novel that the echoic "scared air" of "some meagre, wrinkled" old man amid London's "thronging thoroughfares" seems a phrasing chosen precisely for its antithetical echo of "eager" when released from the lexical adhesion of "some." Drawing on such overridden but still latent linguistic potential, words may at times appear itching to contravene their own truth in the verbal subversions of the Other Dickens.

Or think of it this way: Dickens means what he says; the Other Dickens is urged to say, even if all at once, whatever prose can mean—and is not shy about riding the crest of any tension, even that between graphic and phonetic signs. After poisoning Gowan's dog in the Italian setting of this same novel, the reprobate Blandois puts so bold a face on his denial that his dialogue can indulge in an unheard word game in passing allusion to the ducal epoch of Venice—as if language itself is shuddering in repulsion under the force of his announcement: "Somebody has poisoned that noble dog," he hypocritically repines, even as his own speech rhythms play up the mourned "nobility" into an aristocratic trope and eye-rhyme pun, with the d-o-g said to be "dead as the Doges." Language, too, can play its own dirty tricks on you. While Dickens is here prosecuting a further clue to the speaker's diabolic cruelty, the Other Dickens revels in those almost indigestible moments when one rudimentary constituent of the prose medium plays off, with some linguistic violence, against another. As brought out, in fact, by the first sentence of this very novel—"Thirty years ago, Mars*eilles lay* burning in the sun, one *day*"—where the odd rhyming specificity of place against singled-out diurnal frame (in an entirely typical seasonal heat), while triggering an extended chiming passage full of "staring" and "glaring," is also thickened by its own bilingual mix in "Mars*eilles lay*," with its false alliteration as well as orthographically masked assonance. No Channel, no Continent, imposes a bar on the dexterities of the Other Dickens in the smelting pot of such graphonic phrasing. The playing field of such otherness isn't just English, but language itself.

So it is that one of the best ways to "introduce" one's reading ear again to Dickens is by listening back from the subsequent exertions of literary history in the making of sentences. In *Little Dorrit*, an echo between *doges* and *dodges*, of course, would have been more like it—in DeLillo's vein of slant rhyme, that is: like the phonetic *er*-reflex of *meagre* with *mirrors*. But the perverse graphological exception of Blandois's lexical as well as ethical outrage (dog analogous to Doges, not doggies), or "Marseilles" in both deceptive and operative phonic bond with "lay," only proves the rule of euphony in phrases like the "scared air" of that wandering old man later in the novel. So, too, with the overborne soft *o* (ə) of "the *thr*onging *th(o)roughfares*" through which he moves—the latter inferring, by sheer verbal force, not just a crowding (or thronging) of sounds, but an escalating mimetic jam-up. No surprise, perhaps, that a shorthand protocol in Dickens's early writing career as court and House of Commons reporter, on which chapter 1 is about to look back in earnest—with all its elided (because understood) vowels—would have rendered Boz, the later speed-writing novelist, preternaturally sensitive to such lexical declivities and their consonant rims in the momentum of recurrence. No surprise, but often, again, no little "rapture" in the freshets of reception—in a reading that can feel at once sanguine, half-insane, and altogether elated. And in whose variegated "reagions" for response there is no temptation, and certainly no chance, to "repoge" for long, given more of the same coming.

A contemporary novelist like DeLillo is offered, it should be clear, only as one of many retrospective touchstones in regard to the place of the narrative "sentence" as cornerstone of fictional "writing." The point is mainly that what Dickens reached for, and delved into, in the formative work of wording has the literary staying power of language itself. That is a large part of what the coming chapters are after. In a transversal reading not of single narratives but of linguistic textures shared among the novels, one benefit of this cross-sectional approach is derived from the several temporalities it honors. What is most Victorian about its focus is the way it respects (without, of course, reclaiming or restaging) the original reading aloud of Dickens's serial fiction, his chapters bunched in monthly numbers arranged by frequent cliff-hangers to maximize suspense—and thus too eagerly awaited to be only gradually passed around in print form. What is least narrowly Victorian about it, even in reimagining the oral duration of such family listening, is precisely the *timelessness* of Dickensian verbal forays into the rhythm of syntax across the aural formation of story: in a prose read not just word by word, but word for word—for the word's own inner and resonating sake.

As a work of Dickens scholarship, this book exercises one full-length unprovable hunch about what happened to Boz's writing—from mid-career on—after a second-wind in reading Shakespeare seems to have enhanced his sense of prose's phonic contours, including the central place of those vowel cores that had been restored to his script from their onetime stenographic elision. In this sense, it is the most indirect or broadly suffused evidence that best suits my sense of both this pervasive linguistic recuperation and this literary uptake alike. The bounce-back from unenounced vowels is everywhere, though nowhere for sure. Similarly, though Dickens's allusions to Shakespeare are numerous and often explicit, they are not always the latter. In negotiating the deepest level of his debt, he can put a distance not just between himself and the Bard but between the ingredients of the given intertext, spacing them out into some new exfoliation from a fabled phrase. In *A Tale of Two Cities*, for instance, the vicious aristocrat who has fatally stabbed a serf is annoyed more to have a death on his property than on his hands. For the fastidiousness of power, as the narrator summarizes the case, "it would have been better if he had died"—across a three-word, fourfold assonance—"in the *usual* obs*cure* r*outine*": the said "routine" not (with a further chiming echo) of the general *human* lot, but rather "of his vermin kind." We've just been assured that there was "no touch of pity, sorrow, or *kindred* humanity" in the man when confronting a "different order of creature dying there." All it takes is to hear Hamlet's opening words about his hated uncle and stepfather, "A little more than kin and less than kind," to hear the Other Dickens, alongside an assonance otherwise cousin to Shakespearean sonority, stretching out this wordplay even while putting the etymologically apt "kind" back under an extra weight of negation (phonetic as well as semantic) in the missing "kindred" feeling.

Shorthand redeemed, and phrasing phonetically inflated, by a full Shakespearean license: such a convergence in Dickens of shed regimen and maximized freedom seems to have galvanized the aural aspect of his inner Other like never before. That's the guess, at least—and, in such "a work of scholarship," the analytic wager. As a work of Dickens criticism, however, rather than biographical speculation, this book—in its witness to stylistic density—is a sustained exercise in the undeniable. Its immersive venture is mainly to bring the intuition about shorthand and the evidentiary profusion of sound play into some degree of suggestive alignment. You'll be the judge, yet weighing the stylistic evidence one way or the other, and in one quotation after another, should certainly be its own reward.

But how is it to be doled out, this premium? How best to approach, from the perspective of constructed "sentences" themselves (DeLillo), that "rapture of surprise" (Dickens) they may induce? A note on citational method is thus in order, as of course in evidence already—a "method" that may in fact seem more like the opposite: sheer engrossed sampling rather than, to be sure, any systematic categorization. It's one thing, when discussing intermittent refrains that bridge the flow of event across single chapters or whole arcs of plot (as will be the case, ahead, especially with evidence from *Dombey and Son* and *A Tale of Two Cities*), to compact them for exemplification, without any space made for quoting the intervening prose. It's quite another thing to set off the recurrent girders, phonetic or grammatical, of a single sentence in a way that gives priority to form rather than flow, interrupting the overall drive, or patient drift, of meaning in the name of its sometimes devious means—or, if not deliberately evasive, at least easy to miss.

But let me be clear: clearer here than it is sometimes easy to be in parsing the Dickensian extravagance. There is no dominant performative agenda in this approach, or not in the way that might be supposed: no venture in mimetic form regarding the hesitations or jests of phrase. Analysis is not out to imitate the twists of inscription, merely to honor their often eccentric pace. But just because even the most illustrative and typical effects I have in mind tend to sneak up on the reader of the novels—not just sentence by sentence, but phrase by phrase, often one word (or its equivocal link to another) at a time—there is no reason why they should do so on the reader of this commentary. The effort of analysis is not to overtake and upend attention, but to sort it out. Yet the overlap, and often tighter intertwine, of phonetic and grammatical turns alike, both with each other and with the more obvious tropes of rhetoric ("turns" at that scale), is "illustrative and typical" precisely by defying any clean segregation or typology. My redescriptions of Dickensian description are, let us say, more like those of an embedded reporter than a taxonomist. The effort is to join the Dickensian reader, guard down, in encountering the putative Other Dickens—rather than to catalogue the wild variety (or even continually remixed common denominators) that constitutes such an assumption in the first place.

Instead of standing back at first from block quotations, therefore, to be tackled from the outside in, we will be inching our way across the channels of evocation from the inside out, following along in analysis (which is really only to say "in reading") the unfolding turns of wording, phrase by phrase—and sometimes interrupting the grip of grammar itself to appreciate, before catching hold again of the sense, its festive or nervous false leads. There are no hat tricks here. Except those, at times, pulled off by the Other Dickens. But though readers are invited to anticipate the exegete in a first glance at any given phrasing, I like to think that a close dogging of their steps by the increments of analysis may, at least cumulatively, serve to enact (performative only in this sense) the all-but-simultaneous second thoughts of a keen attention. The effect, then, is to ratchet down the *"slow motion"* dismantling of the realist edifice performed by Roland Barthes in *S/Z* to the level of phrasal form rather than ideologically coded narrative details, including a reading of lexical structure itself rather than of his precoded realist "lexia."[8] In Barthes's effort to dismiss any supposed "innocent" first reading of a text, he gives us terms for a different kind of semiotic interference, or "static" (9, rather than purity), in the lines of communication that a reading of the Other Dickens entails. What is thus detected, beneath the classic plotting of Boz, are those uneven and variable linguistic strata that must be enlisted to generate any and all narrative data. "If then, a deliberate contradiction in terms, we *immediately* reread the text," as Barthes puts it, this is only so as to apprehend it as a "plural text" to begin with: "the same but new" (16). That plurality, that multivalence—in the case of the Other Dickens, that extra surprise from within—is what the equally paradoxical immediacy of the verbal double-take is meant to track here in the sometimes interrupted, if never fully paused, contours of a single clausal span. It is just this skid or slippage that is likely to trip you up, toss you sideways, drop you through to wording itself in formation. And keep you going—back for more.

1

SHORTHAND SPEECH/LONGHAND SOUNDS

To begin this reading of Dickens with a long-ago reading of Dickens, not by me but *to* me, I record that his words were borne in upon me for the first time, unforgettably, from the mouth of a rather ambitious babysitter late in my first decade of existence. "To begin my life with the beginning of my life, I record that I was born." I didn't know "life" in the biographical rather than biological sense back then, but I could surely sense that something at the beginning of *David Copperfield* was swallowing its own tale. I got immediately caught up in such a loop of words answering to each other, *sounding each other out*. My mother took over the task of recitation when time permitted. And in intervals of withdrawal from this addictive listening, I sometimes tried—and surely failed, myself and Dickens both—to negotiate some of the more daunting syntactic hurdles of the print on my own, a prose that I found not just clearer but so much more powerful when intoned. As in fact, when really read, it always *is* intoned.

In any event, alone in spurts or avidly leaning in to another's voice, I was certainly hooked. Even when drifting off to sleep over (or, better, under) the words, the words of my mother's or the sitter's, I could well have felt I was all the more invested in the contours of the tale. I probably identified with both Steerforth *and* David at once when the hero's charismatic school friend gets a sleepy David, night after night, to reproduce certain fictional tales as Steerforth's own bedtime stories in the school dorm—reproduce them not from page but from memory, based on David's own earlier escapist reading—and before him, Dickens's. (I wouldn't discover Martin Chuzzlewit's fondness for passing out—and then into consciousness again—under the spell of oral reading, Shakespeare included, as discussed in chapter 3, until many years later. Nor did I know then how Victorian a thing it was, even at hearthside as well as at bedside, to take one's Dickens by oral installments.) At the time, there was just listening—and perhaps identification. For Steerforth, as well as for me. In any case, summoned in an extreme form of narrative voice only, no print in sight, such was the fabled and animating fiction from a previous century (for David and Steerforth, Smollett, Fielding, and the rest) that *David*

Copperfield constituted then for me. More than half of another century later, the present book is anything, as you might have noticed by now, but the "matured" result of this early fascination. One of its main points, rather, is that Dickens always sends you back to your first half-dreamy sensitivity to language, unguarded and a bit childlike, vulnerable to every undulation. This strange regressive force, this verbal reversion, is often the direct effect of what I am calling the Other Dickens, operating a bit askew to the same story lines that Boz so confidently unrolls.

Not *by* me, then, that first reading of Dickens—but very much *through* as well as to me, with the sentences coursing along the veins of a nascent verbal imagination: an eventual reader born on the spot from the sound of writing. Indeed, it is just that fundamental distinction between hearing and reading, between the receipt and the coproduction of meaning, that is often rescinded when *taking in* such prose. *In*: where, through an almost uncanny process, it seems not just to belong but to originate. Even in listening, language arrives as if from within—registered on the sounding board of recognition. The very phrase "in listening" queries what one might call the *situation* of response. This isn't the special quality of Dickens only, of course. It is the truth of reading maximized, fulfilled, in his prose—yet made unmistakable at times by the obtrusions of the Other Dickens, as if wording could offer up the unprecedented pure voice of language per se. At his most sentimental and unironic, in *David Copperfield* not least, what is infantilizing about reading Dickens is only that we find ourselves learning to read all over again, pupils apt because rapt, initiated each time out into—ah, one of those telltale two-way prepositional phrases the Other Dickens so delights in manipulating—the mysteries of the reading ear. As a child of David's age when first being read to from his saga of dawning fictional investment, I certainly had no sense of the Other as distinct from the writer's name on the title page. Their very commingling, as I would now want to put it in retrospect, was what thickened the listening for me, made it hard—and hard to resist—at once.

But not too hard, which is worth noting: both as the special quality of *David Copperfield* and as providing a glance aside to delights of phrasal extravagance this one novel typically denies to the Other Dickens on grounds of dramatic tact. It was of course in so many ways the perfect text to begin with for a young boy, like me, first encountering the pleasures of expressive language. Partly, this is because David as narrator never goes too far. But there is a more compelling reason for beginning a study like this with *Copperfield*. First chapters should put first things first, and this is the novel that details, in autobiographical retrospect, what I'm proposing as the earliest (if unspoken) training ground for the syllabic sleights and subterfuges of the Other Dickens. I refer, again, to that arduous phonetic compression in the stenographic regimen that launched

David's career, like Dickens's before him, as a reporter—and in whose aftermath one then hears all the floodgates of enunciation thrown back open in the flow of word sounds. One might thus want to characterize the fictional prose of the novels as being released in this way to a lavish phonetic *decompression.*

"Listened To While It Is Being Written"

Indeed, some of the rare commentary inclined to audit the prose of the Other Dickens comes from a novelist himself remarking on the phonetic rhythms of *Copperfield.* "Between Shakespeare and Joyce," writes William H. Gass in an essay called "The Sentence Seeks Its Form," from his collection *A Temple of Texts,* there is "no one but Dickens who has an equal command of the English language"—and he means by this to stress, as it turns out, the aural dimension of the novelist's effects. "Language is born in the lungs and is shaped by the lips, palate, teeth, and tongue out of spent breath. . . . It therefore must be listened to while it is being written."[1] At attention's trained remove, Gass the novelist hears this overhearing, in a signal instance, as functioning to solemnize—or potentially to assuage in retrospect—David's emphatic sense of abandonment in early life. This occurs in a compensatory music of remembered distress conveyed by a run of mournful hammering negations: "From Monday morning until Saturday night, I had no advice, no counsel, no encouragement, no consolation, no assistance, no support, of any kind, from any one." When the increased phonic concentration of "no counsel" returns by way of parallel exclusion in "no consolation," Gass's ear is drawn in particular to the internalized inversion of the long (and long-drawn-out—as well as lamentory) *o* and its virtual phonetic ingestion by what we might term the dispersed sound-script of "*no consolation.*" No solace, that is, except in the sounded precision of this bitter memory and its self-counseled lugubrious sonority. David, the Dickensian persona, drives the point home with the most rhetorically self-conscious of mournful iterations. At the same time, the Other Dickens (the one coming to later fruition, we might say, in David's writerly tongue) effects that extra congestion of negativity within the longer periodic arc of a sentence strung (unmentioned by Gass) between "*From Mon . . .*" to the shifted prepositional sense of "*from any one.*" All told, Gass's example is perfectly chosen to catch the double valence of Dickensian retrospect at this emotional nadir: a monotony of former desolation alleviated only in the fulfilled tonality of report.

A related effect from the same novel, this time in the throes of David's melancholy rather than depression, is remarked in the recent anthology *Dickens's Style,* offering rare good company for the current proceedings in its fresh attachment to the topic. Gass himself has a tacit interlocutor there as well, since an essay by Robert Douglas-Fairhurst entitled "Dickens's Rhythms" cites David's threefold lexical refrain (breaking cadence with one variant elongation) as his thoughts revert sadly to the deserted family home: "I imagined *how* the winds of winter would *howl* round it, *how* the cold rain would beat upon the window-glass, *how* the moon would make ghosts on the walls of the empty rooms."[2] As with the interlaced patterns in the Gass example, one senses further, beyond the essay's own treatment of the passage, how the first slant rhyme of *howl* against *how* (graphically even more than phonically nudged from behind by the alliterating *w* in "winds of winter") also reverberates—more as a murmur or moan than a howl—across the rest of the passage, tainting each of the remaining "how" adverbs with an ambient lament. And then insinuates itself again, across a wider phrasal span, when "how . . . walls" spells out in plural form that same wailing if waning "howl" one last ghostly time. Such verbal bliss—what else to call it?—is certainly subliminal, but if it constitutes something like the guilty pleasure of indulgent hyperattention in any immersive reading of Dickens, it is entirely quilted in, nonetheless, to the general fabric of Dickensian phonetics and its blanketing euphonies.

So it is in *David Copperfield,* as elsewhere—but reflexively motivated there by the fiction of a writer's memoir—that the sentence sometimes "seeks its form" by folding back on its own aspiration to eventual writerly prowess: an *aspiring* in just that breath-borne sense stressed by Gass. In our reading of such moments, as channeled by the subnarrative rhythms of the Other Dickens, the recovery in prose of a former desolate tedium (or of an evacuated and forlorn dwelling place) is, we might say, in some measure recovered *from* by the levitations of sound play alone. As implicit in another and later tedium in the novel, there may well be a partly biographical explanation for this, as already suggested—one that I've never seen explored in commentary—according to which a writing necessarily "born" of breathed sound, once choked back too often by unnatural phonetic constriction in stenography, can come back to haunt a literary discourse. For the grueling shorthand reporting to which David later turned for livelihood would have served to choke back by its own discipline, and thus render stillborn, exactly such an echoic effect as Gass calls out. This is the case because the sixteen soft and long *o*'s that burrow beneath the semantic surface of the passage Gass brings forward would (many of them) have disappeared in the stenographic deaf spots (all internal vowels suppressed) at the center of each consonant frame. Under investigation, this shorthand constraint emerges not merely as an anecdotal exception that proves the later and full-throated rule of Dickensian euphony, but as a partial graphological clue to it all. For to overstate only slightly, it was there—in that phonetically ascetic regimen of the stenographic code—that the very timbre of Dickens's apprentice literary phrasing would have sustained a certain trauma of balked aurality for which a career of indulged sound play was to become the inspired therapy. The vowels that only Dickens, rather than an ordinary reader of prose, could once have "heard" (by reinsertion) in scanning his cryptic script are those the Other Dickens sows so profusely across the palpable phonic turf of the novels.

Gass again: for it is the vowels, not the consonants, that most immediately evoke (when silently vocalized) the "spent breath" of originary utterance shadowing the graphemes (alphabetic marks) on a written page. As it happens, no novel could be more explicit about this expenditure, in the act of speech itself rather than its vestige in writing, than *David Copperfield*—in an episode whose passing comedy produces a short circuit in the airwaves by which utterance is ordinarily propelled from mouth to ear. Earlier in that despondent slough of David's unsupported, uncounseled misery under the Murdstone reign of alternating abuse and neglect, trapped in his room for punishment, he is given hope only by a secret conversation with his nurse Peggotty through the locked door. When she answers his question about what will be done with him, however, he doesn't at first hear that he is to be sent away to school for the education he so craves. "I was obliged to get her to repeat it, for she spoke it the first time quite down my throat, in consequence of my having forgotten to take my mouth away from the keyhole and put my ear there; and though her words tickled me a good deal, I didn't hear them." Slapstick turns to stylistic parable. So, too, are we regularly tickled by Dickens's words in the absence of audition (though not of course recognition): the open page our version of David's porous closed door. For a moment, that is, the hero is submitted to the source of his own presence to us: the partly engaged tendons of speech production under conditions of silent excitation and muted articulation—what neurolinguistics, in the parallel case of silent reading, terms "inhibited" speech. Call it that tickle or tremor in our throat that generates meaning from the silent sounds of all script.

Elsewhere in this novel, the impact of a writing silently "born in the lungs" and "shaped" by muted mouth can serve David in any number of capacities. And no letting the reader forget it. This is the work not only of Dickens—as the ghost-writing narrator of David's life—but of his silent partnering by the Other Dickens. The collaboration can result in the disclosure of the telling itself, including certain digressive echoes and excrescences less closely orchestrated than in passages like the one cited by Gass, with its almost masochistic verbal scratching at an unforgotten wound. Which is to say that the Other Dickens is readily recruited for the prankish as well as the plangent in this novel. One can get high on a certain dizziness of diction—and not least when the subject is drunken overindulgence. In one of fiction's funniest hangovers, our inadvertently debauched hero wakes to "feel as if my outer covering of skin were a hard board; my tongue the bottom of an empty kettle, furred with long service, and burning up over a slow fire." The queasy prepositional levitation of "up over" is a further strain in the prose itself, derived as if from the scorched tongue's implied but unsaid "s-urf-ac-e" stretched only fuzzily across the echoic run of "*fur*red/*ser*vice/*bur*n*.*" In the very furnace of assonant invention, the tongue of the Other Dickens is on fire here too—or at least heartily warming to the novel's local topic. If the organ of last night's slurred speech is the theme, let it do the work of repentance as well.

There is nothing quite like this syllabic *ur*-gency until, a decade later in *A Tale of Two Cities*, such syllabic smelting is deployed in the unique phonemic turmoil of that novel's frenetic revolutionary setting. And again, it is part of the prose of the Other Dickens's surreptitious poetry that such alphabetic byplay would not be exhausted solely by graphic matches, but further sounded out in silent enunciation. Note how the diagnosed "furnace of suffering" that fosters mass violence concentrates itself—in its "averaging" of more soft vowel sounds than meet the eye—into the near anagram of a shorthand-haunted **frns/sfrn(g)**. This trope of oven-level heat in the repeated mention of "boiling" blood among the French populace, together with its further incendiary result, is still on the mind of the prose a chapter later in the syllabic chiasm of the title "F*ire R*ises," and then at the start of the subsequent twenty-fourth chapter, with its "risings of fire and risings of sea—the firm earth shaken by the rushes of an angry ocean." Not only does "firm earth" enunciate and cancel at once the "firm-er" ground thus washed and burnt away, but the metaphor "risings of fire" all but spells out, when countersigned by the Other Dickens, those upheavals of retribution that put the literal "ire" back in the metaphor "fire" by the self-consuming cross-word flicker at "*of f*ire."

Even in the fever heat of *Copperfield*'s hangover scene, however, the humorous outcome of misery and recrimination, as derived from David's association with the indulgent habits of Steerforth, shows its darker side fairly soon—and with stylistic results that recall the long *no*-ing and *on*-ing of Gass's chosen quotation. For that was a passage that can only be outdone in bitter force by a later searing iteration of the "no" in a broken parallelism that reads almost as if it were a death scene—and which, emotionally, it nearly is. Steerforth has just been revealed in his treachery as being the seducer of Little Em'ly: "Mr. Peggotty uttered *no* cry, and shed *no* tear, and moved *no more*." Across the collapse from two transitive phrases under negation to the paralyzed intransitive, the phonic chain reaction is so marked that the links of grammar (entailing the shift of the "no" from adjectival role to its place in an adverbial phrase) seem tightened like a vise.

There is, of course, not even the ghost of lexical jauntiness here, just the skeleton of its normal flexibility and trick articulations. Yet between comedy and tragedy in this novel falls the pure wordiness of rhetoric given impersonation in a single character. Micawber's manic swings of mood are equally grandiloquent at either pole, pulling out all the stops of his elocutionary spectrum in both misery and elation. Among such effects are the self-soothing periods of that improvident man's spendthrift rhetoric in the matter of forced optimism, whereby something suitably lucrative is always, after much verbal decoration of the thought, "about," in so many words, "to turn up." In a kind of rhetorical two-way traffic, discourse borrows back this effect in the case of a chapter's lightly cryptic title, where David is in fact speaking of himself with the titular phrasing "Someday Turns Up." The fiscally undecided is made good on by the rhetorically overdetermined. Micawber's unexpected arrival resituates and anchors the idiom: "Walking along the street, reflecting upon the probability of something turning up (of which I am at present rather sanguine), I find a young but valued friend turn up." As usual with the ingratiating wastrel Micawber, the turn here is that of phrase before fate or fortune.

"Something Real in the Mouth"

But Dickens doesn't always let the garrulous Micawber speak for himself by way of gentle self-incriminating irony. At least in certain treatments of the narrator's rhetorical alter ego, the Other Dickens can intercede with a syllabically mincing belittlement of the delinquent's prospects. This happens when we hear of Micawber—quite deliberately *hear* of him—housed without the rent money. The news comes in a scene change effected by a self-partitioned phrasing of incidental *it*-forms: "It was a *little inn* where Mr. Micawber put up, and he occupied a *little* room *in it*, par*titi*oned off from the commercial room." Mimetic prose has found here an effect richly fit in the diminutive units of its chopped-up syllabic space. In retrospect, it certainly intrigues me to imagine my preteen ear caught by this nesting of belittled locations (and locutions) in the mouth of the babysitter. Not only a "*little in*n," but a "little room *in it*." At that age, I wouldn't have known a chiastic slant rhyme even if I were to have accidentally committed one myself, but I would have heard the sheer fun of it manifest in the voice of reading.

Such "sound effects" can be more than insinuated; at times they can be directly flagged, inflated, and satirized. So back to one of their touchstones in the inveterate bombast of Micawber himself, as it resonates across the writerly aspirations and oral underlay of the entire novel. When he isn't doing his own talking, plot goes so far, midway in its progress, as to turn itself over to someone else more than willing to speak up for him: the public enunciator of his most typical prose. Once Dickens has delegated to Micawber an unstinted taste for verbal expatiation, that is, the stage is thus set for a further displaced send-up. However much his orotund periods tend to come crashing down like a house of cards in an often syllabically stacked deck (with the proverbial "in short" of his last-minute apologetic candor), Dickens does at one point give him full rehearsed voice by proxy. Here Boz lets his comic character, as author surrogate, set pen to extensive paper in a proclamation against the indignities of debtor's prison: a stirring purple screed addressed to Parliament in the mode of that body's own euphonious formalities. But no sooner has Dickens made his parodic orator a penman than he closes the loop by assigning to this discursive agent a character with no other narrative function than to be the reader out loud of Micawber's writing.

Enter Captain Hopkins, buttonholing any potential auditor. If anyone at all "weakly showed the least disposition to hear it, Captain Hopkins, in a loud sonorous voice, gave him every word of it." This ad hoc broadcast is a form of "publication," of mass circulation—a "giving" in the most direct and tangible mode of transmission. "The Captain would have read it twenty thousand times, if twenty thousand people would have heard him, one by one." Such is the intimacy at the allegorized heart of mass circulation, especially when so much fiction in the Victorian era is circulated in recitation at the familial fireside. And it is this oratorical aura of prose to which the voluble Hopkins, following Micawber, is quick to gravitate: "I remember a certain luscious roll he gave to such phrases as 'The people's representatives in Parliament assembled,' 'Your petitioners therefore humbly approach your honourable house,' 'His gracious Majesty's unfortunate subjects.'" Enunciation proceeds "as if the words were something real in his mouth, and delicious to taste; Mr. Micawber, meanwhile, listening with a little of an author's vanity." That participial addendum brings audition (in replay of composition itself) into an unusual proximity with recitation, so that the "mouthing" of expression seems to extend, as if by way of inferred generalization, from any writing to its reading—immediate or eventual. But what even Micawber can't hear—the characterized writer in this return toward an originary sounding of his own speech en route to transcription—is the undervoicing of narrative presentation in its own right. On the heels of Hopkins's "loud and sonorous voice," this involves the quiet rhyming of discourse and dialogue across such an echo as "sonorous" and "honourable," to say nothing of the purely discursive (and recursive) aftertaste of "luscious" in the consonant/vowel cluster of "*such* phrases." The Other Dickens is having his infatuated say along with the good Captain, while in the process turning over the very metaphor of "taste" on grammar's tongue with the slippage between infinitive and prepositional phrase in "delicious to [the] taste."

So unexceptional is this episode that the scene may be called primal. Words are indeed real in the Dickensian mouth. And when delegated to their readers in turn, their sounds are as redundant to sense, as palpable a surplus, as is the very phrase "to taste" after the self-sufficient adjective "delicious." This mouthing of words, this delectation, had once been scourged by programmatic fasting on David's part, limbering him up for the pursuit—hot pursuit, phrase by phrase on the frantic wing—of just the kind of parliamentary oratory that is unleashed here as Micawber's borrowed specialty. Between the petrified phonetics of David's shorthand ordeal and the inflated (breath-borne) sonorities of Micawber's self-pleasuring syllables, then, is released—as discovered by an almost explicit triangulation in this one novel—the true Dickensian undersong. Such is the open secret of the Writing that a closer look at the stenographic occult should help make apparent.

If Dickens's favorite novel is a story about learning to write, it is also a story—or more like a parable—about learning to read. At two levels: for the hero, for us. This happens from the ground up, as modeled obliquely on the acquisition of a tongueless alien script. What David Copperfield calls the "stenographic mystery"—that ordeal of literacy in the contemporaneous shorthand code—is a challenge to whose difficulties both Dickens and his quasi-autobiographical character must submit themselves in their early careers as parliamentary reporters. In the long run, however, the tribulation was as fertile as it was infuriating. Posing at once a hurdle and a springboard for the novice author as writer, the code's at first daunting puzzles amount to a chain of reductive conundrums in which, most prominently, encrypted word husks are gutted of anchoring central vowels, leaving only flanking sketchy consonants in the form of graphic strokes and squiggles. But the code's enigmatic thicket of indicators, its darkest graphological "mystery," is in fact twice *solved* across the imaginative gap between struggling apprentice technician and eventual renowned novelist: once by David's mastery of it, like Charles's before him, as a rite of passage from bafflement to scribal efficiency; and once, ever after, by the detected traces of the code's dis-solution, indeed its sustained antithesis in lexical repletion, across passage after passage in the typical momentum of Dickens's abnormally fluent and openly voweled effects.

The novel's account of this stenographic test of linguistic agility is justly famous—and for more than its autobiographical insight into Dickens's early work ethic. As every biographer and critic recognizes, given the public rhetoric that the shorthand is deployed by David to record, the ordeal of stenography calls up not just the hero coming of age within the arcanum of a paraverbal code but Dickens's own saturation, there at the House of Commons, in the oratorical stretches, the labored flights of phrase, that he was later to mock, travesty, or revamp. As no commentary has noted, however, the novel's send-up of stenography also operates by tacitly evoking a whole range of stunting shorthand effects that a later novelistic prose, especially when tweaked by the Other Dickens, is meant—and sometimes bent out of expected shape—to rectify. Such are the phonic blockages, once so strenuously inculcated in the shorthand regimen of elided vowels, that later give way to vocalities obtruded through every pore of Dickensian prose.

What David stresses, when recalling his stenographic apprenticeship, are precisely the graphic challenges in deploying the code's alien ciphers. Gone unspoken, or perhaps left unconscious, are the deficits incurred in regard to verbal energy itself. And if left unconscious, this is another way of saying: left to the Other Dickens, elsewhere and otherwise, to excavate, vary, and maximize. Centering attention on the translinguistic process involved, the episode about the shorthand regimen begins as follows:

> I bought an approved scheme of the noble art and mystery of stenography (which cost me ten and sixpence); and plunged into a sea of perplexity that brought me, in a few weeks, to the confines of distraction. The changes that were rung upon dots, which in such a position meant such a thing, and in such another position something else, entirely different; the wonderful vagaries that were played by circles; the unaccountable consequences that resulted from marks like flies' legs; the tremendous effects of a curve in a wrong place; not only troubled my waking hours, but reappeared before me in my sleep.

And the autodidact's nightmare continues, inducing a personification of the very "characters" he must commit to memory:

> When I had groped my way, blindly, through these difficulties, and had mastered the alphabet, which was an Egyptian Temple in itself, there then appeared a procession of new horrors, called arbitrary characters; the most despotic characters I have ever known; who insisted, for instance, that a thing like the beginning of a cobweb, meant expectation, and that a pen-and-ink sky-rocket, stood for disadvantageous. When I had fixed these wretches in my mind, I found that they had driven everything else out of it; then, beginning again, I forgot them; while I was picking them up, I dropped the other fragments of the system; in short, it was almost heart-breaking.

That last "almost heart-breaking" is a burst of an unusually undecorated candor—symptomatic, in just this confessional way, of the inner turmoil caused by the disenfranchisement of the young Dickens's own verbal facility when stretched on such an unforgiving rack of unnatural word signs. But, as if testifying to full recovery in the very act of retrospective lament, the passage is, of course, exemplary in its own stylistic turns—well before anything it may help turn up about the deeper wellsprings of Dickensian writing.

The fact that the hint of a cobweb spelled "expectations" doesn't need to anticipate Miss Havisham's web-infested Satis House to aim the whole passage forward toward shorthand's stylistic antithesis in the novelist's later full-bodied alphabetic sound play and its syntactic complements. There is, first off, the "twinning" grammatical figure (hendiadys) in the phrasing "noble art and mystery of shorthand"—rather than, say, the more logical (if still sarcastic) "noble and mysterious art." This is what that past master of ambiguity, William Empson, long ago noticed as the slightly disarticulated "A and B of C" in Shakespeare's most intensified rhetoric, far more relaxed and even comically slack here in Dickens—but to which rhetoricians would still give the name hendiadys ("one from two").[3] This swelling of substantives marks an expansiveness that, at a different scale, the compression of shorthand's artful mystery forbids—even as such an honorific dilation smacks of exactly the parliamentary circumlocution that David will soon learn to glean by stenographic means for the newspapers: "Night after night, I record predictions that never come to pass, professions that are never fulfilled, explanations that are only meant to mystify. I wallow in words." Wallow, that is, in all their insistent wordiness—except, most prominently, for those internal vowels disappeared by the shorthand method in question. For if David were encoding this complaint stenographically, rather than discoursing on it in the narrative present, he would have executed the even purer chiastic distillate (the mirror inverse formed by an *abba* structure) for his present alliteration: a ciphering of his chosen verb in the cryptographic equivalent (as soon to be detailed) of a tongue-tied **wllw**.

Before achieving his remunerative station in the journalistic ranks, David's learning curve has been, as the second segment of the above quotation makes clear, as steep as its backsliding is precipitous. The phrasing "I groped my way, blindly," offers a symptomatic and potentially crippling hyperbole in a process that has subordinated the phonetic to the ocular or graphic, the aural to the visual, requiring thereby the keenest eye for visible signage. Instead, while still struggling for some unblinded clarity in regard to the system, David is beset by a supplemental set of personified (rather than legible) "characters" as new and fiendish enemies, those "despotic" figures that stand, like strict hieroglyphs, for whole long words. With no link to phonetics whatever, the very need for their acquisition confounds at first the main stenographic regime of vowel-suppressing consonant brackets shrinking real but abruptly denuded words. Yet that constricted syllabic effect is exactly what mention of these merely graphic signals summons by contrast, which makes David's initial complaint in the first sentence of this recalled self-tutelage (driven as he is "to the *confines* of distraction") seem doubly fit.

Such are the cramped and muting routines whose effects would seem modestly evaded in retrospect when, after his hero has accessed that "Egyptian Temple" of the code's ramified Rosetta stone, Dickens has David write, not "there appeared" these new seditious "characters," these barbarities, but instead "there th*en* appeared a proc*ession*" of said antagonists. A light cresting of oblique assonance (*en/e/on*)—all of it foreign, except by inference, to a vowel-evicting stenography—thus inclines the ear toward a more rhythmic, a more *processual*, force than any simple *p*-alliteration ("appeared a procession") of the sort shorthand's stressed consonants would have no trouble with. Wordiness in retrospect, if that's how one takes the minor expansion of that noun phrase, becomes a recovered function of *wordness* itself—in even the most modest shape-making possibilities of its internal recurrences. It is the kind of effect perfected (to give instance along with principle in those last two words) in a later and entirely noncomic hendiadys—yet with its compact sound play equally derived in avoidance from the wearying "art and mystery" (rather than artful mystery) of shorthand—in a compound like that describing the "abiding-place" of a personified Hunger in *A Tale of Two Cities* (1859). Amid its many other manifestations, the weight of starvation resides (with not even "offal" available for scavenging) in a phrasing linked by *f*-alliteration to an assonant slant rhyme that thickens the description of a narrow street "full of off*ence* and st*ench*": a pairing that binds effect to cause, reaction to instigation, in the echo chamber of extremity.

Assonance is the truest clue to the stenographic legacy. Lurking there, even at the heart of that fullest narrativization of the author's shorthand training ("then . . . procession"), is a hint of what its various early restraints may have bestowed on so much of the fictional writing that comes after this early enslavement to sheer place-holding graphemes. It's not only that genuine debts of influence (like Shakespeare) get heartily repaid in later writing by Dickens, but that strenuous indentures are redeemed by renounced constraint. Illustrated by that most modest of internal off-echoes, for instance, in "wallow in words": a brief burst of vocalic libido. Such, I'll be steadily guessing, is a matured yearning for all that the young Dickens, and David his delegate, had once learned to check by encryption, to clamp down on by erasure—and all that the Other Dickens ramps up in the aftermath. Even phonetically constrained, what was once "a wallow in words" (to give David's verb a nominal heaviness by back-formation) is all but unrecognizable in its later mutations. The wearying labor of shorthand, centered on the need for compressed traces and tactical erasures, is destined to slough off its constrictions in becoming the flourishes of a marshaled revel in sound forms when allowed their wholesale release.

Put it this way: the Other Dickens, scourge of any such discipline as that represented by shorthand strictures, stages the vehement refusal of all that the pre-Boz Dickens has to keep at bay—or in abeyance—in order to maintain the pace of stenographic transcription. Once having mastered it, David, speaking as well for his author before him, dismisses the epithet "noble," for its "artful" mysteries, by writing instead of the "*savage* stenographic mystery." The Orientalist overtones of that first adjective (mocking a system as exotic and primitive as it is ferociously arcane) complement that nearly "Egyptian" fortress he must scale—and the unsaid *hieroglyphs* that have stood in his way. These, of course, the modern reader can, if interested, reconstruct from the history of short-hand method. In doing so, our discoveries are immediate. For what the quasi-phonetic rules elide in the service of speed is literary texture itself. By an inference so roundabout as to be a contravention and reversal of the whole stenographic premise, this is what I find the Other Dickens more eloquent about than either David or his Author.

In any case, one thing is certain. A demanding convenience (often called "phonographic writing" in Victorian parlance) depends, in fact, on the evacuation of certain letter sounds by a minimalist phonetic code that transfers only the least resonant functions of the alphabet to jots, dashes, dots, and loops—while dropping the vowels that would spread them out and give them breath. David and Dickens join forces in being very funny about this in the passage we've been considering, lampooning both the method's native difficulties and its unique monstrosities—even though not all the peculiarities of the system explicitly emerge there from the skewer-ing. The Other Dickens waits in the wings to help sound out, in resistance, the further principles of the system in their very decimation by Dicken-sian style. This routinely occurs through a delivered uprush of phonation across the lineation of script: an enunciation that might seem to mourn the onetime fate of the vowel by the unstinted resuscitation of assonance in various subthematic patterns.

Subthematic, yes, but often with a low-keyed mimetic emphasis in their own scaled-down right. The crux of the stylistic irony that attends David's discourse in this way (if irony is the right word), descending from his for-mer stenographic challenge, is highly charged, carefully framed, and stra-tegically timed. When David finds himself waxing Micawberish—florid and mawkish at once—in a letter to Julia Mills, his confidante, about Dora, his fiancée, the logic of cause and effect is reversed in suggesting that the speech of an invented rhetorician has influenced the style of his narrator, rather than the other way round. This wrinkle of obverse causal-ity is, in its narrative placement, entirely topical. For it isn't just from long exposure to the "smoothly-flowing periods of [Micawber's] polished and highly-ornate address," nor from Micawber's rising to parliamentary high notes in the formal document of protest doted on by Captain Hopkins, that David has inherited his new tone. The contaminating source is more immediate than this, since the ornate letter is inscribed in the very chapter that begins with David's effort, by parliamentary practice, to master the reigning shorthand method of the day, as outlined in Thomas Gurney's *Brachygraphy* (unmentioned by name). David's own effusive prose thus triangulates the sonorities of public rhetoric and private style via this new training—all en route to the same journalistic career that Micawber will himself eventually enjoy and that Dickens, having survived it as novelist, bequeaths to David for the interim before the hero's own fictive energies take flight.

But that is only the beginning of the issues implicitly bridged in moving from a labored shorthand of mediation and report, in David's training, to the fervid, indulgent, and self-preening aurality of epistolary address put under comic scrutiny in Micawber's case. Besides the minutiae of transcription in the Victorian stenographic norm to be discussed below, broader linguistic issues are also implicitly summoned in the novel—with Micawber their embodied flashpoint. The Latinate Micawber would be nothing without his "stipendiary emoluments" and his "domiciliary accommodations." Unless reinflated by full-bodied verbal transcription, his phrasing, his wording, would suffer as much from shorthand compaction as the newspaper and parliamentary flourishes it emulates. In contrast to the civilized profusions on which the rhetorician in Micawber plumes himself, stenography, even if not "savage" in the ethnographic sense, does imply a barbaric denaturalization. But it is not Voice that is ransacked thereby, but only the phonetic engineering of lexical entities. Whether attending to the One and Only or his Other, or usually the two at once, the emphasis in these pages is never a question of personified speech. The page transmits nothing audible of this sort, nor emits it. Elicits is more like it. So the "issue" is not Authorial Voice but authorized phonetic intuition: a speaking in no sense *to* me, but only *through* me. The full aurality of this is what stenography (in its etymology as "narrow"-writing) tends to stunt, truncate, close out, shut down.

Scholarship is well aware, has in fact virtually mythologized, the impact on Dickensian style of his adept stenography, but mostly, as I say, by linking this mastery to the author's later parody of political bombast and the general fluency of his own periods, rather than to anything specific in the matter of requisite vocalic elision—or its later recuperative dilation. In a broader cultural context of gendered Victorian stereotypes, critic Ivan Kreilkamp has suggested that Dickens's flair in the transcription of parliamentary sessions—his stand-out gifts for this mere clerical work, this strictly secretarial writing—defies the clichéd feminine gift for passive attention and renders stenography a bravura assertion of heroic (and thus masculinized) public energy. So the contemporaneous record might seem to suggest.[4] But beneath the ambitious mastery lurks, for Boz, a kind of phonic castration. In any case, there is another tale to be told as well, less of oratorical bravura by osmosis than of a later recuperation across the silent sinews of prose style: a return and amplified ramification of the once-disavowed vowel.

Questions of docile passivity versus showy virility quite aside, the apprentice writer's labors in the House of Commons, day in and day out, can't help but have placed a strange premium on exactly what was dropped away in his rapid shorthand craft. The man whose talk is modeled on what Dickens heard there—the oratorical Micawber, whose mouthed syllables are, as we know, explicitly "delicious" to the taste, delicious to tongue—reflects a linguistic disposition offered up as countermodel to the shorthand that was deployed to take down its like in the House. With all sonority submitted to a prolonged starvation diet by stenography, its resurgence in the fiction can seem like one long compensatory indulgence, feasting on what another kind of graphism once held fast against. And when not comically deployed in narration's own intonations, the effects can be targeted as a satire of rhetoric itself. The prosecuting lawyer in the trumped-up case against Charles Darnay in *A Tale of Two Cities*, for instance, takes delicious relish in accusing him of "pernicious missions"—as if there could be any other kind, or any other epithet for them, in such a calculated denunciation. Oratorical cadence has, in short, a long afterlife in the novels, with Micawber's speech patterns only an early part of it.

Voided Vowels

Certainly far more seems at stake in the shorthand tutelage of David and Dickens than just a practiced ear for parliamentary color and expansiveness in the general brand of rhetoric transcribed. Whatever Dickens learned (and happily forgot) of encryption's "mystery" on his way past reportage to fiction, the Other Dickens has retained like a kind of negative imprint. The vowels discounted by the consonant brackets of shorthand, in the interest of compression, are restored and multiplied—say, extended by the trailing aura of assonance—in the novelistic longhand to come. Dickens the satirist learned the inflations of bombast firsthand, even as he muted them in his lightning notations; the Other Dickens, if only later able to make good on this in full-blown echoic patterns, was all the while tutored under constraint in the eventual ballooning of vocalic pattern within—and across—the ridges of script.

But this career-spanning difference, this tension between certain excised phonemes and their restored prominence, also follows a timeline far narrower than Dickensian writing's long and evolving commitment to either the quiet or the high-strung sonorities of prose. Even in the throes of the "stenographic mystery," rejected vowels have to be reinjected in the very process of decryption. Phonetic material must be wedged back into the glyphs of reportage, to turn the dictagraph of the pen back into the textual reproduction of speech on the page. This constitutes the greatest hurdle of all, as David's temporary impasse makes clear. On first try, even after much practice and escalating confidence, he can't keep up in Parliament with the actual momentum of rhetoric. More home study is needed. But having eventually prided himself on being able to follow his friend Traddles in a decelerated recitation of such oratorical rhetoric, he then confronts, disastrously, the very chasm between writing and reading on which all communication, let alone all style, depends.

Everything has been going swimmingly, he thinks, in regard to the graphic dots and dashes of this complex cursive telegraphy. But when the time comes, it is as if there is no one there, certainly no cognition, at the receiving end. Lines of scrawl confront him, but they haven't achieved the status of a known language. The notes would seem to annotate nothing, for "as to reading them after I had got them, I might as well have copied the Chinese inscriptions of an immense collection of tea-chests, or the golden characters on all the great red and green bottles in the chemists' shops!" At this point, in the intended utility of self-reading, the scribble that might as well be pictograms or chemical formulas leaves him no way back to the sounds it may or may not—who knows?—have properly encoded. He must start all over again in the effort to read back from mark to articulate sound. In a more particular way, this is what the Other Dickens never stops doing—by teasing us to do.

The broader our sense of these ultimate reverberations of the stenographic episode, the nearer we come to appreciating, in their aftermath, the once-impenetrable molecular abstractions of the shorthand method. That strained decoupling of writing from reading is the key. By the first achieved stage of his heroized writerly career, in getting public rhetoric into mass newsprint on a salaried basis, David (as seen by contrast with his early fumblings) has had to become in his own right a conversionary *medium* for speech, enciphering a variable path between sender and receiver. Even in his subsequent turn to fiction, this condition of text production never goes away. It is only the lag time that narrows, so that the emergent novelist in Dickens was to hear what he himself composed even as he wrote it (Gass's point again: "listened to while it is being written"). As inventive writer rather than automatic recorder, he thus decodes script with a keen ear for the underlying vocality that spawns it—and that, in stenography, used to yawn mute within the unmarked valleys between consonant peaks. Another way to conceive this, from our historical point of vantage in the *techne* of inscription, is to note that "word processing" as such is nothing new, with shorthand only a case of inordinate technical "compression." On the tympanum of the literate ear rather than on the cursive, stenographic, typeset, or backlit page, all wording is microsoft: fast, fungible, and evanescent.

For this reason, the more closely we imagine our way back into that nest of graphic twigs, clue-withholding curlicues, and vowel-free clefts faced by David Copperfield in his crisis of self-illegibility and balked reading, the clearer a sense of comeback we might entertain in the auto-auditions of the Other Dickens later. We know, for certain, the primer, the textbook, from which Dickens worked, quite apart from whatever euphonic finesse it might have served to sponsor in recoil for his own subsequent books. As noted, the stenography manual purchased duly and rather dearly by David, anticipating the exorbitant work required by its method, was implicitly (as in fact it was, biographically, for Dickens) the Thomas Gurney volume called *Brachygraphy* ("short writing"), mainstay of shorthand craft from the preceding century, its latest revision by his son Joseph in 1825.[5] It is essentially, like all variants of stenography, a minimal graphic coding of phonetic speech by strokes and curves, stressing the definitive consonant framework of words and filtering out the internal or "medial" vowels that can be derived—or, we might now say, reverse engineered—after the frantic moment of recording.

"Stenography" ("narrow" writing) was the generic term in Dickens's day as well, but the Gurney volume used the older designation. Nomenclature aside, the "mystery" consisted in the "savage"—and phonetically ravaged—shortening of words from the inside out, their narrowing in the middle so the structuring absence could be bracketed by slashes, swirls, and dots. This rule of elision included most prominently the internal suppression, along with the lateral truncation, of vowel markers. It is, indeed, the implied "narrow" squeeze of stenography (as opposed to the merely "short" writing of brachygraphy) that is etymologically more to the point here, in regard to those vowels *sqzd* out of script (exactly as Gurney might have illustrated the process for beginners) in deference to their ready inference in later decoding. Such is the narrowing work of a spatial, and hence temporal, contraction—a speed writing—that amounts, in acoustic terms, to the scouring obverse of literary assonance, especially in connection with what the linguist Roman Jakobson tracks as "nuclear phonemes" under the sign of their "poetic function" in recursive schemes.[6] Or, otherwise: under the sign of prose poetics—and thus under management everywhere, or at least covert manipulation, by Boz and the Other Dickens in cahoots. In broad cultural terms, brachygraphy represents a kind of

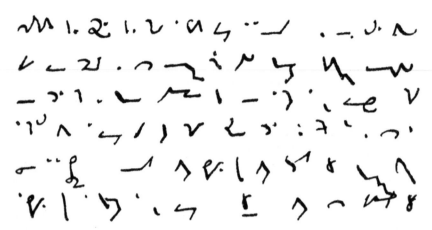

Figure 1. Page 68 from R. E. Miller's *Lessons in shorthand on Gurney's system (improved): being instruction in the art of shorthand writing, as used in the service of the two Houses of Parliament.*

Miller's 1884 *Gurney's System (Improved)*, from Rider University's digitized books. Louis A. Leslie Collection, Rider University. Digital image copyright 2011. Identifier: Z56.G87 M55 1884.

millennial reversion: lapsing as it does—through the expedient priority of its consonant indicators—to a voiceless state before what Roland Barthes saw as the ancient Greek "miracle" of vowel signs introduced into the inherited Phoenician alphabet.[7] In this sense, Gurney and company are found leveling what once elevated writing toward the embodied pulse of speech.

Stngrphc Mdls

Models or Muddles? That is the STeNoGRaPHiC question. And it all depends on the syllable-grounding vowels suppressed in their MiDDLeS. So, before lending an ear to how this mining of once-buried phonic matter might work itself up and out in prose fiction, a more detailed look at Gurney should give one a sense of the anti-Dickensian cramp of such notations. For it is only by sustained inversion of the shorthand method that the pattern of evicted vowels is upended, at which point such alphabetic sounds can be returned to new dominance in novelistic word chains, submitted there to recurrent subliminal transfusions across equilibrated syntactic spans. In the terms of Jakobson's poetics, recall the vowel nucleus of a phrase like the one we earlier lingered over from *Martin Chuzzlewit*—where the abstraction of "sanguinity" seems phonetically as well as semantically inflated to a fissuring break point in order to

generate the very phrase "s*anguine* to *ins*anity." If it seems like the bulking up of an overstuffed lexical portmanteau, it might also be thought of
a "concertina." (To this metaphor, not my own, I return in a moment.)
The lexical process bears immediate comparison, for instance, with the
later Victorian transformation—in a poem by Thomas Hardy called "In
Front of the Landscape," about the remembered dead and their revenant
visualizations—that first twists a normative adjectival "ashen" into the
macabre "*ash n*ow" and then reverbs the unspelled core term further into
the chiming telescopic expansion of "with *a*(ngui)*sh*." In his shared revi-
sionary debt to Romantic sonority, the Other Dickens can often be recognized in this way as performing the poetry of Victorian counterpoint
itself.

To do any justice to intuition here in working back to plausible causes
outside of literary history, however, I'll need to offer my own shorthand
version of the brachygraphic system: a kind of halfway house of ab-
breviated signage making clear its general tendencies in retained alphabetic indicators. The point of departure, codified by the tutor text from
Gurney, is clear. Consonants block breath, vowels expend it. Typically,
this contrast is routinized in language—until submitted under duress to
what one might call the shutter speed of stenography. Gurney himself
gives alphabetic renderings of his "essential" phonetic "reductions" before translating them into nonlettered shapes, including the words **esnsl**
and **rdxn**—all so as to **cmpr** (another of his instances) such accordioned
consonants with the mere graphemes (upstrokes and down, curves and
miniature full circles) of his code. (To sample the method once passed
from an illustrated principle of reduction to its actual swifter instances
in nonalphabetic jotting, one can find many of his cuneiform-like
markups on the web.) Gurney would be the first to admit, though,
the lurking potential for uncertainty—as when the thought of *camper*
or *compeer* above, for instance, would derail our insured recognition
of *compare*—in anything but a close consideration of context. In the
intuitions of decoding, a difference like that between *despise* and *dispose*, say, cannot be dispensed with just because it is ambiguously rendered in the brachygraphic equivalent of the alphabetic **dsps.** (with that
period-like dot as punctuational placeholder for the missing final *e*, in
one of those "changes rung upon dots" that maddened poor David).
Dickens learned all this painfully; David transforms it to comedy; the
Other Dickens makes it a mainstay of later slant rhymes—caught halfway between eye rhymes and genuine echoes while proliferating everywhere in the inertial momentum of prose's syllabic sequences. And
finally, such coded compressions surface again—not from the memory
banks of expertise, but from the underside of illiteracy itself—in the
young Pip's halting letter to "Jo"(e) in *Great Expectations*, with its

cryptic salutation "BLEVE ME INF XN PIP." There, the letter-form enunciation of alphabetic characters at "eff ex" helps spell out "affection" against the more normal phonetic onset of "infection," which is, in fact, closer to the noxious premonitory truth about a coming change of heart in Pip's exit for London. It is as if this deserted forge-side affection were actually predicted by the homophony of "leave" as well as "lieve" in the (also rebus-like) *b*—for "be"—of the doubly misspelled "bleve."

Years before *Great Expectations*, when David bemoans the frantic variability of those infuriating "dots, which in such a position meant such a thing, and in such another position something else," he is no doubt referring to the way final vowels in a word—sometimes silent, of course—are indicated by different positions of a mobile pinprick ink mark abutting the previous consonant at one telltale height or another above the line. In my simplified sketch of this, however, or of its implications rather than its actual execution, I'll simply continue putting that pesky "dot" at the end to evoke this disappearing act of the understood final vowel. In contrast, internal vowels typically drop out altogether, unmarked among their determining consonants. Thus might the resonant core of a word suffer itself to be *deleted* on the stenographic page—/or *dltd*, or, more to the point,/ \ll\, given that *d* is distinguished from *t* only by the slant of a single backstroke for the former (\), as against the upright stanchion (l) of its "dental" (its tooth-tongued) counterpart. Note, therefore, that the word *dote* would be distinguished (barely) from *dot* roughly as follows: \l. versus \l (with English lexical competence filling in the blank). Concerning the rippling aurality of Dickens's own prose, recall the unnamed woman from *Copperfield*'s opening page, who—though buying David's caul at auction, with its rumored protection against death at sea—thought the better prevention was never to leave shore and so "never drowned, but d*i*ed tr*i*umphantly in bed, at n*i*nety-two." The tongue-tipped bridge at "di*e*d *t*riumphantly" (\\ lr) only further latches the internal buckling of those long *i* phonemes ("d*i*ed tr*i*") in the mention of her achieved landlocked apotheosis.

Nearer at hand, in the very passage about stenography, we can almost detect its fossil forms in witty resuscitation. In the first stages of his trial by cryptographic ordeal, we hear how David is galled by the staggers and fits of his dimly personified "imbecile pencil" (the epithet transferred, or displaced, from its wielder) in not being able to keep up with the parliamentary flow. On alert from the historical record in the matter of brachygraphy, what's to keep us from hearing, in just David's way of putting it, an undertone of phonetic liberation from the **imbcl. pncl** of those former exactions—and their phonic excisions? And what then? Might this not suggest further that the searing memories of stenographic discipline run deep enough in the Inimitable himself, as tweaked by the quietest surprises of the Other Dickens, that some of Writing's best flashes of inspiration in this novel, and others, can be felt to descend, by rectification, from its once-curtailed phonetics? To grant as much is to help stave off any sense that the Other Dickens is not, in fact, the one most readers might indeed readily recognize in the fillips and flourishes of the One and Only. In assessing Dickensian sonority, one would never wish to say, of course, that a recoil from stenography was the long and the short of its motive. But just as the method's vocal gulfs, its gutted medial vowels, could only have informed the writer's sense of diction's inner valleys and ridges, our recalling the method's alphabetic compressions aids in gauging the opened-out contours of echoism and its like in the shaping work, whether reverberant or more covert, of both Dickens and his Other.

One critic, Douglas-Fairhurst again, does analogize the Gurney experiment to Dickens's descriptive habits at large, but just so: at a scale a good deal larger than implied here—a matter of descriptive "style" but not of word forms, or word formation—despite the fact that the same critic elsewhere, not in his role as biographer, has shown his own keen ear for phonetic accordion-play in that "how/l" passage from this very novel.[8] In his alternate focus on the young Dickens, rather than the young David, Douglas-Fairhurst quotes Gurney's sample sentence (in alphabetic characters rather than shorthand strokes) from a parliamentary speech, with all but the necessary disambiguating vowels dropped out. Yet in his "mst al dply afd w so s los" (62), the powers of alliterative association (or perhaps just an ear for cliché) would be needed to reconstruct the epithet "severe" when the phrasing undergoes decompaction as "must all have been deeply affected with so severe a loss." For Douglas-Fairhurst, the modeling noted in such recovery actions takes this form: "Learning how to 'concertina' writing in this way appealed to the side of Dickens that enjoyed extrapolating stories from tiny clues, or from pictorial details in the real world, while having the confidence to skim over those parts of it that did not merit a second look" (62). The parallel is ingenious and in its own right convincing, but for me the "parts" at issue are more linguistically particulate. Certainly skimming over missing word sounds was scarcely Dickens's way—but rather filling them in with a relish ("something real in the mouth") for tapped possibilities and harmonic repletions. Not just in scenic elisions or more expansive rhetorical expansions, then, it was this still-phonetic way to "concertina" such undue stringencies, to unfold or accordion the syllable itself, that made for the subsequent performance art of Dickens's insistent verbal play.

At Dash Speed

But more than this familiar richness of vocality—comic or not, but always a little "funny" even when not overtly festive—also lies latent in the matter of a negated (or recalibrated) stenographic legacy. Beyond the strategic and complex elision of most medial vowels, set off by a differential inflection of the consonant-indicated graphemes that close down on them, there is another main contributor to speed in stenography's compressed transcriptions—especially valuable in getting down the maundering elaborations of the House of Commons. This we have touched on already in anticipating those narrow channels of water-treading repetition with which Dickens often makes so merry, Micawber's written address to Parliament included. In response to such dilatory iteration, the extra feature of economy in the Gurney bag of tricks depends on the elision of whole words and phrases in a manner uniquely serviceable in the grips of that rolling parliamentary oratory (loosened, recursive, self-perpetuating) whose cyclic variations are to be honed later, when not openly lampooned, in the striking anaphoras of Dickens's fictional rhetoric. In an important convergence of critical perspectives, here then, especially, is where the often-cited debt of Boz to elocutionary cadences might well meet head-on the overlooked internal dynamics of the shorthand system mobilized to record them in telescoped form—a meeting, in this case, that highlights their shared vanishing point in a silent speech deferred to eventual unpacking in the reading act.

It is therefore time for another actual illustration from the shorthand bible on hand. In sample ellipses, the Gurney primer weighs in with a grandstand iteration waiting for compression: "Whatsoever things are honest, whatsoever things are pure, whatsoever things are . . . ." That's Gurney's example of a parallelism (technically, again, an anaphora) to be dispatched with long elliptical dashes, once the auditor catches on to the mechanics in play, of course. Again, in this light, we can find in *David Copperfield* the return of the suppressed in fancier dress. What Dickens in reportage learned to bundle by reduction, Dickens in the parallel editing of syntactic montage learned to unfurl again with a commanding snap. Try this, for instance, as written about the misery of the brutal Murdstone regimen: "What meals I had in silence and embarrassment, always feeling that there were a knife and fork too many, and that mine; an appetite too many, and that mine; a plate and chair too many, and those mine; a somebody too many, and that I!" Grammar refuses to give way in the end to the immediate alliteration of the more colloquial "many, and that me," but instead holds out long enough to round out the long *i* of the three first-person possessives ("m*i*ne"). Yet isn't it likely that the very inspiration for the syntactic sweep of this passage might have sprung to mind, in collaboration with the Other Dickens, from the verbal synapses of a former Gurney student? On this model, imagine the flesh of David's rhetoric at the moment of its gestation on grammar's skeletal bones: "What meals I had in silence and embarrassment, always feeling that there were a knife and fork too many, and that mine:—appetite—, and—;—plate and chair—, and those—; a somebody—,—I!" Once install the template, and the iterated "that mine" is mechanically rotated through the series until achieving its assonant rather than alliterative variant in "that I." What the remembered stenographic brevities of such schemata might have suggested in generating this passage, to Dickens and his Other at once, is that even the bitterest of routines can be reduced to abstract pattern, lamentory flow to cognitive grid, with misery routed through the imitative treadmill of syntactic constraint. And rectified in retrospect by just such expressive dexterity.

Then, too, there is a further inference lurking here about parallel phrasing in the novels, as such prose was once short-circuited by the ellipses of stenographic abbreviation—cutting off the cadence in its first detection, leaving the informed decryptor to fill out the framework with only hinted iterations. As it happens, in that same early passage about the Murdstone oppression, we encounter another variant of Dickens the veiled autobiographer speaking through David his first-person surrogate—even while the Other Dickens, as emancipated erstwhile stenographer, is arranging for certain linguistic wrinkles to be voiced through the "phonography" of both. Again there seems hovering in place a certain recognition of a shorthand logic when we hear a dental consonant clicking its teeth around what would otherwise have been a swallowed vowel. For while the ongoing parallelism of a tacitly exclamatory "what" ("What meals I had in silence . . .") continues from the preceding paragraph, this time the prose hits a wall of its own mimetic impasse: "What evenings, when the candles came, and I was expected to employ myself, but, not daring to read an entertaining book, pored over some *hard-headed, harder-hearted* treatise on arithmetic." Thus does **hrd-hdd, hrdr-hrtd**—as if generated (dental bumper to bumper) from its even more schematized form as **hr\-h\\ hr\r-hr**—enact its own insistent dead-ending of desire.

Such impacted iterations, skimped on by the elisions of Dickens's early stenographic expertise, but always latent nonetheless—lying in wait for expansive deployments, as above, in the coming prose of the novels—can seem all but archetypal in the semantic slippages and collisions of the Other Dickens. Indeed, chapter 3 will contemplate briefly, amid various manifest extravagances and their stronger probabilities of influence, a quite indirect way in which stenography's most efficient expedient—the linear ellipsis of the mere dash—might come back to haunt, or taunt into deeper irony, the disrupted seriality of the novels' comic compounds. Such are the blurted diversions (every sense, grammatical and comic) of the Other Dickens, as brought out in the prose's most characteristic bravura tricks with serial grammar. Here, however, we are working still at smaller scale.

Nuclear Reactants

What we've noted linguist Roman Jakobson calling, among his many "figures of sound," the "nuclear phonemes" of certain poetic patterns is precisely what goes unwritten in shorthand, which treats only initial and final vowels by standardized marking, as discussed, and lets the swallowed openness of sound in the medial vowels gape unsaid between consonants. The parliamentary diatribe that would lambaste an opponent, via kindred attributes fused by an elongated and chiastic *u*, for his "obdurate and ruthless" stance on an issue (**.bdrl. & rthls**) releases its sonority to the underscore of the Other Dickens in just such a phrase as that. So it is that we find Dickens contrasting the false impressions generated in just those paired words concerning Mr. Jorkins in *David Copperfield*, the silent partner of Mr. Spenlow. Jorkins is eventually recognized, instead, by alliteration and a looser assonance, as "a *m*ild *m*an of *h*eavy tempera-*ment*." If taken down in shorthand rather than imaginatively concocted for the page, the bonded temper of the last two words, their togetherness, would be sunk to silence in stenographic code, awaiting the return of the suppressed *eh*-mphasis only in decoding.

And the minor syllabic chiasmus of the vowel-tuned *ur/ru* in that compound "obdurate and ruthless" can, at full phrasal span, have far more pointed thematic results in later novels. *A Tale of Two Cities* lights a slow fuse for this in a minor assonance that quite figuratively ignites, in full detonation, only later. In the underlit streets of a destitute Paris, a "feeble grove of dim *wicks* swung in a *sick*ly manner overhead" — including an explicit premonition of the mass revenge that would one day see as many aristocrats hung from these same stanchions turned to gallows posts. The Inimitable, recognizably enough. But later in the same chapter, the sickly wicks, fanned by energies other than Boz's unmistakably ingrained assonance, mutate further into an urban demographic register conveyed first of all by rhythm per se. This transpires syllabically when Lucie and her father are driven away across disyllabic prepositional contraries, "*under* the feeble *over*-swinging lamps." The immediately following grammar of the next paragraph devises a mimetically flickering assonance broken only by comedown in the last monosyllable and its noneye chime: "Und*er* the *over*-swinging lamps — swinging *ever* bright*er* in the bett*er* streets, *ever* dimm*er* in the worse." We follow, after the dash, that fading *ver/*

ter/ter/ver/mer/wor sequence through a kind of fragmented tracking shot across alternate precincts of wealth and destitution as the phrasing pivots grammatically on a phonetic chiasmus ("over-swinging — swinging ever") cued less to the music of transit than to the beat of history as destiny.

The aural syncopations of the Other — or say, the enhanced sprocket clicks of syntax itself — are in perfect service there to the immediate shot plan of the cinematic Dickens, as they are at smaller scale, as well, in the metrical tick-tock (or swing-song) of a watch's "sonorous sermon" earlier in the novel, with something of the same pressure building in the thematic of a revolutionary time coming. For Mr. Lorry's admonitory watch seems to beat out an ingenious memento mori of its own when, in a cadenza of chiastic syllabics that pivots across the threefold "ity" rhyme ("gravity" / "longevity" / "levity") with a more elusive see-saw of vowel sounds, his inexorable timepiece "pitted its gra*v*ity and longe*v*ity against the lev*-*ity and e*v*anescence of the brisk fire." No sooner does "levity" wriggle itself free from "*long*e*vity*" than that four-syllable lexeme of duration is answered and thinned by another fleeting four in "evanescence." Mimesis is no more rarefied here than it is unmissable. And in the ultimate syllabic gyrations of revolutionary carnage, as far from the phonic frolic of Dickensian comedy as language can come and still be doing its job as lingual invention, one suspects the ghost of Gurney at work in some of the novel's strangest phrasings: evoking, for instance, not just the prison's "horrible smell of foul sleep" but its amplification a sentence later by the jolting, multichannel synesthesia of "noisome flavour of imprisoned sleep" — where the stertorous stench (**nsm:** noisome, or nosome?) can almost be tasted ("flavour") — and then elsewhere, too, in the even more arresting grammatical implosion (and vowel displacement) of the fiendish wood-sawyer's maniacal "See my saw!"

One can audit the larger issue of such "sonorous" synchronizations this way: the cognitive premium on vowel sounds, deduced from the blanks of shorthand, now seeking its return, at the level of Dickensian longhand, as a recovered chance of prolonged echoic (and often mimetic) aurality in the forward momentum of narrative prose. While the motives for journalistic reporting that first sent Dickens (and David after him) to Gurney were of course financial, the results, as we've begun to see, enter into a broader stylistic economy in the fictional Writing to come. According to its checks and balances, the discounted vowels of the stenographic system, squeezed out by the "narrowing" ("brachy-") frame of consonants, return at a new pitch of iteration — and compound interest — in the rolling vocalic dividends of both the rhetorical Dickens and his alphabetic Other. In this way does the "vowel nucleus" enter upon its own atomized and assonant chain reactions across the detonated phonetic flashpoints of a given phrasal series.

To stress this here, in connection with the vocalic stintings of stenography, is only to note how the imagined damage done to a Shakespearean soliloquy or sonnet by the expulsion of vowel sounds should help us conceive the ground Dickensian prose had to regain—however effortlessly—once released from the deafened trenches of brachygraphic discipline. Just contemplate, in "to be or not to be," the manhandled, dash-marked parallels of **lb. or nl**—, with the dash-marked elision of the second "to be" pointing up a momentary syntactic doubleness in Hamlet's own halting speech. For he has already posed what seems the self-sufficient antithesis of "to be or not" before, by way of counterforce, the subsequent precipitous ligature of "no*t to*" (**nl l.**) kicks in—toppling forward into the famous second *be*. Or think (without hearing the "oh" refrain) how the throttled drive of **lmrw, &—,— —** would elide three sets of escalating medial vowels in the phonic terracing of Macbeth's to/mor/row speech, to say nothing of its phrasing's already mimetic evanescence in overrun via the merging **an\ l** ("and t-") forms. A Dickensian equivalent seems likely. The crash course in Shakespearean "speechifying" we know to have been under way at the same time as the young Dickens's court-reporting assignments might well have made Dickens's Gurney-schooled service there, and later at the House of Commons, seem in hindsight (or hind-sound) all the more straitened and denaturalized—and all the more completely to be overthrown by a fictionally unprecedented onset of vowelization in the novelistic prose that later emerges. And so to reiterate: in the inner auditorium of print fiction, it is the frequent subversive role of the Other Dickens to aid in outplaying the once-strangled core of wording with what can only be called at times, with Shakespeare in mind, a truly histrionic assonance. Here, then, is prose—recovered from the choke hold of sheer mark—intoning itself to the gallery for all to hear.

To treat such matters, if we're so inclined, like a time-travel adventure across collapsing temporal nodes in Dickens's career, it is as if—once vacuumed into the medial black holes delimited by the linguistic event horizons of marked consonants only—the imploded zones of the vowels are extruded again years later and distributed across the tenacious assonance of a new fictive force field. But no need for such an overheated metanarrative of stylistic evolution. Indeed, the main point to be made needs no causal narrative at all. Suffice it to say that at one point Charles learned to write without major vowels while at the same time combing his Shakespeare, and then quickly thereafter began to write that other kind of script (neither stenography nor dramatic poetry) known as prose fiction, and from then on achieved the prose brio we recognize in his full-blown (forget mature) style. Just to bear these relations in mind contributes to the issues at play in the verbal crossfire of sensed influence and linguistic intuition that reading Dickens elicits—and that *David Copperfield,* its hero taking us back to the very scene of remembered verbal consternation in the grips of brachygraphy, so readily exhibits.

All this convergent aural self-consciousness, along with its tempting explanatory trajectories in the progress of the writer, recalls quite directly that matrix passage on the "noble art and mystery" of reduced and denuded phonation. For in David's complaints about its byzantine and "savage" rigors, the most telling point, as noted, is that even when our hero thinks he's on the verge of mastering the speed writing, it turns out he can't read a word (back out of its scribble). It isn't language at all that he's writing, just lingual code. Language is instead the saturated context for this inset satire, where even the most minor tilling of phonetic soil—in fairly inconsequential instances of phonetic play—keeps the ground fallow for more daring incursions of assonance rising to the surface of the legible script in dramatic transaction with the mind's ear. If so, the soil can be fertilized with the most ephemeral and furtive instances. In David's besotted fascination with Dora, the romantic comedy of sexual fixation may seem to trigger the verbal libido itself in the indulgence of its own compulsions: "Dora was talking to an old gentleman with a *grey* head. *Grey* as he was—and a *great*-grandfather into the bargain, for he said so—I was madly jealous of him." The real "bargain" here is largely phonetic, and pays itself back in kind—even as it seems to be servicing yet again that long-term negative debt to Gurney when, against all tactical "narrowing" of the brachygraph, the **gr. h** of "grey head" condenses across two fully sounded monosyllables into the **grl** of "great"—all in the blur of a misplaced jealousy figured as a kind of aural suspicion.

If shorthand was once for Dickens the shortchanging of all sounded language, it entailed as well, so we've noted, the imposition of undue demands on the mental ear in its subsequent decryption. The scratches and hatchings of the code represent the gatekeeping of the consonants, not the muted explosions of the nuclear vowels. Stenography is the stand-in for palate, tongue, lips, and glottis, not for the pathways of throated air, shut tight by its unremitting economies. One is tempted to say that the Other Dickens never lets the Inimitable forget what his writing had once been reduced to—instead, celebrating its freedom at every chance, as if from within the vestigial brackets of its remembered former constrictions. And we are further tempted, therefore, to call up the Other Dickens when noting even the most minor obtrusions of vocalic nuclei, as, for instance, with the five-syllabled insistence on "uncongenial" brushing up against the monosyllable it describes when the dreaded Miss Murdstone presented an "uncongenial *cheek*" in greeting. Think the nonalphabetic equivalent of **ncngnl chk,** where everything is missing that would, once reinjected by the translating eye and ear, make for the withering rightness of that epithet/noun pair.

Some nearly subliminal moments, however, even passing ones, are more thickly orchestrated and densely resonant, evincing the true sinuous instincts of the Other Dickens at their most adamant. Early in the novel, still at the misnamed (because deserted) Rookery of David's first home, shadowed by the prenatal death of his father, the sounding oscillation between inscription and its described scene cues us to the peculiar "burden" (in the musical sense) of "some *w*eatherbeaten ragged old rooks'-nests, burdening their higher branche*s, sw*ung like *w*recks upon a stormy sea." The prose line, in subtending lexical boundaries, has more lilt to it—and more alliterative ring—than mere spelling might seem to actualize. For in the seesaw of syllables, the *w* takes an extra breath when the mention that "some" nests in "higher branche*s, sw*ung like *w*recks" is directly evoked by ligature in the prose's own swing-song rhythm. In the process, the "some/ung" oscillation only buoys (by varying) the figured nautical thrust—as if by some free association with "crows-nests"—across the cresting *rag/wreck/ rook* pattern. Again Gurney in reverse: the Other Dickens regurgitating once more those swallowed vowels of pure phonetic reduction in **rg wrk rk.** By a further stretch of the narrative imagination, one might sensibly wish to find prefigured, in just this phrasing, the means by which the deserted domestic nest at the Peggotty boat later, abandoned by Little Em'ly in her amorous flying of the coop, will result in two deaths by shipwreck (one fulfilling, by way of nomen est omen, the symbolic fate of the morally rudderless Steerforth). Or maybe not. Always the reader's call. Yet if all this may indeed be supposed weighing on the writer's encompassing mind in an early elegiac turn, it is certainly the extra strokes of Writing, at the hands of the now phonetically untethered Other Dickens, that bring this immediate figuration to life in the evoked local color (and vacillating half-tones) of a transient seafaring simile deployed to render memorable the scene of paternal loss, long before the familial separations and resulting later deaths. No need to overallegorize the *collapse* from makeshift home to ruin within the phonetic bracket linking "*r*ooks's-nest*s*" to "*w*reck*s*" to find, in this aural falling off, a calculated fit with the evoked mood.

Note how different in affect, yet how comparable in phonetic tenor, this is to David's later timidity in approaching the Dover household of his aunt, where, rebuffed by the maid, he "was on the point of going away, to think how I had best proceed." Stepping back to go forward, okay—good enough, until he thought better of the wording. For David through Dickens—and this in a rather atypical revision at the manuscript stage—shows his own stylistic pluck (and latent heroic destiny as man of words) by introducing a half-comic internal rhyme instead of the flat-footed "going away, to think." With the almost mimetically entwined revision of "slinking off, to think," it is as if cogitation were harbored in the very verb of retreat. In the double temporal vision of this novel—abandoned child under the lens of the accomplished writer he doesn't even yet aspire to, but already is—here, then, is the Young David, wordsmith in embryo, biding his emotional time until the right nurture might present itself. Here is the novelist waiting to break out across just such linkings—and slinkages—of phrase as he can slip in. In the process, words are already doing their own thinking for him. One is of course grateful to Nina Burgis's edition for noting the manuscript fix in this case.[9] Yet once other favored stylistic instances are checked against the footnotes—in this case, as well as in the sifted manuscripts and proofs of other novels—our awe can only be compounded when realizing how rare it is that these little niceties of phrase, and the serious zingers to boot, actually derive from second thoughts. It is frankly astonishing how many of Dickens's best things don't get fiddled with, but hit the page straight off—at least after conference with his Other in the compositional mind's ear.

In direct contrast to any such links and kinks in the chain reactions of vocalized prose, stenography narrows the field to lexical markers without the music of speech on which its decryption still depends. With the Master exercising his overarching control, the Other Dickens is forever unearthing the tacit concatenation of speech sounds in prose. I spoke early in this chapter of the "openly voweled" effect of such writing. It is the "open" sound of the vowels themselves that this entails. And in being released from the prison house of speed-facilitating code, they open onto each other as well as out, feathering together across the dovetailed pace of script. After the "short writing" of *brachygraphy*, that is, come the lengthened-out and slowed-down energies of a convergent rather than suppressed phonetics. But what, then, can we make of the stunning disclaimer in chapter 43 about David's particular script? No reader could have expected this, even as it comes brushed by the long-standing clichés of the "found manuscript" in the framing of fictional dissemination: "I feel as if it were not for me to record, even *though this manuscript is intended for no eyes but mine*, how hard I worked at that tremendous short-hand." Surely it is only the "tremendous" compression of the full phonetic register in stenography—rather than anything in the language of the serial fiction we're in the midst of—that is intended only for the scribe's eyes, where it requires reverse transliteration back into "vocalized" script. In another sense, of course, that is what reading, even silently, accomplishes in the more general case—and what a published novel institutes.

The Auditory Warrant

Further, why wouldn't it be the case that the vowels once taken for granted in that shorthand transit, syphoned off from lexical code, might well return in fictional prose by way of a recursive impetus that spills over from word to word—rather than being drained, as before, from each word in turn? Posing that speculation more pointedly yet, as we've implicitly been doing: might not the onetime trauma of aurality be therapized by later play? Certainly, after the former hollowing out of vowels, prose has often seen them come hollering back, or at least whispering, in new silent groupings along the line. After such strictures in the rigorous concisions of brachygraphy, we might want to say (in Jakobson's terms) that the formerly shorn vowels can seem almost militantly renucleated in even the quietest turns of phrase. The economies of elision are reversed in a teeming repletion, not offsetting or redemptive in any deliberate way, but nonetheless—if only at some unconscious level in the drive of Writing—speaking back to a once-straitjacketed syllabics with defiance and abandon. That back talk is the signature sound, beneath the flair of character and plot, of the Other Dickens.

So let me bring together two last examples, from early and late in the novel: atmospheric passages that mark David's Shakespearean sense of a father's ghost, on the one hand, and that, on the other, mature him toward becoming a potential father in his own right with his second wife, as his love for her gradually takes focus. On the way to the lyricism under scrutiny in the next chapter, spurred by Graham Greene's evocation of it in *Great Expectations*, consider, then, the first of these two loaded moments of aurality in *David Copperfield*. It comes upon us as if triggered by David's mother reading aloud from the Bible in the "doleful" best parlor where mourners had once gathered, the boy's been told, for his father's funeral. In one of the novel's present-tense recursions to a past never fully put behind the narrator, there is this: "One Sunday night my mother reads to Peggotty and me in there, how Lazarus was raised up from the dead." Continuing in the present-tense (and presently felt) enunciation of memory's not wholly shed anxiety: "And I am so frightened that they are afterwards obliged to take me out of bed, and show me the quiet churchyard out of the bedroom window, with the dead all lying in their graves at rest, below the solemn moon." Not just "under" earth but "be*low*" a "*sol*emn" cosmic oversight, where, beyond that unvocalized graphic link, the irrelevant etymological nucleus of "sol" for the parent sun, antithetical here, is still within the orbit of the unsaid yet embedded *mel*ancholy of the scene. With that richly Bardic "solemn moon" (further remarks at the start of chapter 2 on this "sequestered" legacy from Shakespearean theater and sonnets alike), more than just such a middle space—between eye and ear rhyme—rounds out, in a Dickensian lexical economy, this picture of the moon in its emotional fullness. In Gurney, we would have to endure the eclipsing pictographic equivalent of *slmn mn*. In the Other Dickens, we help produce a ballooning from within of solemnity's objective correlative—or say, the "concertina" spread from syllable to substantive. The fact that growing attuned to such back drafts and undertones in reading the Other Dickens thrusts one further into the kind of curious graphonic syncopations that make "b/elo/w" seem to the eye a better preposition for "s/ole/mn" than "under" would be is all of a "secret" piece (more soon) with the aural oscillations of everything from "hard-headed, harder-hearted" to "solemn moon." And at this point of syllabic investment, who is to discount the diurnal microdrama by which "moon" may seem released—freed up from lexical eclipse in the phonemics of *sol/mn*, with its ghostly etymological hint of solar impingement—by the doubling and upward pitch of its own inner quasi-hieroglyphic *o*?

Near the book's end, we come upon another delicately piercing example from a novel that frequently reprises David's learning curve in such wording. It is an example detached from any immediate context in the shorthand gauntlet described much earlier—even while fulfilling it via a generous redemption, in the economic sense, of style's incurred debts (if debt is quite the word) to a former phonetic suppression. In David's return to Canterbury and Agnes (with all the influence by which she seemed to "pervade" the place), description moves, across a single paragraph, from "airy voices" of birds in the cathedral towers—making them "more retired than perfect silence would have done"—to the airy phrasing of a perfect prose silence floated on internal rhyme. For "everywhere—on everything—," as the ineffable calm of Agnes is felt to descend, "I felt the same serener air, the same calm, thoughtful, softening spirit" that Agnes has always radiated, with the second comma momentarily installing "calm" as a noun, in a rephrasing of "serener air," before it is adjectivally diffused into the rest of the evocation. Indeed, after "everywh*ere*," there is just that moment's breather until the airy breath of silent harmony is thematized again in the uptake of "ere" by "air"—and by the harmonic re-description to which it leads. And just before that subsequent evocalization (the folding over of "ah" and "ough" onto "oft" in "calm, thoughtful, softening") brings phonetics unmistakably to the fore in an unscribed prolongation of the sound of "awe" itself, the very idea that this phrasing unpacks, in apposition, has a way of naming the silent expenditures of aspiration that produce its rarefied emotional air. The adjective "serener" has been not so much a transferred epithet for David's dawning affect in regard to Agnes as it is a testament to her distillation of the entire peace of the scene via the almost Miltonic overtones of a phrasing like "serener rare." In "phonographic writing," by contrast, the phrase would be scraped out by the stylus in an approximation like **srnr. r**, thus losing the beautiful—and almost graphically visible—chiastic balance of the three-*e*'d "s*e*ren*e*r."

In auditing these phonetic inferences of the Other Dickens, the list has been woefully partial, but suggestive at least in its variety. Obdurate ruthlessness, ragged wrecks of rooks'-nests, a solemn moon, figuratively serener air, to say nothing of those imbecile pencilings so thoroughly addled by their task, or, for that matter, poor David's burning tongue as if furred with undue service, and of course the "sanguine to insanity" send-up upon which, earlier in the introduction, we zeroed in: these are the fervent and assertive returns of phonetic lettering from within the ongoing service of words. From what unnatural regimen, in the trials of stenography, these letters return intact, we've amply considered. With what true force that return is accomplished remains a question demanding one more attempt at generalization—and the further examples that await, of course, in later chapters. We know that "phonetic shorthand" worked to shortchange nothing so much as the phonic place of speech sounds, leaving only the diagrammed infrastructure of their interplay in traced difference. And we have wanted to know what difference this might have made for Dickens the writer in the long run.

As usual, David the novelist sheds his characteristically indirect light on this. As soon as his inaugural book, his unidentified version of *Sketches by Boz*, renders him financially independent, it frees him first of all from the reporter's grind. With an adroit play on the personified *windbags* of the House, he is happy to announce that very soon thereafter he "noted down the music of the parliamentary *bagpipes* for the last time." Insisting that "I have never heard it since," he admits, however, that it lingers cited in the newspapers still, where, with a typically sensitized assonance and dental (teeth-tapping) latch, the "ol*d d*rone" (as if in dissonant chime with the shaded-off *o*'s of "note*d d*own") returns in just such evolved "music" of the Dickensian turn. The dismissive monosyllables thread together as one slurred and belling monotony, but only so as to vouch for the force, yet again, of that negative stenographic training-ground for the generative invention of Dickensian prose. As made obvious in the prominence of those linked, tongued *d* sounds in ol\ \rn., as well as in nl\ \n, the definitive English vowels I've been stressing as first casualties in the onslaught of brachygraphic compression only symptomatize in their absence—whenever orotundities are "noted down"—the wholesale ban on linguistic enunciation in David's gruelingly acquired scribble.

How a budding fictionist might have stocked both his word hoard and his syntactic arsenal by eavesdropping on the stentorian politicos is no surprise. But how the greatest stenographic reporter of his day became the most phonetic novelist of the century has required attention at a different scale. Dickens can't be said to have taken down those public debates word for word. He had quite literally to ob-literate their words on the way to temporary storage in code. As such, brachygraphic process is decidedly extreme: as alien at first as its procedures, when reversed, can become eventually reacclimating—and intensifying. Before that, however, all normal aggregation of the English alphabet had to be unlearned under the tutelage of an arduous code that inculcates at the point of decryption, nonetheless, a fresh lesson in English words: a lesson in Dickens's case residual, persistent, and enlivening. As the dissevered and pulverized lexicon is re-membered (in subsequent transcription) according to the stems and affixes of actual syllabic speech, wording thus comes into new relief in its differential constitution. And is highlighted as such in David's case, tacitly, by the plot itself. To this end, when David's first book-length publication is read by his "old friends," they are said, in effect, to translate its typographic code after their own fashion, and thus to "read my book as if they heard me speaking its contents." It is as if David, in replay of Dickens, has invented a personalized system of phonetic transcription all his own, literary rather than clerical. For the actual sound of Dickens's voice, of course, not to mention David's, we have no such vocal touchstone as claimed by his fictional circle of readers, no such aural memory trace. All we hear is our own voicing, along with the undertones of the Other Dickens, in prosecuting the text—including all those inward sighs of relief, so to say, that breathe life back into syllabification.[10]

And sometimes scramble it in the process. Phonetic centers of gravity are certainly among the playthings of shadow phrasing, time and again, in such prose. So vigilant in the matter of vocalic contingency is the Other Dickens that he can even play on the Master's own name. A passage demolishing the Romantic pretensions of literary nature worship in *Our Mutual Friend* stresses almost obsessively how the "grating" and "sawing" spring wind—shaving and shredding the cellulose debris of London into a worthless "paper currency"—is not the work, with its chiastic epithets, of "gentle spring ethereally mild, as in Thomson's Seasons, but nipping spring with an easterly wind, as in Johnson's, Jackson's, *Dickson's*, Smith's, and Jones's Seasons." With the fivefold series deliberately thickening the possessive sibilance there at the end as a kind of alphabetic stunt, still any personal witness meant to clinch this demotic sentiment only slips in by way of the phonetic anagram that records \ksn's for \kns's. Earlier in this last novel, as less a joke than an intensification of visuality per se, there is the more easily misread graphic anagram unfolded from the consonant scaffold of **trd** in comparing the eyes of Mr. Venus, the taxidermist, to the "over-tr*ied* eyes of an engraver"—so that the very sound of things too-long *eyed* has spectrally appeared, as if by optical fore-image, in the suppression of *tired* by its given causal form.

All told, the wholesale dialing out of sound in "phonographic writing," to adduce again a Victorian term, and the need for voicing it back in, may put one in mind of Paul Valéry's characterization of poetry as "a prolonged hesitation between sound and sense": an internal insecurity turned to an aesthetic hovering (or balancing act).[11] In view of what stenography clamps down on, we might say that the resultant prose poetry of the Other Dickens, streaming beneath larger spans of discourse, is the sometimes "hesitant" delay of sense (a comprehension slowed rather than just oscillating)—or, alternately, the suspected residue of such sense at play in the *betweenness* of the sounds themselves. After Gurney, that is, only when vowels are retrieved to inhabit again the lexical shell of encryption can the words be put back into full intonation, jarring or harmonized—and in either case sparring against each other with no holds barred.

And the more discrepant—as well as outrageous—the evidence, the better, a reader of this chapter might agree. Moon-drenched and *moon*-wrenched solem*n*ity is the outlier rather than the rule in Dickensian rhetoric, whose lyricism is typically marginalized by farce and melodrama alike. But unlike the decided comic bias in the deliberate surprises of splayed grammar to be sampled in the third chapter, the afterlife of shorthand in vocalic restoration would seem to crop up everywhere, cutting across all facets of narration, from caricature to melodramatic ferocity, satire to sensationalism. The resurgence of vowels that may be thought to result, however disruptive, is extraordinarily evenhanded in this respect—scribed by the underhand script of the Other Dickens in any given mode of prose event. Even Boz must sometimes barely have known what hit him. Two final examples, then, at the far poles of deflating comedy and impending tragedy—and at the far edge of either stylistic tact or logical coherence. Though it is surely happenstance that each bizarre enunciation involves an anatomical appendage as well as a phrasal extremity, it is no accident—once granting the incorrigibility of the Other Dickens—that writing like this should emerge, should be virtually exuded, under the comparable pressures of satiric animus or violent dramatic impact. Though only the dire comedy of *Hard Times* (1854) gives discursive credence to a quite outrageous pun, half a decade later an unnerving vocalic gesture in *A Tale of Two Cities* doesn't lag far behind on the roster of improbability.

In the earlier novel, Gradgrind basks in gratification when his star pupil, Bitzer (nomen est omen), has delivered himself of a namesake atomization—this, of the linguistic substantive "horse" as a kind of zoological exhibit: " 'Quadruped. Graminivorous. Forty teeth, namely twenty-four grinders, four eye-teeth, and twelve incisive. Sheds coat in the spring; in marshy countries, sheds hoofs, too. Hoofs hard, but requiring to be shod with iron. Age known by marks in mouth.' Thus (and much more) Bitzer." Note especially the vocalic abutment of "sheds hoofs, too" against "Hoofs hard," since this bluntly colorless iteration has already, if one may put it this way, shed an extra echo in advance, as picked up inadvertently as well (no poet Bitzer) in the phonetic bracket "shod." At this point, no doubt, the "hard" double *oo*'s seem under typical Dickensian control as a kind of tone-deaf mechanical free-association across Bitzer's bite-sized, pulverized taxonomy. Thus (and much more) Dickens, the One and Only. But only the Other Dickens could have anticipated this in so slapstick a fashion that even before Bitzer is called to his feet, we've watched—make that heard—Gradgrind mock the horse rider's daughter Sissie, fresh from her circus world, for her failure to render up her intimate personal knowledge of horse flesh in a language befitting (as Gradgrind has phrased it) "the minds of reasoning animals"—those human "pitchers," as he also calls his students, waiting to be filled to the brim with information. For it is "on behalf"—but not quite—of such creatures that facts must be enforced as facts. At just this moment, every sensible lexical instinct on the reader's part recoils from the biped (or two-syllabled) rear-ending to which attention must now submit. For, instead of having Sissy humiliated "on behalf of" her peers, idiom is caught laughing out loud in the prose describing Grandgrind's snide dismissal: " 'Girl number twenty unable to define a horse!' said Mr. Gradgrind, for the general behoof of all the little pitchers." Behoof! How dare the prose? Thus (and much more) the Other Dickens.

Even after being slapped silly by such diction, one may still not be prepared for an even more macabre oddity in the building revolutionary intensity of *A Tale of Two Cities*. The narrative locus in question—the cultural geography inferred—amounts to a figurative axis joining the most frenetic precincts of the Revolution to a quiet domestic cul-de-sac in London. As rage mounts, the St. Antoine region of the Defarge wine-shop is increasingly personified as a body politic of sanctified uprising, the eponymous saint's very throat hoarse with the litany of injustices, his fateful footfalls unconfined to any neighborhood or nation, but communal in their tread and transnational in reverberation. Even across the Channel, the noise of trouble, and of the saint's vendetta, resounds. Like the spreading news they figure, the "loudly echoing footsteps of Saint Antoine" (the preposition of ownership now, rather than place of origin) collect like a tainted atmosphere in the corner of the heroine's London house, massing in her domestic enclave like the sonic fog of war. Lucie thinks she hears the tramping of doom, that is, even in her deliberate retreat from it.

And what do we hear as a counterpoint to her justified paranoia, given that her husband is soon to be consigned to the guillotine? We hear the Other Dickens at work, in an anatomical monstrosity comparable only to the Parisian beheadings themselves—indeed constituting a metaphoric dismemberment all its own. For these echoing footsteps, as sonic metonymy for the enraged mob of St. Antoine and, in turn, for the national body up in arms—these foreign and entirely estranging sounds—capture and bracket an inexorable progress in their first iteration here: "Headlong, mad, and dangerous footsteps to force their way into anybody's life, footsteps not easily made clean again if once stained red." Several pages later, in the chapter's last paragraph, the scheduled refrain is completed in a single "echoing" footfall of discourse with an internal grammatical adjustment: "For they are *headlong*, mad, and dangerous; and in the years *so long* after the breaking of the cask at Defarge's wine-shop door, they are not easily purified when once stained red." Intensified by that new chiming between adjective of present force and adverb of traversed temporal distance, the tracks of such footsteps map again the violent storming forth of the enraged saint not only upon the bastions of state power but upon the overseas hermitage of the implicated heroine.

But this time, with little hope still of ablution and purification, these tramping body parts have found their metaphoric status warped in transformation. Synecdoche has displaced metonymy: part for the whole rather than the looser association of lower anatomy with forward mobility. For it is now "these feet," not the "footsteps" (as antecedent of "they are headlong" in the preceding sentence), that are, in clambering iteration, themselves "headlong, mad, and dangerous"—as if in some bizarre corporeal inversion (headlong feet!) of motion and motive. And even if the entirely neutralized anatomical figure lurking in the idiom "headlong" (for this frantic and footsore progress) were written off as inadvertent—an accidental grotesquerie under the momentum of this loose-limbed refrain—that would not displace or abate the further, more disruptive aural irony that has just been unleashed by the Other Dickens. To stumble over this is to recognize that while Lucie, in the common sense of the phrase, is hearing things, so are we. To wit (and without the license of any obvious wit to mitigate), we note how the resonant nonsense, or countersense, of the single exacerbated sentence at the crux of this scene, pivoting into the one last quoted, unfolds across its subsidiary alliteration and assonance: "Now, Heaven *defeat* the *fancy* of Lucie Darnay, and *keep* these *feet far* out of her *life*!" Exclamation mark indeed! Blood is thicker than water, and prose than both, in this punning defeat of bloodstained feet.

Why let prose risk such freaks of surreal phrase? Or ask: what is the Other Dickens gambling on in this game of chance, this charade of syllabic false leads? There may be no telling, but ask we nonetheless have to. Crazily uncensored in its own aural phantasmagoria, one wavering valence of this phrasal violence in the dissonant echo of *defeat* (contravening the "fancy" of these hydra-headed headlong feet) may find itself justified by the all but bilingual sense of *defait* (from the Latin *defacere*), implying to *unmake* more than to rout or root out, to vanish more than vanquish. But the martial sense lingers, gathers, and gains sway, in what can only be called a counterrevolutionary turn—where the most militant of defenses may be, just so, to swallow the monosyllabic threat whole (de[feat]): a defiance by narration per se from amid its call to higher powers yet ("heaven").

Or there's perhaps another way to think of this—given the chapter's third iteration of the "echoing footsteps" motif, beginning with the title. It could conceivably fall under the protocols of Dickensian rhetorical extravagance to let echo itself become openly contaminated—in a kind of delirious auditory hallucination suffusing even the passage's own diction. No telling, finally, how the Inimitable came up with this, or let it stand, any more than with its quirky equivalent in the high-stepping "hoof" of *Hard Times*. But we may well guess, or at least this chapter is inevitably destined to do so, what the Other Dickens was disposed to hear in the equal-opportunity deployment of such shameless punning across two such different texts. For embedded there yet again are phrasal shades of the bad old vowel-crushing days. The phonetic differences deduced or reconstructed from such systemic scrawl are subsequently induced upon normal speech rhythms: **bhf;** /fl or \fl—BeHalF or BeHooF; T(h)e FeeT or De-FeaT. If the lexical shoe fits, wear it—at least for the length of a lateral shuffle between consonant brackets. Writing, featured as such in moments like this, operates on its own unabashed behoof. In this way, though here in lexical extremis, has the return of the medial vowel become the very medium of echoism in the dexterous hand-ear coordination of the Other Dickens.

2

SECRET PROSE/SEQUESTERED POETICS

What kind of verbal stealth fails to withhold itself from notice? In the forward current of wording, what kind of secret pact—or compact—leaks by definition from word to word? And what is the effect of such underhandedness when worn on, rather than hidden up, the sleeve of verbal event? I ask in the spirit, or at least in the vocabulary, of a notorious gauntlet once thrown down to Dickens criticism in the passing mention—and lone example—of Dickens's "tone of secret prose, that sense of a mind speaking to itself with no one there to listen."[1] It is an idea long ago lobbed into literary-critical discourse by the novelist Graham Greene—to become the source of a minor cottage industry of speculation ever since. In an essay from 1950 called "The Young Dickens," Greene's vaguely metaphoric emphasis on this cast of writing (exemplified, as it happens, only by the older Dickens)—figuratively, a prose more indirectly *heard* than read—is part of what is so suggestive, yet overgeneralized, about his formulation.

Offering a renewed point of departure for our considerations—since one is always beginning again in taking the elusive measure of Dickens's cagey style—Greene's throwaway insight about one facet of a resonant "music of memory," an inward cadence of rumination, should not take readers of *David Copperfield*'s lyricism by surprise, even though our preceding concentration on that novel took us mostly elsewhere. Beyond Greene's focus, soft as it is, the present chapter is more broadly concerned with effects that one assumes the Other Dickens to "secret away"—in an earlier, more Victorian verbal usage—from moment to phrasal moment. Beneath the bustle and showmanship and verve, these effects texture Dickensian Writing in any mode or mood, from satire to reverie. In and beyond what Greene terms the "secret" (privatized) discourse of memory's "music," or even its dissonance, what his evocation therefore helps us listen for is, in effect, the unexpected reticence, and resident nuance, of the novel's least plot-driven moments—and their internal verbal generators.

I suppose that if Greene hadn't made his opaque sense of the term "secret prose" so famous in connection with the rhythms of memory, it would have been a tempting phrase for the teasing, oblique, sometimes even cryptic (and regularly nonthematic), mysteries of the Other Dickens, especially in those sequestered pockets of prose's own reflexive irony: prose, that is, ironizing its own excess or deviance. These, we know, are the little open secrets bursting through the very surface of narrative description with energies almost counter to it, turned inward on their own oversensitized "memory" of sounds previously emitted by alphabetic signals—and this in patterns of marked, if not always harmonic, recurrence: the jogs of short-term textual memory, one might say.

To the Shakespearean Ear Endeared

But there is a longer-term "music of memory" to which I've several times alluded, well beyond actual allusions to Shakespearean characters and plots. This is the demonstrably probable remembrance on Dickens's part of his saturation in the palpable aurality of the plays and sonnets alike—to whose timbre it is time to lend an ear, lean in, listen up. Examples in Shakespeare that sound "Dickensian" don't prove a conscious debt, of course, but collectively they are hard to discount in any circulatory system of literary-historical phonetics. Anywhere you look, you hear it. Still in memory of David's "solemn moon," one may call up the way Prospero follows one labial off-rhyme, in "so*lemn temple*s," with another in the same speech, "dis*turb*ed with my in*firm*ity," where in the second case the plosive comes first (*b/m* rather than *m/p*). Either phrase would seem typical enough in Dickensian discourse, anomalous most anywhere else in nineteenth-century narrative. Just a little too much extraneous music for normal storytelling.

And of course what writer of prose fiction other than Dickens—and not just when, in parody, modeling his own decrepit Cleopatra in *Dombey and Son* upon her theatrical archetype in a novel emerging in the wake of his concentrated Shakespearean immersion—what novelist could ever have been expected to take more from Enobarbus in this most "purple" (indeed) of consonant and assonant clusterings?

> The barge she sat in, like a burnish'd throne,
> Burn'd on the water; the poop was beaten gold,
> Purple the sails, and so perfumed, that
> The winds were love-sick with them, the oars were silver,
> Which to the tune of flutes kept stroke.

Long *u*'s are certainly a favored sound in Dickens's ear, even when built toward by their "shorter" cousins, as when a character in this same Shakespearean play explains his advice as "a st*udi*ed, not a present thought, / By d*u*ty r*umi*nated." In the book even nearer than *Dombey* to Dickens's American travels with his portable Shakespeare, we read this: "He continued to sit in gloomy rumination by the stove." Cont*in*uous *in* dejection, that is, himself unrelieved by reading amid the clamor and vulgarity of his translatlantic sojourn, the eponymous Martin Chuzzlewit submits to a "gl*oomy rumi*nation" that may also put the reader in mind of one of the great graphic as well as phonetic anagrams in Shakespeare, enhanced in Sonnet 64 by the unmodernized spelling in which Dickens may possibly, at one point or another, have encountered it: when, that is, "ruine has taught me thus to ruminate."

One hopes (in some utopian phonoverse) that Dickens didn't just know this line in its updated spelling. For not only vowel cores, but missing final vowels, would always have had a special extra force for the lapsed Gurneyite in him. In any case, even just by the internalized reverb of "ruin" in "ruminate," the apprentice Victorian writer would have been taught, of course, a further lesson in mutability at the level of phonic nuclei. Indeed, syllabic expansion from two to three syllables in such a splayed-out rhyme is a Shakespearean specialty not likely to be lost on Dickens. These internalized recurrences can stage microdramas all their own. Remember Lady Macbeth apostrophizing her lord in his absence, about the squeamishly self-imposed limits on his ambition, contemptuous that "What thou wouldst *highly,* / That wouldst thou ho*li*ly" — as if mocking, with snidely rolling tongue in cheek (or, rather, flicked against teeth and palate), the intrusive hollow syllable as well as the sentimental qualm. Macbeth's own later complaint is delivered in a similar key of incremental phonetics, though this time across, rather than just within, lexemes, when lamenting that fate has placed "a bar*ren sce*pter in my grip, / The*nce* to be" — as the tensed echo thickens — "wr*ench*ed."

Better yet as speculative precedent for Dickensian aurality in this vein of cross-word blurring — because closer yet to the slippery fiber of woven vocables when reformatted for curious lexical echo in the tugged phonetic threads of the Other Dickens — there is Cleopatra's own military Antony, Marc, not Major Anthony Bagstock, saying of Pompey (across a chiastic reshuffling of assonance and alliteration) that he "hath laid strange courtesies and great / Of late upon me." With a pre-Dickensian abandon, the phonics are here laid on in such a way that the withheld second half of the phrasal verb "laid upon" is not just postponed but almost wholly reiterated by "late upon." The ghost of a Gurneyesque conflation yet again: l\ . . . ll. And then, of course, there is the most famous line of all about Antony's paramour in the play. Enobarbus in testimony again: "Age cannot wither her, nor custom stale / Her infinite variety," the last a phrase used to describe the hallucinatory modulations of landscape in the eyes of the failing Betty Higden in *Our Mutual Friend* ("what infinite variety of forms of tower and roof and steeple the trees took"). Yet aside from (or alongside) the seven-syllable fricative and dental buildup of those two Shakespearean words, it is the metrically determined redundancy of the first "her" (rather than a grammatically cleaner "Age cannot wither, nor custom stale") that anticipates many a shifty mystery in Dickensian syllabic expansions. It is as if the almost imperceptible elongation of "er" into "her" (easily misheard by elision, under the sign of time's great "witherer") is caught performing, in aural fashion, something of the very wilting away, in phrasal momentum, that is put under negation in descriptive terms. The effusion thus seems buoyed by the exertions of a subtle syllabic confusion.

For a more climactic foregrounding of phonemic interplay, listen again to the way Albany's concluding speech in *Lear* releases an enhanced antinomy in its nuclear vowels by varying the trope of biblical payback ("the wages of sin") with a symmetry weighed in the scales of syllabic justification as much as martial justice:

> All friends shall taste
> The wages of their virtue, and all foes
> The cup of their deservings.

It isn't just the aural (and heavily rhetorical) balancing act of "virtue" against villainous "deservings" that "sounds Dickensian" here, but the faux etymological undertone of negation itself in an inferential "de-service" to the Crown. Bracketed by the formulaic alliterative antithesis of "friends"/"foes," the "taste" of adjudicated fates feels conveyed to the ear on the very tongue of enunciation.

By no means last, and certainly far from least, in any roster of Shakespearean hearings to be easily imagined on the part of the avid young Dickens—and never afterward forgotten by his Other—are those that gather to a head in *Othello*. The flashpoint for such audition isn't just the obvious double entendre of "Put out the light, and then put out the light": the kind of straddling grammar that is to become a Dickensian stock-in-trade. Before that climactic moment in the play are sounded certain signal appearances of the victim's name (the etymologically "ill-fated" Desdemona) that are shortened under metrical constraint (as editorial glosses repeatedly have it, and this more often in the First Folio than in later "normalizations"): for meter's sake alone, that is, rather than for morbid punning. This syllabic truncation of the "a" in "Desdemona" operates, so the inference goes, not to install a swallowed play on "demon"—even though that feels almost half intended by the murderous Othello's "Have you prayed tonight, Desdemon?" In any case, the libeled wife's gathering panic at this point, in its choked cadences, seems to trigger its own lexical byplay by anxious free-association: "These are portents, but yet I hope, I hope / They do not point on me." In the phonemic lengthening across the *i/o* repetition "I hope, I hope"—like a ghostly inverted diphthong on phrasing's contracted way from "portent" to "point"—it may well also seem that the aberrant preposition of "point on," rather than the idiomatic point at, has deployed its faint oftecho (*en/on*) with the feared disyllabic cadence *port/en/d* to keep fate at bay in phonetic foreclosure itself.

These last effects are all easily subsumed to, and thus lost in, the basic plosive alliteration of her outcry, of course. Harder to miss are the vocalic ironies that haunt the mutable last syllable of the heroine's name when, even after metrical syncope, it appears by osmosis from a tandem vocable. Such lexical contaminations precede the final pleading with Othello in two alternate ripples of phonetic give-and-take that certainly can't be laid at meter's door alone, since they depend on the ligatures of operable phonetic ambiguity. One emerges way before the murder scene, with Cassius seeking, ominously enough, and here in the Folio version, some "brief discourse / with Desdemon alone"—as if to say, with an adverbial double valence, "Desdemona lone and only." Available as sound play even in the later standardized format that Dickens is likely to have encountered (with the still-sensed aspirate elision of "Desdemona alone"), this giddy little wrinkle has become monstrous by play's end. For such is the excruciating musical dissonance sounded (both rung out and plumbed) when Othello turns a deaf ear to her frantic attempt at exculpation. He does so oblivious no doubt, at least consciously, to the way the emitted sigh (of his own "ah"), if only acted on feelingly, might return to her the full stature of her once good—and beloved—name:

> DESDEMONA. To whom my Lord?
>   With whom? How am I false?
> OTHELLO. Ah Desdemon, away, away, away. . . .

After inadvertently anagrammatizing "Desdemon-ah" in dismembered form, he then strives to put that "ah" of devastated regret out of earshot at the receding threefold horizon of "Desdemon, aw-." It is the essence of the tragedy that Othello won't hear more. Even, or perhaps especially, if the phrase reads (without metrical clipping) "Ah Desdemona away" in the text Dickens would have known, it is the essence of the Shakespearean legacy that the Other Dickens would have been listening in to the phonic omen beneath such nomenclature.

Onward Words

When Othello puts his all but involuntary "ah" so cruelly "away" from recognition, his killing gesture draws its force from vowel flow as the very lifeblood of speech. In just this regard, the last chapter's main proposition was a simple one, and aptly summed by the kind of question one calls rhetorical. Can it be any wonder, after Gurney's audially dulling rigors, that Dickensian prose would allow for its vowels to breathe deep and frequently within the full alphabetic sequencing once denied them? Surely, after the contractions of stenography, writing "out loud" again would have seemed its own breath of fresh air. Yet it's none too soon to enter a caveat about any such intuition, however dearly held I wish to keep it. Nothing in the quirky phonetic exertions of Dickensian wording depends on my hunch being right about their source in overcome stenographic fetters—whether by Dickens, in either subliminal or conscious craft, or by his Other, as liberated scriptor. However derived, direct from the hand of Shakespeare or by recoil from the clutches of shorthand—or from both, of course—the sound play is simply there for the hearing. Everything depends, in the test of response, on the effect of such sounding prose, whatever the cause. To hypothesize one dimension of its impulse—call it stenophobia—is only a way of keeping awake to the volatility of its subvocal force.

This is a force that is often tinged with mimesis, if only because, once noticed along the grooves of plot, it seems naturally enough to belong there. Between *David Copperfield*—which we've seen, at least speculatively, working to fictionalize one secret source of its own prose style in a wholesale suppression of sonority by shorthand constraint—and *Great Expectations*—where Greene (former spy and sometime spy novelist) locates his scant exemplification for the secrecy claim—a middle novel like *Little Dorrit* is full of many stealthy maneuvers in the trenches of inscription, where sound gets a curious march on sense, stealing up on it through the inner ear. Having explored certain ripple effects of the stenographic "art and mystery" in the one novel that satirizes it, we can thus turn to its entirely unspoken (but no less audible) legacy. In stepping back from the particulars of Gurney's stenographs to illustrate the general endearments of the ear (Keats) inherited from Romanticism by Dickens and augmented by his assiduous reading of Shakespeare, we can do so by dipping in almost anywhere. Such phonetic substreams in *Little Dorrit* serve to structure the onward wording of narrative by phonetic microdramas of their own, now minor, now incorporating whole swaths of theme. At the negligible end of the thematic spectrum (in the haste of inner voicing I had here mistyped, originally, and symptomatically enough, the accidental but not inapt "negligible lend") there is no stopping the domino effect of phonetic drift and its mounting syllabifications. Or say, the passed baton in wording's aural relays. In this—and almost any—Dickens novel, at least after *Martin Chuzzlewit*, to be "a lit*t*le *l*onely" is all but inescapably, by vocalic transfer within the same completed phrase, to be "a lit*t*le *l*ow."

Just as, also in *Little Dorrit*, "weakness and wickedness" go together—as if by vocalic cause in its developed effect. In this way do we listen to the listing of one word into another by collusions made audible just under the various taut or loosened fabric of plot.

At the broader thematic level in *Little Dorrit*, the contagion of speculative market investment associated with the corrupt banker Merdle carries its critique over from one word to the next when the bad advice is—by the most insinuating of cross-word inf(l)ection, as if in a subtle stutter of rumor's own re-iteration—"car*ried* into ev*ery ear*." Such is an epidemic of mass fiscal hysteria related to its quiescent opposite in the staid mire of Circumlocution (the Office, as often accompanied by the verbal tic as well), which in its bureaucratic torpor is shown to defy all justification. So it is that its institutional logic is thereby, after a long stretch of actual circumlocution concerning its byzantine functions, said never to be "made appar*ent to* m*en*," where the internal rhyme is quietly abetted by a flicker of dental elision. Victim of this procrustean Office, the gifted machinist and inventor Daniel Doyce is driven to the Continent to realize his engineering plans, for in England the transgressive nature of his genius, indeed his "industry," is conveyed, by a parity of sound as well, when we hear that "in*vention* is on a par with"—is in a lexical sense reduced toward— "*felony*." By contrast to the wonderfully homely "*vigorous clink*" of the engines in Doyce's machine shop back in London, there is the industrial metaphor for the "mill" (the treadmill) of the superficial proprieties embodied by Mrs. General, a social machination that is all of a fabricated piece in being a "trans*cendenta*lly g*enteel* mill" in the very complacency of its leveling sameness. And even in a different mode of lexical irony—in the grammar of unexpectedly shackled grammatical objects (technically, again, syllepsis, with examples awaiting us en masse in the next chapter)—we come upon phrasings that fork in separate directions, doing so in regard to their phonetic (along with syntactic) prongs as well. Note, for instance, the boisterous boys in recess at the Cripples Academy, who, accosting a visitor at one point, "*burst* into *pebbles* and *yells*": both plosives and sibilants obtruded together in their aggressive hiss across the binding *l*-alliteration.

Where can one possibly stop—stop the ears—in picking such things out in the aural lingerings of Dickensian phonics, these little secret pockets of syllabic gradation and dilation? *Little Dorrit*'s is not a prose to make easy any such determination of limits. The novel's organizing site (and symbol) of the prison, in one of its earlier descriptions, involves a de-compressed aurality in "the *string* of people already *straggling* in"—including a further and distended phonetic straggle in the subsequent sing-song shuttle of the "*errand-bearers*." Just before this, in describing the exterior of the prison, we have already heard tell of the outer detritus of nonhuman waste swept by rain against the prison wall, including the personified and also phonically intermingled phrasing (in a play between silent and sounded letters to which Dickens frequently gravitates) that buffets the syllables themselves in "*wai*fs of *stra*w and dust and paper, the *waste* droppings of the pump, and the *stray* leaves of yesterday's greens." The pileup of extraneous debris is thus registered by a vocalic clutter of syncopated long and short *a* sounds amid the more orderly *w-s* pattern. It is as if the real sedimented residue here—and who could doubt it?—is verbal before (otherwise) material.

These descriptive indulgences have turned strained, darker, more melancholy by the time the hero Clennam finds himself imprisoned—but no less phonic in their subterranean charge, their almost subdural resonance in the silent reading brain. This time, the words are clamped tight, inextricable from each other, so that his "*low, slow* fever," from which he briefly emerges on a "*moist*, hot *misty*" day—both these examples easy to imagine as part of a facile exercise in the early stages of a stenographic primer—is anticipated by an assonant contamination, a kind of affective entrapment all its own. This occurs in the phrasing of Clennam's "*dread* and ha*tred* of the place"; the very fear arrived by repetition in the (lexically) fated articulation. Backstory operates in concert with the main plot in just these ways. Clennam is a man, we find, whose father had "no *voice* in his *choice* of a wife even," where the failed speech of desire seems almost mocked by the very voicing of that lack in present echo. And in the brief retrospect on the heroine's growing-up in prison, the summary "this was the life, and this the history" (as if it were recalling the biological/biographical divide in the paired words of "to begin my life with the beginning of my life" at the start of *David Copperfield*) elides "this *the his*—" (shades of the Shakespearean "wit*her her*") into a second redundant iteration of the demonstrative pronoun—with the further suggestion, no doubt, that the constrained life and its diminished history are yet again so much one and the same that they can't evade the stuttering rut of their own phrasing. Even as all these little echoes and skids may be imagined simply to trip off the tongue of the Writing, they may still trip up the reading act with a transferred phrasal self-consciousness.

No details are too minor to garner phonetic treatment by the Other Dickens in such syncopated ways, each a little secret twist harbored and obtruded at once. With *Little Dorrit* still open before us, if there's the least hint of the anagrammatic in a phrase like "*crazy* stair*case*," its audible effects are soon be heard when it "*creak*ed under a *quick* tread." Very much in the vein of shorthand differentiations left over from Boz's Gurney days, the vowels breathed back into one word, to return it to life, can inflate the next as well, as in a character's "ruddy puffiness" of face—where the verbal interface of this representation inherits by association its own phonetic inflation. Or sometimes, on the score of a tacit mimetic charge, the phonetic turn can fail to enact the signified, but quite markedly so (and despite alphabetic links), in a syllabic torsion like that when Fanny Dorrit sits "an*grily* t*rying* to *cry*"—as if the monosyllabic infinitive might all by itself wring tears from the adverb and participle that anticipate it. Such a somatic impulse—borrowed back in this case from its frustrated attempt in the story line and transferred to the corporeal production of the wording itself on the reader's throaty part—is later carried to an explicitly diabolical extreme. Fanny again is the focalizing narrative energy, and we enter her POV shot of Merdle, leaving on foot from his latest (and last) tedious visit, just before suicide. Here the tears of "vexation" ripple and distort (or refigure) her view—as if compounding this cinematic ingenuity of focus with a filmic (quasi-photogrammatic) sense of piecemeal jump cuts sliced up across phonetic texture itself. Filtered in this manner, it is not just the view of the exiting villain that is found shimmering with the prismatic effect of tears, but the warped audio-optics—the graphonics—of the phrasing itself. The result is to render Merdle's receding image, in derivation from the "*vex*" of her mood (its nuclear vowel, that is, as well as its subsequent sibilance), as if he might be, which of course he is, "po*ssessed* of *several devils.*" Can phonetic writing, can the sound of wording, ever be more effective than that—even in effects more or less secretly inculcated on the run? That's all commentary needs to stress in suggesting such lateral sound play as a case of "flicker fusion" (a term from the filmic apparatus) that would, in this pointedly visual instance, have its Victorian correspondence in the oscillatory work of such optical toys as the hand-spun thaumatrope or the slotted seriality of the rotated zoetrope—where process is not quite invisible in the ocular result.

So, too, still sampling at random from *Little Dorrit*, the phonetic substrate can appear equally vexed, at the lower end of recognized motion, for the paralyzed Mrs. Clennam. Only at the end, when the deadlock of her rigidity is broken by the first tremors of panicked movement, do we hear that "a c*urious* st*ir* was ob*servable in her*"—indeed an insinuated "inner" compulsion before an outer mobility. Even her "wheeled chair" offers another curiosity of cross-word enunciation. Sometimes, yes, phonetics can provide an etymological tunnel vision through the mere eye of an alphabetic needle, with "wheeled chair" anticipating its eventual philological contraction into "wheel chair," or elsewhere in this novel, with "ingrain differences" reminding us that such differences will eventually reverse the course of historical compression to become, in more modern usage, the unelided and more passively participial "ingrained."

But while we're at it, and listening again to the "curious stir . . . observable in her" (Prospero's "disturbed with my infirmity" an "ur"-text, so to say), the concept of "ingrain differences" is perhaps a good way to think, further, of the granular "inner" lining of "in her." Or, in an opposite tonality, to account for the way such a preposition can operate in the mode of an advertising jingle when the Merdle investment craze invites everyone to "go in and win"—as if the latter were vocally inevitable in the wake of the former. But the sound form *in* can just as soon undergo satiric modification as a kind of punning thud of retribution, as when the depersonified joke on Pancks's part about the Casby Head, the beaming noggin of his slumlord boss, leads to that hypocrite pate as the deceptive signifier of false advertising personified. In this description, the faux Patriarch is lambasted, by a kind of cross-word hiccup stuck in the craw of contempt, as "an Inn signpost without *any Inn—an in*vitation to rest and be thankful," but whose phonetic bridgework is further undermined by the obtrusive monosyllabic (and plosive) fact that "there was no *p*lace to *p*ut u*p* at." In contrast, when calmed down after his revenge against Casby, Pancks attends the closural wedding of hero and heroine, there is the sibilant and assonant byplay of his "*sin*king the *Incend*iary in the peaceful fr*iend*"—as if with the hiss of remission for a submerged red-hot rage. We may wish to think of this as rounding out, as well, another bout of the Other Dickens's frequent revenge against Gurney in the open syllabic secret of liberation and phonetic revel.

In just this respect, the later novel that Greene himself cites for its introvert "secret prose" is every bit as inclined as is *Little Dorrit* toward the onward topple of syllabic matter, whether with or against the grain of sense, including those cross-word incursions of sound that we will be returning to among the straddle effects called out in the next chapter. The many disarming charms in *Great Expectations* include, in their tweaking by the Other Dickens, such phrasing as the poststenographic expansion of "*lost* its *lust*re" in describing Miss Havisham's yellowing bridal gown. Even before this, the actual exit of the captured criminals in the novel's first episode tones itself down to a rudimentary anagrammar of fixation when "the *p*ri*son*ship seems to be *iron*ed like the *p*ri*son*er." And if the rather obvious effect of this iterative manacled chain of sound seems enhanced by pulling the final guttural "er" into its nexus, this is only the sober version of a farcical phonetic allegory when the volcanic Mrs. Joe erupts with a plosive rumble in raspy address to her husband and her brother Pip, "oh a pr-r-ecious pair you'd be without me"—the sound of "pair" already there in the growl rather than purr of sarcastic contempt. In prose like this, what could a clerk introduced as a "*s*mel*t*er who kept his pot always boiling" possibly be expected to do but "*melt* me anything I pleased"? And what could anyone naturally be said to do in transit from a "*slui*ce-keeper's" but "come *slou*ching"? This is the kind of prose in which familiar adjectival logjams can even find an additional twist—as when the chiming pivot at "oth" redirects the suspected next epithet to a participle in depiction of an "old weather-stained pea-green hammercloth motheaten into rags." And amid the stench of decay at Barnard's Inn, what could finally be extruded as example "from dry rot and wet rot and all the silent rots that rot in neglected roof and cellar" but an erstwhile stenographic baffler like "rot of rat"?

Back again at the comparable decay of Satis House—the name itself, of course, a secret Pandora's box of cryptograms ("Enough house" for the anagrammatic stultifications of Satiety, Status, and Stasis all at once)—there is the cobwebbed epergne on Miss Havisham's decayed banquet table, overrun with insects, both beetles and "sp*eckled-legged*" spiders, where that last spindly eye rhyme tapers off from the tongue-twisting hinge of the hyphenated epithet. A minor touch. The assertive brilliance of the scene, however, is to envision this infestation of spiders as a social network stirred by collective concerns—and thus to embed in comic microcosm, at the center of Miss Havisham's festering desolation, the very world she excludes. But the inserted further brilliance of the Other Dickens is to picture the mildly echoic "blotchy bodies" rushing in and out of this clot of cobwebs "as if some circumstance of the greatest public importance had just"—wait for it!—"tran*spired* in the *spider* community." In building toward those final paired aspirates, the public rhetoric of a faintly parliamentary circumlocution has given the writing just the needed extra space in which to draw its best vocalic—anagrammatic—breath.

Such are quite minor ironies of phrasing when compared, in this same novel, to a semi-literate and unwitting excoriation by the blacksmith Joe, whose tongue-tied articulation in connection with the removed world of Satis House seems answering, at one point, to Pip's earlier Freudian slip in mentioning a plan to visit "Miss Est-havisham." When Joe wonders if she's been "rechristened," Pip insists impatiently that it was a "slip of mine. What do you do think of it, Joe?" He means of the planned visit, not of the telling portmanteau, but what Joe might well think of the slip itself comes out in his own tortured grammar later. In his contorted efforts to speak with propriety in connection with such gentry, his solecism is eloquent when he is expected to be the medium between Pip and, as it were, Miss Tavisham, the chilling fairy godmother linked by false expectation to the better "witch" of a man named Magwitch. Of this spoiled fairy tale we are reminded when the Other Dickens has Joe splutter, in ungrammatical formality across more subordinators than necessary, and as if with his own failed attempt at a high-toned and fastidious circumlocution: " 'Would you tell him, then,' said she, '*that which* Estella has come home and would be glad to see him.' " Even the inadvertent homophonies of dialogue, let alone of descriptive prose, have a hard time keeping the darkest secrets in this plot of erotic bewitchment.

Then, too, in contrast to that previous anagrammatic slant rhyme of "-spired/spider," the same *i-d* matrix crosses between lexemes in another context of recoil (and defensiveness) when Pumblechook, silently hectoring Pip, "*eyed* me severely—as if *I had* done anything to him." In this phrase, the italicized first person lends an extra degree, or angle, of attention to the polarized (yet otherwise secret) linkage of "eyed"/"I had"—as if this cross-word echo were also cross-eyed. Pumblechook is the same bully who later, true finally to the hidden destiny of his name, induces in Pip the wish to "fly at *Pumble*chook and *pummel* him all over," the hypocrite being, no doubt, too obnoxious to be merely "shook." Hidden destiny, was it? Not really. Nomen est omen once more, typical in Dickens—as, for that matter, with the faux promise of Havisham. Certainly this time the "secret," such as it is, has been in plain view, or earshot, from the man's first patronizing physical aggressions against Pip. And there are aural aggressions too, beginning with our first introduction to Mr. Wopsle, who, in lording his would-be preacherly intonations over the assaulted boy, "punished the *amen*s tre*men*dously." The Other Dickens often intervenes at this more oblique angle, rather than in the outright punning of "Pumble" and "pummel" or "that which" and "that witch"— even doing so, as we'll see, in those very different moments Greene has in mind from this very novel. Moments drawing, no less, on that same thickened vocalic texture of a counterstenographic rhythm—as, for instance, in Pip's version of David's "solemn moon": a luminosity absent rather than present this time in the context not of a father's graveyard, but of the clandestine mission to save a father-figure from the gallows. At a turning point in the plan to spirit Magwitch away, the conspirators have time for "a little counsel" under cover of a darkness evoked in its own semisecretive channel of slant rhymes, for "night" was, by convenient symmetry, "*fast fall*ing and the moon, being *past* the *full*, would not rise early." Prose alone seems to have opened the needed brief window, phonetically hinged, for the scene of action.

Internal Reverie: Chord Changes of Memory

Without deigning (and certainly without laboring) to pinpoint his sense of the phrase "secret prose," Greene does seem to have something more specific in mind than his lone example might evince. Secret? Encrypted? Or just private? What does the adjective really wish to evoke? It isn't easy to say, because Greene doesn't. He simply alludes to a self-evident "music of memory" in *Great Expectations*, with its "delicate and exact poetic cadences," a music "that so influenced Proust."[2] It amounts, somehow, to a special kind of secretive transcription—and here he sums up and shelves the point—meant to capture the rhythm of "the mind speaking to itself with no one there to listen." No one? No one *else*? Or, in a more radical sense of self-evacuation into text, no one left there at all on the scene, at the site of articulation? It takes a moment to ponder this, since Greene doesn't do it for us.

But another moment of potential clarification—and intertextual association—first. The seeming hyperbole of "secret" (rather than *introspective*, say) for the timbre of such burrowed monologues has, quite possibly, a certain further provenance—and thus a curious reverberation when applied to the Inimitable by a former British spy. Quite apart from his own undercover history, however, when this modern novelist writes so cryptically about language unlistened to in this one high Victorian author, it's easy to imagine that he has the formulation of another Eminent Victorian in mind, John Stuart Mill, when Greene moves in similar terms to distinguish, one might say, the Poetic (or Proustian) Dickens from the Rhetorical Dickens, let alone from the Narrative Task Master of high-voltage narrative prose. With a glancing apology on Mill's own part for what he flags as the facile rhetorical finesse of his own distinction between rhetoric and a preferred verbal poetics, this Victorian arbiter of literary taste nonetheless influentially cordons off the audience for eloquence from the eavesdroppers upon the inward work of verse. This is the ubiquitously earmarked passage from Mill's "Thoughts on Poetry and Its Varieties":

> Poetry and eloquence are both alike the expression or uttering forth of feeling. But if we may be excused the seeming affectation of the antithesis, we should say that eloquence is *heard*; poetry is *over*heard. Eloquence supposes an audience; the peculiarity of poetry appears to us to lie in the poet's utter unconsciousness of a listener. *Poetry is feeling confessing itself to itself, in moments of solitude*, and bodying itself forth in symbols which are the nearest possible representations of the feeling in the exact shape in which it exists in the poet's mind.[3]

Between Mill's and Greene's proposals, the correlation is hard to avoid. Memory's music spoken to oneself with no one there to listen; feeling confessing itself only to itself: as such, the defining features of "secret prose" and true Poetry, however impressionistic and debatable the claim in each case, speak to each other rather directly. But if both introvert prose and its cousin intimacies in verse eventually come into contact with the reader, we need further to ask: in what material form, exactly, is such speech found "bodying itself forth"? Or bearing down further on Mill's terms: what "bodily form" of "symbols"—the alphabetic characters of symbolic language—could possibly render the "exact shape" of confessional reflection?

Dickensian prose is full of tacit answers to this. But only if there *is* someone there to listen. To count as language, secrecy must have its say after all. And not in Dickens alone. In this respect, his name is a placeholder for literary reading personified, somatically articulated. Or put it this way instead: Dickens's words, more obviously than most, are the symbols of a writing "bodied forth" in the pulse of the reader's own audited enunciation, silent or otherwise. This is why the Mill prototype offers our own point of clarification, if not Greene's. Whatever Greene may have seen, or heard, in the lone passage from *Great Expectations* he offers up, it has been left unguessed by further commentary, which seldom even mentions this free-floating example in the many allusions over the years to Greene's pithy descriptors. There must never have seemed much of anything to do with the passage Greene once read into evidence—and that is introduced here again in its adduced but underspecified music, sustained in the key of remembrance's own trance. One might at least have thought to *read* it:

> It was fine summer weather again, and, as I walked along, the times when I was a little helpless creature, and my sister did not spare me, vividly returned. But they returned with a gentle tone upon them that softened even the edge of Tickler. For now, the very breath of the beans and clover whispered to my heart that the day must come when it would be well for my memory that others walking in the sunshine should be softened as they thought of me.

The summer weather that comes "again" is, of course, a recursion in two time scales at once, annual and biographical. Pip is back: back in the past, back at the home he has forgone—and this in a pastoral ambience of agricultural recurrence, all fruitfulness and nurture, with the bitterness of the past no sooner summoned up in recall than dissipated. Pip has returned for his cruel sister's funeral, and everything feels for a moment more relenting than she ever was. For "as I walked along, the times when I was a little helpless creature"—not one survived period of time, but the many separate episodes ("times" plural) of mistreatment—"and my sister did not spare me, vividly returned." The last unrhythmical twist of that sentence is like a snap of grammatical recoil as well as emotional reversion—as if to say, "And believe me, my sister never spared me!" And then the crux of this revisitation is transacted across the close repetition of the verb itself: "But they returned with a gentle tone upon them that softened even the edge of the Tickler"—blunted in recollection, that is, the former sting of the sister's punishing weapon, even as the long voweling of "tone" (in emphatic variance from "returned") is lightened, visually as well as aurally, by the anagrammatic embedding of "s*oft*ened." Yet by the end of the passage, in the two-way street of retrospect and return, that figure for alleviation—the half-pictorial, half-musical "gentle tone"—has descended upon the landscape as a psychological inscape.

Maybe the laconic Greene chose a good example after all. The inference of this temporal complexity can build only gradually in the cadences of such "secret prose," or say, in the manipulative grip of the Other Dickens. After the muted and unusually homely (homey) personification of "beans and clover" as advisers who "whispered to my heart," the content of their overheard motion is further audited, though with no one really there to listen still, by actual reading: a reading articulated along the double path of memory and premonition. Carried lightly on the air, that is, and this in the "secret" enunciation of nature's own tongue (think Wordsworth's "language of the sense") is a complex responsiveness matched to a palimpsest of past, present, and future. For the whispered message is "that the day must come when it would be well for my memory . . ."—what?— to recover these better feelings? To fix on some such amelioration? So we would expect the sentence to go, based on an idiomatic model like "it would be well for me to bear in mind." But the temporal swivel of the whole passage is actually hinged on the unwritten shift from "my memory" as subject to "the memory of me" as object, the very crux of autobiographical retrospect rehearsed in this one musical chord change. The logic of an entire genre turns on a phrasal dime. For memory can be made "well for me" again only if "others walking in the sunshine should be softened"—like Pip's own purging of the Tickler as scourge—"when they thought *of me.*"

In rounding out this passage, the alphabetic curvature of "softened" (already having absorbed a soundless echo of the legible, if unsayable, anagram "tone") is reverbed in turn against the very sound of the compressed monosyllable "thought" (*oft/thot*). And this happens only after an earlier and closer juncture of diction within that uncertain figure of "tone" as conjuring up either coloration or the phonics of its evocation—or both at once. For the double vision of this return (of past into present) is further blurred, in this attenuated as well as extenuating moment, across the phrasing "gentle tone upon them"—not "tone to them," in association, but "upon," as if more palpably "bodied forth"—which softens the harder edges of diction itself across the fused word break, transforming the effect of appeasement into its own cause in the unsaid but nonetheless whispered "gentle(*d t*)one." Unsaid but inherently intoned: or say, in-toned. By such an evanescent flutter in the flux of syntactic time, the narrated past is made still latent in its own restoration—as if through the faintest of kinetic "dissolves" that closes out so "vivid" a flashback, gentles us out of it, by the route of a formal relaxation and return. In this microfilmic (rather than broadly cinematic) sense, such are the special effects in the laboratory of Dickensian frame-advance.

Here is where secret prose meets the secret force of reading halfway, on wording's own terms. The hush-hush of silent, inward reading is, in other words, never more than half-operative, never in its essence fully shushed. And if there is no self there to listen to such writing, this may be because subjectivity is imagined, in psychic fact, to be *embodied by* such prose—if only in the sense of engendered through it from phrase to phrase. In Greene's sense of inwardness, the audial secrecy of such style, and of its reading in turn, consists only in not *breathing a word*—hardly in not *sounding* it, since we are always closely, if passively, engaged in taking the silent audial pulse of a given phrasing. And yet the tacit "eavesdropping" metaphor (Mill's "overheard," Greene's intercepted "speaking to itself") may well still apply—in what Joyce would eventually come to call, in punning self-exemplification, "a*n ear*sighted view."[4] Eavesdropping in this sense is nothing like wiretapping, of course, but it is nonetheless a way of tapping into the very line of prose in the course of its unfolding—and in some cases into the verbal calisthenics of its high-wire acts. In a point I'll return to after further examples, it is this that again invites the filmic more than the cinematic analogue—but only as a way of clarifying the plastic substrate of prose in the file of phonemes. Looking at words and seeing (rather than just recognizing) what they name: hallucination. Looking at such symbols and imagining their referents in the so-called mind's eye: reading. It's an everyday version of the sixth sense. But there is another uncanniness with which reading is laced, the Other to its phenomenology of description. Not unlike the model of eavesdropping for the participatory "overhearing" of poetry rather than a more passive response to elocution, the intercepted secrets of prose do entail something like a further seventh sense available for "hearing things," the things called words, in the full heft and waver of what they "body forth" along the reeling track of phrase. Another version of the question at stake in this chapter, then: if "secrecy" is mostly construed as the opposite of full-bore rhetorical presentation, what other "lyric" effects attend its muted prose poetics, its sequestered musicianship, in the vocalic arpeggios and chord changes of the Other Dickens?

Discords of Retrospect

In wanting other instances that would count as, and help account for, the "music of memory" that Greene finds so *secretively* evident in Dickens's prose—maybe that's the point of underexemplification?—it is irresistible to return to *David Copperfield*, that most monumental of memory books.

And what we quickly find in its most elegiac pages isn't just the mind speaking to itself with no one there to listen, but the unconscious talking back by way of free association. This is an effect captured in scenes not just of nostalgic fixation but of drunkenness, exhaustion, or nightmare, any episode of cognitive waver or derangement—including the deliberate language not just of dreamlike depths but of their onset in sleepiness. How else could a writer, fully awake and vigilant, not have censored out the echoic overkill of the following semioneiric rhythm in the very matter of drowsy hearing? When David is first shown his little bedroom at the Yarmouth boathouse by Mr. Peggotty, he attends to it all "in a very luxurious state of mind, enhanced by my being sleepy," a mental state indexed by the way he "listened," among other nocturnal stirrings, "*to him and Ham hanging up two ham*mocks for themselves." Such a fading "luxury" of mind relaxes into an overflux of iteration—yes, all but ham-fisted—not unlike the swaying of those described slung bed-works. Yet the imitation at play here is less a mimesis of the scene than of the semiconscious filters and drowsy syllabic loops of its rerun in the coils of memory.

Looked back on from the bitter turning point of the Yarmouth plot in the elopement of Little Em'ly and Steerforth, this rhythmic fillip of the Other Dickens, here and elsewhere, retains the sing-song cadence of a better day. Once Em'ly has "fallen," time is entirely out of joint, the "music of memory" with it. David is hesitant even to phrase to himself his own memory of having once inwardly wondered, at his most Victorian, whether it would have been better for Little Em'ly to have been dead rather than disgraced. He has ruefully admitted—to begin with, in the first manuscript draft of this passage—that "there had been a time since when I have asked myself the question." In Dickens's hands, that was David's first confessional version. However much later, but still at the manuscript stage, the Other Dickens rose to the occasion with this hedging insertion: "a time since—I do not say it lasted long, but it has been—when I . . ."[5] Mental revisitation seems generating in its own key a textual revision. Inhabiting the brief plangent dilation of that insert, as the reader does, there is a strange hanging sense—in the isolation of the phrasing—of a time, a temporality per se, that is caught locked, abstracted, into a distilled mode of its pure perfect (or absolute past) tense in the "has been." The very grammar of tense, by which the temporality of all human action is marked in speech, seems in this displaced phrasing to have been swallowed up in its own reflex definition, thus secreting away the metaphysical short-circuit of a more idiomatic tautology like "the time was when . . ."

All the more reason, then, with this pending misery for the Yarmouth cast, that the "music of memory" would try to wrest some earlier moment of respite from the track of the inexorable. One passage seems to achieve this with an unusually clear reliance on a nonfinite grammar of perpetuation rather than on the ironies of "been-ness." The reverie begins:

> I don't know why one slight set of impressions should be more particularly associated with a place than another, though I believe this obtains with most people, in reference especially to the associations of their childhood. I never hear the name, or read the name, of Yarmouth, but I am reminded of a certain Sunday morning on the beach, the bells ringing for church on my shoulder, Ham lazily dropping stones into the water. . . .

And so forth: *-ing*, *-ing*, the prose itself ringing against its own participial forms in a cadence timed to that of the church bells. What comes forth invites description, to my mind, in an unusually specific version of filmic analogy. But it also has a more strictly linguistic set of parameters. In tenth-grade Latin class, I learned about the ablative absolute. In college, when there were still such courses, I learned in Literary Stylistics that this syntactic format was known in undeclined English usage as the "nominative absolute," one of the mainstays of the "cumulative sentence." Then in graduate school, I tracked its fortunes in a History of the Language course. Its history in this one sentence of Dickens is a drama—and a course of study—all its own. For here are the harmonics of memory in a suspended legato span, "absolute" in its own terms: lifted out of time but not in negation (as with "it has been") but in levitated preservation, "the bells [still] ringing, Little Em'ly leaning . . . , Ham lazily dropping . . . ," all in echo of the "morning" (in its faded gerund form) these phrases elaborate.

It is in this respect that this fixed, mentally encased memory, this morning-in-amber on the "beach," leads by the least strained of alliterations to "bells" among its first recovered impressions. The absolute construction, not a participial phrase, has caught and held the moment: noun plus verbal form but (deliberately) with no freestanding claims, all impressions associational rather than subordinate, a gathering rather than an arranging. Nothing is predicated anew, just recovered as it was, but ongoingly. So, too, as the passage ripples out from its belling core: with (again) "Little Em'ly leaning on my shoulder, Ham lazily dropping stones into the water." After these "quick cuts" between fixed impressions, almost "freeze-frame" snippets of the nonetheless grammatically "progressive" action, how rhythmically perfect it would have been to end with the panoramic long shot—and iambic rounding off—of an elliptical and verbless fixity like the limpid simplicity of "and the sun away at sea." Instead, by the operation of a descriptive zoom lens, in fact this central noun "sun" absorbs two more amplifying phrases into its prose orbit. It does so in the rapid widening of the stylistic aperture with another absolute suspension rather than a last receding cadence: "and the sun, away at sea, just break-ing through the heavy mist, and showing up the ships." A further curious phrasing, certainly, that last: not "setting off" or "lighting up," but a little of each—though with none of the usual sense of competition or eclipse in that chosen "showing up." In any case, the *show/ship* chime preps us for what's coming—as "*sh*/ow" widens to contain phonetically an effect (once again, in the associational logic of such sound play) found positing its own cause: "*sh*owing up the *sh*ips," that is, and with shades of Plato's cave, "like their own *sh*adows." The Other Dickens isn't stressing silhou-etted forms on the horizon, but placing emphasis instead on the ships as secondary manifestations of unseen originals, anchoring in their turn all derivative and remembered sense impressions of that iconic day—as if in some idealizing daydream conjured by prose alone. The cinematic telephoto shot gives us the image; the prose of simile, with its internal "filmic" iterations and distensions, refocuses that image at a secondary depth of perspective for this subocular vanishing point in the mind's eye only. More broadly, it is that play between quasi-filmic seriality and pro-tocinematic angle—between syllabic aggregates and descriptive vantage points, between molecular alphabetic increments and narrative shots, frozen or otherwise—to which discussion will come back again in just a minute, directed there by the uniquely "secret" counterpoint of flashback and phonetic disjunction in this same phase of the novel.

In just a minute—or so. The time can be well spent with a brief look at both manuscripts and proofs of that same last sentence—as logged in their emendations, though without comment, by Clarendon Press editor Nina Burgis.[6] As luck would have it, this turns out to have been an unusually rough patch for Boz in transmission—and, I would add, a stylistic pres-sure point, and breakthrough opportunity, for the Other Dickens. The manuscript had originally put it much more simply, with the sun "showing up the ships like shadows." All backlit outlined solids, no nautical detail: abstracted as if by distance itself. The point would have been clear enough that way. But this intended phrasing suffered a phonetic collapse at the first proof stage: narrowed to "showing up the ships' shadows" (sounding like a slipshod phonic variant, via borrowed sibilant, of "ship shadows"). Easily corrected—but prompting the afterthought of an analogy-enforcing comma: "showing up the ships, like shadows." Yet a minor chain reac-tion had begun—and the ultimate detonation seems no less than inspired. The clarifying space pried open by that comma may seem to have yawned wide to the ear of the Other Dickens when next the proofreading eye passes over this nettlesome simile. For in the first revised printed edition, from 1849, the full reflex intrusion has been effected in final revision: "showing up the ships like *their own* shadows," with that telltale extra twitch of discrepancy between phenomenon and epiphenomenon. The ships are no longer just shadow-like, but second-order ontological traces of themselves. As Dickens mulled this wording one final time, we might think to overhear the Other Dickens putting in a vote, helping to turn the serviceable breather of the comma into something closer to quietly breathtaking.

Elsewhere in this primal Yarmouth episode, and also under the shadow of foreboding in retrospect, the prose of David's ignited boyish passion for Little Em'ly does its "secret" service in a wish-fulfillment fantasy that begins with wide-awake exclamation—even as it moves on, with a sub-liminal candor, to image the intimacy of a sleep unto death. Here is the Other Dickens sabotaging the "music of memory" from within its own delusional cadences:

> Ah, how I loved her! What happiness (I thought) if we were married, and were going away anywhere to live among the trees and in the fields, *never* growing older, *never* growing wiser, childre*n* *ever*, rambling hand in hand through sunshine and among flowery meadows, laying down our heads on moss at night, in a sweet sleep of purity and peace, and buried by the birds when we were dead!

The parenthetical "I thought" is the one overt sign of an ironic judge-ment in retrospect—spoken by the writing David rather that his pro-jected younger self. This is part of a protesting-too-much that does itself in across the iterated participles of the fanciful "never" (neither "grow-ing old" nor "growing wiser"—like an expanded, noncomic version of a more typical split phrase like *never growing up or wise*). This repetition lays the tracks by which "childre*n* *ever*" falls under its own negation in the very posing of its delusory perpetuity—as if to say, in the full secrecy of a speech never listened in on aside from its written form: children once together but never more as fantasized.

And that's not all—in this evanescing of past fantasy under what one is tempted to call the auditory gaze (or textual "overhearing") of retro-spect. Word borders succumb, as well, in the summoned lyricism of the next sentence—and this in the very act of isolating David's blissful future prospect as a mirage, a "picture," no sooner figured as such than treated cinematically, as if in a telephoto shift from backlit gleaming focus to astral long shot: "Some such picture, with no real world in it, but bright with the light of our innocence, and vague as the stars afar off, was in my mind all the way." But to put my estimation that way, in overt cin-ematic terms, is only once more to call out the serial and cellular as well as panoramic facets of the self-eroded vista, the differential and dialectic as well as the pictorial: again, the substrate of phonemic flicker beneath the scene. The so-called "cosmic zoom" of Hollywood optical rhetoric, as if, in this case, sweeping from the moss banks of idealized sleep to the distanced stars of indifference, is accompanied, as well, by a marked telescoping of sound across the slant rhyme between "*of our*" and "afar" — and then again with the third phase of this vibration fading away into "off." Every little word counts, as well as every adjacent phoneme — or iterated preposition — in this alphabetic micromontage. The lack of a "real world in it," the sheer fantasy of the vision, finds its perfect topographic contrast in the implicitly spatialized idiom "in my mind," where residence is taken up instead, with one "in" displacing the other. No prose could be more secret than this undercurrent of the Other Dickens in the felt effects of an ironized lyric ripple along the vanishing strip, and stripping away, of single alphabetic increments. The power of the phrasing has been floated into "earsighted" view on the sequestered scalar chiming (*uh/suh/tu*) by which the seemingly formulaic "*Some such picture*" actually builds from within, layering its own hallucination in the words of its ex post facto conjuration across the inspired vocalic fade-out, and final chiastic clinch, of "*vague as the stars afar off.*" How in the world, to coin a phrase, does he do it? Whomever we mean by the personification "he."

Secret prose, as the subcutaneous pulse of Writing itself, can be lifted to a level of even greater intensity (and narratorial self-consciousness), if never quite outdoing a passage like that last, in the later novel to which Greene actually looked for his sole example. In the process, *Great Expectations* can again evoke, for us, the private screening room of a narrator's mental cinema — along with the subconscious cellular proliferations, loops, and potential subversions that gather toward the image generated. In the famously revised ending of the novel, Pip's first-person discourse reverts to its own phrasing in pressing forward toward connubial resolution. But we have, as it were, heard this coming — and not just in earlier false notes of secret yearning but built toward as well in the less resonant dexterities of phrasal (rather than psychic) self-division.

Dissonant Ligatures

What the next chapter will examine in the divided syntax of split predication, where one often seems to hear Dickens and his Other vying for coherence in a single comic arc of phrase, is found as well in Herbert's report of Miss Havisham's jilting: "The day came, but not the bridegroom," a temporality doomed to fixation by the missing spatial sense of a physical arrival. Pitting movement against time in this way introduces a profound discrepancy in the very a prioris of narrative duration and event. Such a rhetorical effect keeps company in this novel with a more minor verbal splintering. The correlation of pace and space captured in an urban stroll, where "Wemmick and I beguile the time and the road," is mostly just a swift phrasal economy (barely idiomatic at that) like the time-passing nature of their conversation. But on Pip's later homecoming, his return to the scene of emotional crime at Satis House, time and space are again rendered equivocal by just such cloven (or self-straddling) grammar. The summons to a last audience with Miss Havisham and Estella together is anticipated, in its residual delusion, when Pip, in an ineffectual cleansing of both distance and its soiling, "washed the weather and the journey" from his person—or so he tried to do. But the journey has been long.

This splitting of material and abstract objects, grime and transit itself, is a far cry from the buoyant double-pronged confidence at the outset of—the setting out for—Pip's anticipated London career. But even there, an awkwardness grammatical as well as psychological sets in with "farewell, monotonous acquaintances of my childhood, henceforth I was for London and greatness; not for smith's work in general, and for you!" Despite the confident parallelism, the syntax cannot be said to unpack itself with any certainty. Such, clearly, is the transitional moment when, in welcome farewell to his past, Pip projects himself "forth" across the supposed unforked path vectored by "henceforth I was for London and greatness," a place and a station guaranteed. But this burst boil of prideful enthusiasm drains away into the grammar of something like a Freudian slip. Pip's manifest destiny, according to the patronizing sense of his broad-gauge apostrophe, is decidedly "not for smith's work in general, and for you!" But whether (instead of the clearer "or for you") the grammar simply covers in negation the "you" of his past home scenes only, or breaks away—given the immediately following sentence of reiterated obsession—into a shaky positive for an irruptively addressed Estella (in a subtending "for London and greatness . . . and for you!"), we can't definitively say. This is itself a defining touch, since the very ambiguity bespeaks the way Pip's whole consciousness is potentially directed toward Estella at every benighted turn.

As is next made explicit in this very passage. In his aiming away across the double prepositional vector of "for London and greatness," and thus distancing his old domestic associations in the vanity of his valediction, even the certainty that he is not "for you (all)" leaves open the question, yawning in the world of dreams, whether in fact he is "for Estella" after all. All told, the brisk concisions, or outright comedy, of Dickens's sylleptic straddlings are so true to the bivalent instincts of Dickensian grammar that the jokey yoking that has recently had the vainglorious Pip planning for "everybody in the village" a "dinner of roast-beef and plum-pudding, a pint of ale, and a gallon of condescension" can, in its syntactic waver, be repurposed for the ironic cleft between Pip's being "bound" no longer apprentice but for London and maybe Estella. Finally at ease "to consider the question" about his beloved (in that pompous downbeat of ratioci-nation), Pip drifts off from daydream into oblivion when lying on the old Battery. It is there that he, meditating on "whether Miss Havisham intended me for Estella, fell asleep." For one thing, his ego is particu-larly well symptomatized by the tunnel vision of that preposition: not "in-tended Estella for me," for her own sake—but "me for Estella" as one of my several upward destinations. In just this way has Pip always mapped his own borrowed desire onto another's for another. But the Other Dick-ens, holding true to this logic, would naturally want Estella evoked there at the end of the prepositional phrase, lying in wait for the predication that it (she) would contaminate. The dissonant reverberation of her name at this point ("for Estella, fell asleep") has a precedent many chapters back. Just after first meeting her at Satis House, Pip learns her name only by being asked to call it out, as if on his own behalf. Miss Havisham has commanded him to summon her, but since the imperious old woman was merely mumbling toward her own mirror image, Pip—in an unlikely assumption—guesses at first that she was prompting her own need to call for her charge. Instead, when soon wised up, three times he must sound out its fated etymological cadence—until, in reference not solely to her candle, Estella's "light came along the long dark passage like a star." With the first syllable of "Estella" sounded there, aslant, in "a/st," it is then, instead, the last two syllables that return much later with lyric perversity in the iambic falling off—as if into the unconscious itself—at "for Estella, *fell a*sleep." Some secret prose may be so sequestered in its essential pho-netic coincidence that it remains unrecognized by the erotic consciousness itself, registered only as a kind of syllabic dreamscape.

Or is it perhaps that this tinny rhyme is somehow secreted in the prose as Pip's own self-mockery, rather than a strictly authorial dissonance? Toward the end of the novel, and even when looking back, Pip certainly knows better than to retain his early fantasies, and, with the music of memory turned sour, spells this out. He denigrates himself for the humili-ating way he still "hoarded up this last wretched little rag *of* the robe *of* hope that was rent and given to the winds." Woven there into the non-eye alliteration of "wretched" and "rag," together with the assonant, plosive, and thus overblown "robe of hope," the phrasing "rent and given" evokes the idiomatic overtone of that everyday redundancy "rent and riven"—even as the distended phrasing seems about to shred and unravel on its own choppy terms. But one may still want to ask whether the retroactive narrator and protagonist, rather than just the Other Dickens, is fully in charge of "Estella, fell asleep." Any version of that question, as applied to any number of passages in the book—as well as any related sense of language resting on its own unsaid—leverages a certain extra measure of fascination.

In this respect, we may well hear the Other Dickens rising to the aid of Boz, in the latter's prodded second thoughts, for the equivocation of the novel's revised ending. Writing to his eventual biographer, John Forster, about having "resolved" to take his friend Bulwer-Lytton's advice about a less downbeat resolution of the story, Dickens allows as how he has "put in as pretty a little piece of writing as I could, and I have no doubt the story will be more acceptable through the alteration."[7] More than pretty, even—but at points a little less, too, a shade darker, less settled, than one might have expected:

> "We are friends," said I, rising and bending over her, as she rose from the bench.
> "And will continue friends apart," said Estella.
> I took her hand in mine, and we went out of the ruined place; and, as the morning mists had risen long ago when I first left the forge, so the evening mists were rising now, and in all the broad expanse of tranquil light they showed to me, I saw no shadow of another parting from her.

Yes, internal echo achieves a balancing act of its own there at the start of this cadenced finale, but after all the downs and rare ups of the relation with Estella, the phrasal parallelism and internal echo of "rising and *bend*ing . . . as she rose from the *ben*ch" can harmonize only so much. Many a "ruined space" in the psychic topography of the novel would not, it might seem, be so easy to get "out of," to leave behind in any real way, but neither is this desolation at Satis House. Indeed, the only vista opened is the absence of any certain finality. The "no" of that absence had been much juggled in Dickens's own revisions, and even more worried and debated since by critics. Closure arrived in the manuscript under the shadow of the valley of death, with "no shadow of another parting from her, but one."[8] It is as if Dickens couldn't easily give up the stark aura of finality even in the open-ended revision. But he finally struck the last concessive phrase before the first edition, giving "the shadow of no parting from her"—as if that prospect of nonseverance had an impending gloom all its own. Even in a subsequent revision of the "no shadow" ending for the 1862 edition, that implied double negative of final consolation (no parting, no further nonpairing, so to say) is retained with the almost deliberately wish-fulfilling focus of "saw no shadow of another parting from her."

Niceties and phrasal resistances aside, there is no doubt about the attempt, on prompted second thought, to wed the destinies of these two damaged characters—if not to ceremonialize their union with an actual marriage scene—rather than send them on their separate chastened ways. The latter option is, of course, exactly what Dickens had originally intended with the last closed-circuit grammar of Pip's exit line, when, after meeting Estella again years later, he recognized that suffering "had given her a heart to understand what my heart used to be." Not the idiom "given her heart," as in the courage to admit all she had thrown away; and not what my heart "used to feel," but instead what had once constituted it ("used to be"). Furthermore, in bolstering this first ending, other phrasal vestiges are recalled by that final "used to be." The reciprocity of painful tutelage that Pip finds verified in this later Estella, a woman "given . . . a heart" like the Tin Woodsman by the very ordeals of plot, recalls the earlier Estella who has had all emotional affect, even all apparent sexual appetite, bred out of her as a tool of Miss Havisham's revenge against men. This was the Estella who warns Pip that "she has no heart"—even while relenting, under his objection, that she means this only in a figurative sense, as that term is usually associated with feeling. Otherwise, she owns to the biological organ in which the very verb of existence seems housed—this, in her echoically truncated and neo-Shakespearean admission that if it "ceased to beat I would cease to be." Many chapters later, there is little to celebrate in the revised ending by which Pip is told by a softened Estella that he has always "held a place in my heart." If that's in any sense true, it was for too long a place of negation.

In this respect, the many more words it takes to earn (or at least secure) closure in the revised version of the ending testify to the strain on tone needed to unite the cloven pair as lovers and helpmates after all. The words are tasked now with a curious intrigue all their own—a secret prose in almost more than the usual sense. With Dickens attempting to relax the disquieting "music of memory" at this point, as well as its more grating discords, still its sequestered poetry must work its wiles, and overtime, in the very pace of normative grammatical reading. The alternating lift and descent of symbolic marsh mists is always a bit ambiguous in its refrain across the novel, as to whether they're rising into view from the marshes, or rising higher up to free the view. In this case, however, it grows clear soon enough that their ascent gradually opens an aperture to the light—though it is not by any means at first clear what is predicated (let alone spectated) in that availed space and perspective. For grammar does not press straightforwardly to its goal, but retraces its own ground instead. Yes, "the evening mists were rising now, and in all the broad expanse of tranquil light they showed to me . . . *my best hopes made possible*." Something like that is the transitive grammar we might anticipate from the launch of the sentence, broadened across the wide-angle lens of assonance itself in "exp*an*se of tr*an*quil." Instead, disclosure is relegated to a subordinate clause, recognized as such only after the fact: "in all the broad expanse of tranquil light [that] they showed to me, I saw no shadow of another parting from her." In this way we find subjectivity taking over as grammatical anchor for the final visionary reach, whether it comes up shadowy and half-hearted or not. For "in all the broad expanse they showed to me," it was up to Pip alone to find something, however speculative if not specular, to focus on. It is only the secret Other of Pip's closing gesture that links "showed to" and "shadow" more closely than negation might desire.

That aside, grammar has already undergone its slippery side step. The syntax of secret prose, uttered to no one, takes even the nonlistener by surprise at the novel's final turn. By what we might call a microloop in grammar within an otherwise stationary POV shot of the clearing marsh vista, once again the filmic Dickens passes unfilmable (by standard means) within the too facile lure of the cinematic analogy. And once again I adduce the technological comparison less to enroll such effects on the pages of media history than to appreciate the unique temporal plasticity of their stylistic drive, traction, and recursive pull. The real issues are strictly literary. So deep is that elemental verbal realm in Dickens that it structures the whole spectrum of effects, from comic through satiric to lyric and elegiac. The various double takes that throw attention back on a phrase's own punning alter ego, in giddiness or denigration, are the same syllabic and grammatical second thoughts that can elsewhere recast a sonority in the image of its lexical successor or undermine a syntactic vector with its semantic back draft. When in Pip's last moment, what is "showed to" him is no revelation at all, but only the optic field of his own negative *speculation*, the rug has been almost as thoroughly pulled out from under narration as in a comic pratfall of grammar or a starker ironic disjunction like *he saw what was in front of him and no future*. In such wavers of phrase, the wedge of doubleness is driven straight into the linguistic precincts of the always still possible—not emotionally, but phrasally.

In Pip's story, the same flexed language that can deliver a verbal joke can also equivocate an ethical quiescence even under the sign of emotional reward. What we read in that last sentence of *Great Expectations* Redux is not the syntax of restitution but the transformational grammar of subjectivity itself ("they showed to me/I saw"). From page to reader's engagement, and like so many turns (including about-faces) in the prose of this incomparable novel, such phrasings of the Other Dickens—whether in Wordsworth's "still sad music" of memory or its attempted override—are words *brought to sound*: not themselves only, but something else beneath their own wavelengths, including a frequent interference in transmission that can adumbrate whole linguistic paradigms on the wing. They are words to be sounded out in the very process of their reaching further in and down. Enunciation becomes its own plumb line, even though few previous approaches to Dickens have tried sustaining this measure of linguistic attention. So it has to be said again. If featured here is simply the volatile stylistic aspect of Dickens that everyone somehow recognizes, that recognition arrives only beneath the skein of character-driven action and its more strenuous—sometimes even strident—rhetorical organization. This is the irrepressible Other Dickens known, if not regularly owned to in commentary, by readers seldom tending to slow, in notice, over the most fleeting, circumscribed, and definitive effects thus generated—so in that case no sooner known than forgotten, let go. Certainly the narrative *surface* as such, however defined, will not yield up its mysteries unbidden, since it is from hidden linguistic springs that we find prose drawing continuously on an otherness banked within its own forward-spinning forms: a tireless potentiation of verbal force from the reservoirs of its own linguistic source.

Clear by now is the thrust of the present chapter in this regard: that Dickens reaches to a deep formative *poetics* at his least versified and metrical, his least "poetical"—in passages where what is at stake is the inner shaping of the word form, often with one syllable lending (or b-lending) itself to the next in the meld of utterance. In this respect, those minor pockets of off-echo we began with in that random sampling from *Little Dorrit* are continuous, in their sly passage under cover of plot, with the more commanding transformations examined since. Hence the further service provided by Greene's coinage. However quirky or mystified in respect to narrative discourse or psychology, still the epithet "secret"—to the extent that one does intuitively see what it might mean, might be *getting at*—sheds its preciousness by contrast with certain current trends in so-called surface reading.[9] When pitted against anything superficial or manifest, the term "secret" stages a clarification. What needs penetration, rather than just apprehension, cannot be figured, or treated, as strictly two-dimensional, available simply to the examination—cursory or not—of words in sequential appearance on the page. Taking the pulse of phrasing is also taking its depth—even if only in transformational grammar's sense of a variable deep structure, with syntax lifting to light its own branching root system, entwined syllables included. No outward skating across a given track of text can begin to crack the stylistic code, lay bare the enigma of creative force. Irruptions of the Other Dickens keep us aware of this. So in reading on, one must, though not in the normal thematic and pejorative use of the term, read *in*. This is only to say that we collaborate in letting language in Dickens, at uneven depths beneath the equivocal surface of things, speak eloquently for itself. In the Writing's everywhere taut and bristling formations, such is the always blithely betrayed "confidence" (both senses) of Dickens's sequestered poetics—and the true unkept secret of a prose beyond both restraint and compare.

3

PHRASING ASTRADDLE

What kind of writer does his work not just across a sentence but between and astride its phrasal gaps, here lexical, there syntactic—where even *here* versus *there* can be rendered uncertain en route? What kind of writer, that is, would leave his enunciating readers, from word to word, unsure for a moment exactly which of the successive words they were busy with, still or already—with one lexical unit leaching part of its syllabic matter from the other in the very work of their silent articulation? By the same token, at the grammatical rather than syllabic level, what kind of writer would let his readers be hung up on one prong of a compound predication in the sudden need to broad-jump the *and* of phrasal linkage in order to sort out a divided semantic sense? Unsure, hung up: only for a split second, of course, but that splitting of an instant's difference is exactly what keeps us on verbal edge.

As usual with this book's field of attention, such questions about authorial motive default to a more integral recognition. None of this is definitively a writer's ploy after all, so much as it is the unhindered, and sometimes momentarily unhinged, work of Writing. It is the Other Dickens at play—in exactly that sense of "play in the engineering sense" so perfectly said of Shakespeare by William Empson: evoking the give and slack that are at one with writing's tensile force.[1] In the Other Dickens, from phrase to phrase, this play is often manifested as the gift, not that keeps on giving, but that immediately takes away again and remakes on the run. Before encountering once more—with some further attempt at distinction—the overlap of these two (in themselves overlapping) skids of wording (syllabic and syntactic, alphabetic and grammatical), it should help to appreciate the "pure" form of each energized slackness in separate instances, each with its particular way of being semantically distended into the counterpart of a lexical portmanteau (where two word stems interpenetrate both graphically and phonetically). But that's only one among many metaphors that may serve to compass the phrasal binding in question. Binding or stress fracture—and sometimes the two together in a kind of syntactic splint. Metaphors like this keep coming to mind in order to keep in mind the discrepant registers in play. None has priority in the always ad hoc fascination of these divisive or transfusing formats. So another figure offers itself as well. Since the straddle in question is always a kind of bridge or latch, a join, at one scale or another—ranging from the least pleatings of adjacent words sounds to whole discrepant syntactic compounds—we might distinguish between cuff-link phonetics and handcuff grammar. It is in this way that the Other Dickens traverses a sliding scale from surprise syllabic mash-ups to the abrupt reining in of serial sprawl with a forced tug of idiom.

By any designation, and yet returning for a moment to the portmanteau metaphor (and model), there is certainly much overpacked syllabic baggage under satiric pressure in the inflections of Dickens and his Other, manifest at times in the formation of word sounds out of mere inchoate phonation. In *Little Dorrit*, we find an extreme example of this last tendency in the paradoxically embarrassed false pride that increasingly besets the mumbling speech of William Dorrit in his Grand Tour grandeur, where it is tempting to hear his "ha-hum"ming as the hinted humbug of his false values as well the inbuilt "ha" of mockery rather than just the "uh" or "ah" of mere distraction or chagrin. The nervously self-aggrandizing Dorrit runs the whole gamut, or slurred arpeggio, of such sheepish aspirate throat clearing when explaining his eagerness to "show by any means, however slight and worthless, the- ha, hum- high estimation"—in fact the cross-worded "high est" deference—"in which, in-ha-common with the rest of the world, I hold so distinguished and princely a character as Mr Merdle's," where even the sycophantic object is abstracted into his reputation ("character" in that sense) rather than his person. In another ventriloquizing by the Other Dickens, the balked nature of Dorrit's blather can speak volumes from within its own intermittent voids. In mouthing the man's contemptible pretensions, that is, Writing opens a space in the quasi-aphasic babble for a more pointed enunciation of what he would renounce in his prison past—or what he would, in a more *letteral* etymology and metaphor, seek to *erase*: "a painful topic, a series of events which I wish—ha-altogether to *obliterate*." In this fantasy of wiping the slate clean, putting a stop to all his daughter's nostalgia, so total is his blindness to past affection that his debilitated ("halt"-ing) language seems swallowed up in a stumbling portmanteau version of "wishaltogether."

This is the satiric version of phonetic slippage that finds its counterpart in a more melancholic clinging of word sounds in the description of Amy's prison past. Enlisting the alphabetic rather than grammatical end of the spectrum (the phrasal straddling) that we've begun to sample, incarceration has been somatically internalized by the heroine before being figured as a synecdoche for the world at large. The latter trope—the sublunary prison of the living world—is enhanced, to begin with, through the tactical metrics of Dickens's iambic prose leading off a prolonged inverted grammar: "Far aslant across the city, over its jumbled roofs,"—with the beat relaxing briefly next, "opening" up a bit in its cumulative build—"and through the open tracery of its church towers, struck the long bright rays, bars of the prison of this lower world." In an appositive overspill from the arriving grammatical subject, however, the newly stressed and oddly syncopated phrasing "long bright rays, bars" entails a staggered monosyllabic beat that momentarily overrides the shift from visual phenomenon to emblematic resonance at the abrupt comma pause—after which, in immediate recovery from this slipknot sequence, the tripled beat of "long bright rays" seems precipitously mapped upon the otherwise awkward threefold phrasing to come, with its lumpy genitive cadence in those "bars of the prison of . . ."

Border Raids

In connection with such slanted and slatted "bright rays"—in their more immediate focal point from within the Marshalsea prison itself—there are odder soundings yet: internal to wording but not wholly constrained by lexical borders. If the world is its own kind of prison, so does imprisonment offer its own way of seeing the world, a deep theme in the novel that infiltrates not just another striking figure of speech but the very word forms of its depiction. Here, then, earlier than that apocalyptic cityscape, is how the heroine, child of the prison, images for herself the space of all she is *barred from*, where exclusion itself leaves its own optic imprint: "Wistful and wondering, she would sit in summer weather by the high fender in the lodge, looking up at the sky through the barred window, until, when she turned her eyes away, bars of light would arise between her and her friend, and she would see him through a grating, too." That friend is the turnkey, keeper of the lock, guardian of her little world, and thus in her vision included within it, enclosed by the supplemental "grating" as well as the bolted gate.

All this is Dickens to a tee. What the Other Dickens has superimposed upon its carceral logic and striated optic—in the very description of an ocular afterimage—is the multiple phonetic aura of an aural afterglow as well, a kind of syllabic aftershock. The reverb heard at this level exceeds even the epithet of "high fender" as it propels the assonant move from "sky" to responsive "eyes." Nor is it exhausted even by the stranger way yet in which "fender" seems to make "friend" inevitable (**fndr/frnd**), a kind of consonant anagram (only thickened further by "her and her friend"). In a similar fashion, and even more readily attributable to Gurneyesque fallout, the fact that the heroine is said, just two sentences back, to have "*wander*ed about the prison-yard, for the first eight years of her life" makes her "*wonder*ing" curiosity now, about what lies beyond, all of a phonetic piece (**wndr**). Further, as part of this pervasive lexical claustrophonia, so to speak, the "bars of light," if heard not as an equative genitive but as an objective genitive, preventative rather than mimetic, strike the ear (rather than eye) as "bars of flight," obstacles to any such mused-upon release. More that this, in precisely the turn of prose itself when blurring letter-forms across the interstices of textual vision, it is only when Amy "turned *her eyes*" that, in the uncanniest of echoes, this ocular trace "would *arise.*" In one of the great cinematic POV shots in Dickens, yet again it is, nonetheless, the "filmic" (serial) sequencing, rather than the optical vista alone, that undergirds the instantaneous frame-advance of Dickensian—how else to put it here?—phonotography.

Deserving a place amid the test-case vocalic densities scooped up from *Little Dorrit* at the start of the previous chapter, an example like this last, under concerted thematic pressure, puts separate word forms, and their syllabic materiality, not just into muted conversation with each other but into phonic debate and abrasion, while in the process loosening up new lexical undertones. The raiding of word borders may thus come in further aid of depicted image. And in contexts more ominous, as well. There is, for instance, the nongraphic assonance that makes a ravenous crowd at a treason trial in *A Tale of Two Cities*—as if to say "stewing over" their disappointment at not being treated to an execution—turn into the more figurative "h*u*man st*e*w that had been boiling there all day," and that only now "was straining off." Worded there in that last sibilant phrase is a sieving perfectly thinned out between the written "wa*s* straining off" and the half-sounded and more obvious, if less culinary, sense of "was draining away."

Sometimes such phonic slack, when delegated to a character's speech instead of the momentum of narration, is foregrounded as involuntary, a sheer accident of sequenced enunciation. In *Bleak House*, for instance, we hear Esther Summerson's memory of the chilly goodbye conferred on her by the housekeeper, Mrs. Rachel, who "gave me one cold parting kiss upon my forehead, like a thaw-drop from the stone porch—it was a very frosty day—." It is as if Dickens knew this perfect phrasing turned on an impression (and covert onomatopoeia) too ingenious by half for his straightforward heroine—and normalized it, contextualizing its metaphor with that midstream explanatory insertion. What might have been an unsaid but implicit "iciness"—superbly congealed into the twice-assonant simile "like a th*aw*-drop" from a "stone p*or*ch"—gets a "the" for "porch" instead of an "a" as if to explain away the figure as less than sheerly "clever," which Esther always says she isn't, but influenced instead by ambient connection and attentive recall: "it was," as she immediately adds, "a very frosty day." As usual, though, given the collaborative work of the Other Dickens, no good stone turned is left unrewarded by an extra plus in the pulse of phrasing, since the "the" assures a further fit with "thaw." Moreover, no reader can be expected to believe that the pitter-patter of *aw/ŏp/ōn/ōr* is the work of sheer visual notice and association rather than minor phonetic inspiration—including the way it captures cause in the effect through the cross-word ligature of "thaw(ed) drop." As often happens in *Bleak House*, the Other Dickens seems to be whispering in Esther's modest ear.

And not least next, during the similar chill of her arrival in London, where, though she remains sheltered from a "raw" morning, "the fog still seemed heavy—I say seemed, for the windows were so encrusted with dirt that they would have made midsummer sunshine dim." Ensconced in this temporary domestic setting, nestled between the off-echo of "midsummer" and "discomfort," rests a more powerful stylistic touch: not just the syllabic inversion of "*mid*summer sunshine *dim*," which frames the gloom between a luminous zenith and its chiastic negation, but also the novel's lone released play on the heroine's obviously allegorical tag-name. The effect is no less a syllabic ingenuity than the obvious satire of phrasal implosion in the novel's opening chapter, where "My Lord," amid the figurative muck of Chancery, indoors and out, is slurred—liquefied—to "Mlud." Later now, into a miserable domestic atmosphere that could becloud even "mid*summer sun*shine," one Miss Summerson—spelled only slightly otherwise—enters dispensing aid, comfort, and her usual brightness of disposition. So primal is the release of lexical energy in this syllabic overlap that the phrase itself can be read two ways at once: not just as written, but, in another renegade spacing, as if it were "make midsummer sun shine dim." Tolerable only within the "engineering sense," as it were, of a cross-lexical tolerance, a lateral "play" again, the beaming pun on her name would be ridiculous if made more explicit, let alone explicated. Instead, for the first and last time in the novel, it is woven into a phrasing other to it on the run.

In this respect, Esther's encoded nomination is a striking case in point—maybe the perfect exemplar—for a prose force field operating beneath plot or characterization, where the Other Dickens is the true protagonist. At the same time, of course, the name Summerson sustains its bonded overtones in freestanding contexts—as if released after portmanteau christening (reimagined here) to its concretized substantive form. So once again, as manifest early in our evidence with Mrs. S/Nagsby—and in an effect also snagged on the run with the affrighted Affery or with Est/ella as "a st/ar," quite apart from the dissonance of "Estella/fell a[sleep]"—the proper name (even in the case of the rogue nurse Mrs. S/Gamp, perhaps) can operate as a kind of frozen lateral wordplay. Though this occurs most blatantly in a one-off pun like "The Lord Knows Zoo" (a mishearing of "the Lord knows who" in the dying Toby Chuzzlewit's answer to a question about his grandparental ancestry) is a phonetic meld that is typically (and more mutedly) cemented for repeated denomination—like a kind of syntactic skid in recurrent freeze-frame.

In any case, the valorized atmospherics in that example from *Bleak House* are certainly largely phonetic. "Sun" adheres to "summer" while releasing "shine" from its own compound noun in a lexical dispersion where words do indeed straddle each other in generative disarray. Less intrusive and diffusing, and again in delegation to Esther, is her notice of the wordy lawyer Kenge as "a portly, important-looking gentleman." The true weighted core of this description, its center of phonemic gravity, comes bearing such a heavy assonance (*port/import*) that one suspects the Other Dickens of slipping in a portmanteau trick across the elided "y/i" difference, thus suppressing the comma and ballooning the compound, in the conflation of worth and girth, to "portlimportant-looking"—in a ponderosity matched to the man's own orotund sonorities in coming dialogue. Aside from the phonetic hitching point of elision, we are only one step away from a phrasing that would straddle syntactic rather than lexical increments across a broader span, as if the seated Kenge were said, in taking his chair, to have *given a rest to his portliness and importance at once*—in a swivel between conditions physical and mock-ethical.

Twin grammatical objects, twin epithets—in neither case do the twain quite neatly meet. Even twin phonemes as well: spilling over into notice from one word to the next. In Esther's actual phrasing, this results from the open-voweled *i/y* sounds making their separate (if also fused) mark on attention. To recall here the spectral cross-word compression of "d her eyes" into "d arise" in *Little Dorrit* serves only to spotlight an effect—let us say an audio-optical aftereffect—far more subliminal, in its border transgressions, than are the overt acrobatic "splits" of double-jointed grammar that may be more easily recognized as turns both of phrase and of plot. Those latter syntactic gestures are the exertions that, rather than blurring two words into one, are found—just a split second after the fact—to have spun one verb out in two different senses across competing objects or complements. After many instances in the *Sketches by Boz*, there is the first full-bore example in *Pickwick Papers*, when the title character "*fell* into the barrow, and *fast* asleep, simultaneously," with recognition—as if respected by the first comma, even while sped along by alliteration—involving a shade more lag time than the described coterminous falling.

So far, we have been lingering over "sound defects" that go beyond any such low-key alliteration to a structural dissonance in the delimitation of word borders themselves: effects we will find operating in frequent collusion, beyond their own alphabetic collisions, with broader arcs of semantic leapfrogging in compound grammar. Spanning both scales of effect, the overall perspective should be coming clear by now. At some level of attention, I've insisted that the Other Dickens is the one everybody relishes, dazzling us right there alongside the narrative showman: that unflagging vocal coach in unmistakable league with the immortal maestro of inventive set design, casting, costuming, and plot. The inveterate phrasemaker is the one any teacher or critic, like any reader, knows on contact, but knows as well to forget, or must learn to, in getting on with the *point*—whatever argument it is that needs making, in or out of class. Here in this book, instead, it is the making, or makeup, of such wording that *is* the point, called out free of thesis, theory, or even fictional theme. The lens of attention is focused not on the novel writer but on the novelty of the Writing—as well as its developing routines.

To the general rule that such effects are expeditiously sidelined in commentary, one recent exception bears comment, especially for the way this critic's willingness to be upended momentarily by the Other Dickens operates exactly within the close quarters of those single syllabic transitions whose cross-word phonetics have most recently concerned us. Alex Woloch, a prominent theoretical critic of Dickens's fiction within the "character system" of the novel as genre, delivered an unpublished paper at the annual Santa Cruz Dickens Project, in the summer of 2015, when *Martin Chuzzlewit* was the text of the season.[2] He took to noting, among other things related to dilated middle spaces and lacunae in the narrative trajectory of that novel, certain odd gaps and catapults at the level of style as well as storytelling continuity—and sometimes a matter of style almost in defiance of plot, including at one point the cross-paragraph bridgework between a single vowel sound in inadvertent recurrence within dialogue. Woloch's general point was the tendency in this Dickens novel, as in Dickens at large (if often more subtly), for discourse to get out ahead of its own story world, or, in other words, for the telling to exceed and even override the told.

One result was precisely that Woloch's ear picked up on things, very little things, usually missing from the roster of critical evidence—their being beyond both critique and all thematic utility. One might identify the phenomenon Woloch was after in his discourse/story split as a case, in prose fiction, of prose trumping its own fiction. To crystallize this Dickensian inclination, Woloch instanced a quintessential, if almost infinitesimal, moment at the level of "microstylistics," where the lack of relevance to story (or call it a character's own potential obliviousness to the spoken effect in question) throws us back on phonetic process alone—and the ambivalent zone of its audition, neither definitively here nor there. With Gurney in mind, it is a case of stenography's lost vowels returning on steroids, and all but in stereo, to solder the eccentric crevice of this interchange. Triggering a kind of a portmanteau moment both degree zero and maxed out, here is Mark Tapley to his friend Martin, with surprising vehemence on a minor point: "Why, then I answer plainly no." Without dropping a beat, but merely prolonging a legato note: " 'Oh!' said Martin, in so exactly the same key as his friend's No, that it sounded like an echo." Resembled an echo in whose mind? Nothing is made of this—except by Woloch. In the passage as given, who's listening but us? Not *seemed* (to anyone in particular) like an "echo," but, yes, "sounded" like one. And beyond the quasi-cinematic sound bridge installed by this narratively irrelevant inflation of the letter *o* into a homophonic rejoinder, there is (I would want to add, in the very spirit of Woloch's evidence) the Other Dickens also at play in buckling—just one extra notch tighter—the cross-syllabic aural hook between "*so* exactly" and "*Oh, said.*" Such is a further and flanking border raid of discourse upon story. Suffice it to say that, in the hand-tooled bag of tricks that is the Dickensian portmanteau—in all its scalar variance, from single fanned-out letters to whole interfaces of conversation—the internal pockets of demarcation can fold and invert as well as swell and telescope. The aberration braces the norm. Even in this tiny "No/h" drama, there is an energy in the wording—a force one couldn't call style—that bestrides the gap, and does so with the contingent byplay of sounded letters operating astraddle, yet again, to sense. To reiterate, therefore, this chapter's initial cross-examination of such cross-word distraction: what writer writes this way, so that his readers can't even tell whether the characters are in on what the narrator depicts about the very sounds they make? The wrong question, again, for it is the Writing itself that executes the effect at this point of interchange, bridging this strange cantilevered gap like an improbable prose enjambment. It is the Writing that writes itself out, out into the open, in such cases, self-propellant in both its verbal fetishism and its unabashed semantic irrelevance. The Other Dickens, we may come to think, is simply the scribe of this writing drive, taking dictation from the originary matrix of his own word forms.

One grows so attached to Woloch's idea of auditing such minor volcanic phonemes, as if erupted not just from gaps in the prose line, but from the breach between discourse and story, that it is tempting to apply such a bipartite model, one level down, to that cross-linguistic play between signifier and signified noted in the introduction, for instance, in the first sentence of *Little Dorrit*. There we see/hear the Other Dickens taking visible as well as audible delight in a covert intrigue between spelling and meaning in cross-lingual assonance and phantom alliteration ("Mar*seilles* l*ay* burning in the sun, one d*ay*") before shifting from this public oven—melting pot as boiling cauldron—to the inner prison plot.

It's perhaps to be expected, then, that in the next novel, *A Tale of Two Cities*, the English-French bilingual play would be even more pointedly recruited, as in the mayhem emblemized by the "*coarse garb* of the *Carmognole*" in its switches between long and short vowels, diphthongs, and hard and silent *g* sounds, the last playing its strictly English-speaking part in the tightly intertwined "rage of conflagration" elsewhere described in the novel's mounting violence. With Woloch's more particular example in mind from *Chuzzlewit*, we note that even the fused bipolar *o(h)* sound returns in *A Tale*, not in the lingering negative of dialogue, but this time in the rhetorical address of apostrophe. For the same passage that mentions the daily delivery of bloody "wine" to slake the "devouring thirst" of La Guillotine, rendered up from the punning "cellars" rather than *cells* of the prison, later narrows its play to a single amplified phoneme when adding—this time in the artificial address of discourse alone—that, compared to liberty, equality, or fraternity in the mantra of the Revolution, the threat of "death" (its mandated alternative) was "much the easiest to best*ow*, O Guillotine!" In phonic transference from French to English: uill = ee; ine = een. From "bestow" forward, then, at the heart of another chiasmus and its trailing after-echo here—ee/o/o/ee/o/ee—the bilingual waxes all but metalinguistic.

Then, too, the nervous energy of rhetoric in this novel is so strong that the unspoken inverted cliché of turning swords into plowshares joins with that other avoided biblical allusion, about *reaping what you sow*, for a further disruptive syncopation concerning the guillotine's vinoculture. This happens in a phrasal blindsiding by the Other Dickens when the Revolution is compared to the yield of more natural cycles. In the final scene of martyrdom, the motif begun with "the Farmer, Death" is summed up in suggesting or seeming about to be (in my conjectural italics) that "there is not in France, with its rich variety of soil and climate, a blade *other than the guillotine whose fruition is more inevitable*." Such mordant wordplay is what we might have expected in a phrasing that in fact swivels away from the easily misread steel "blade" of violent outcropping to the extended agricultural series of "a blade, a leaf, a root, a sprig, a peppercorn"—all singled out as no more certain of "fruit" than the sown "seed of rapacious license" eventually brought to harvest by none other than the otherwise unsaid, but here hinted, vertical blade of the true Grim Reaper.

As should be apparent by now, the Othering from within of Dickensian phrase can take place not just across the straddled gap between grapheme and phoneme, or between bilingual registers, but between one word and its entirely dodged but nonetheless immanent—or echoing—alternative, not to mention (though I'm about to) between punning syllables of otherwise more neutral surnames than ones like Summerson. Analysis resists protesting too much on behalf of the most "secretive" of such wordplay.

Certainly, a reader doesn't have to think that the disused agricultural "carts" mentioned in the first chapter of *A Tale of Two Cities*—as destined for repurposing as those tumbrils eventually rolling (or, more to the echoic point, "rumbling") to the guillotine—are meant to shadow the syllabic Cart-on (to death) of the martyr-hero's name. Nor is it inevitable, in the relation of nemesis to victim, to hear the click of Madame Defarge's knitting needles in the name of the threatened and antithetical Darn-nay. Even the slipperiness of the Other Dickens, if I may put it this way, is usually on firmer ground. And, to be sure, no such obsessional parsing is necessary to respond to unmistakable tag-names, nor to register the phonetic cresting that may come in their lexical wake.

When Carton complains to the allegorically misspelled Stryver of always being withered in the face of the latter's gross pushiness, spelling has other oblique work to do: first by forcing some phonemic elbow room of its own within the very phrasing of a shouldering bully's progress, then by the offstage slant rhyme of an absent idiomatic word with its oblique and dehumanizing substitute on the page: "You were always driving and riving and shouldering and passing, to that restless degree that I had no chance for my life but in rust and repose." Carton once responded to this claustrophobic ambit of ambition as a sheer slacker, and prose here follows suit. Straddling text and vernacular intertext, the psychological corrosion of "rust and repose" chimes with a formula like *rest and repose* (across the vestigial stenographic **rst** bracket) just as the iterative emphasis (though not phrasing) of "driving and *(d)*riving" serves perfectly to derive a divisive effect from its indefatigable cause. To complement Empson's engineering sense of verbal "play," both tension and give, with another explanatory trope from mechanics, we might add that the gaps straddled at various scales by the Other Dickens are often fluctuating syllabic or phrasal valves—between word sounds or senses—that become the revolving doors of this play, this circuit of interplay, in cases both phonetic and syntactic alike. In *A Tale*, the results can range from the Cockney mispronunciation of Jerry Cruncher's "I'll out and *announce* him," speaking more accurately than he intends, to a prose overstepping its phonetic bounds in a quite different fashion. The latter occurs, notably, when the blood-red "stain dyeing" everyone who comes to sharpen their blades at the Paris grindstone—saturating in the process the fabric swatches that bind up the broken weapons ("ligatures various in kind, but all deep of the one colour")—involves a dye matched, more closely than anything but phonetic echo can intend, "by the same red hue" that "was red in their frenzi*ed eyes*." All told, the crush of desperation and brutality in this novel seems to release the heady rush of the Other Dickens as never before, so that in this case the frenzy, like the blood, drenches the ligatures of prose in even the fleeting bleed between syllables.

Lending a Shakespearean Ear

Following on from our last chapter's auditory excursion into the perfected and unchecked thick of vowel sounds that were once, under high-speed stenographic policing, thinned to silence, one way forward is by returning to the double Shakespearean influx first detected in *Martin Chuzzlewit* but more heartily at work from the next novel forward. This traceable, almost tangible, impact can be felt, beyond character formations, in everything from phonetic to syntactic intricacies and iterations, from sly sonorities to manifest rhetorical amplification—including, as we'll be realizing, certain kinks and overheated linkages of grammar that are largely unique, before Dickens, to Shakespearean intensity. Between *Chuzzlewit* and *Dombey and Son*, and with stagings of *Hamlet* fresh in Dickens's mind, we've noted already the uncharacteristic joke that rises defensively to Scrooge's mind in *A Christmas Carol* in order to beat back superstition, trying as he does to blame dyspepsia rather than ectoplasm for the risen ghost ("more of gravy than of grave")—as if, beyond the crisp dichotomy, alliteration and assonance were in themselves an index of nervous free-association. In a related manner, our preceding chapter emphasizes a certain centripetal force at the core of Dickensian *wording* generated from the vocalic nuclei of his echoism—however much given to further syllabic pickup across a given prose terrain. We turn now to a tendency of more marked centrifugal overflow from a manifest whole *phrasing* into its semantic spin-off. One stylistic difference that results: where the stenographically inflected (or shadowed) inscape of single words tends to stress their phonetic center of gravity, the expansiveness of sound and syntax in the complementary habits scanned from here out in this chapter operates as if to straddle phrasal alternatives rather than to concentrate sense in recursive or displaced sonority.

Shakespeare hovers over all of this, even when no specific rhetorical tics are brought to mind from the plays. Well along in *Martin Chuzzlewit*, in a wholly digressive sidebar, one of the lowlifers gathered around the scheming Montague Tigg (a name whose vocalic core is easily flipped later, under alias, to "*Tigg* Mon*tague*") agrees with an absent acquaintance that "There's a lot of feet in Shakespeare's verse, but there an't any legs worth mentioning in Shakespeare's plays." Bared limbs and sexual theatrics aside, there's a good deal of metrical footwork in Dickens as well. Beyond this, too, and not unrelated to the doublings and phrasal distensions of Shakespearean rhetoric, there is, as noted already, that disruptive form of comic phrasing that has, quite deliberately, either two legs or none to stand on: its conjoined associations bowed open, rather than knock-kneed, within a bracketing syntax gapped across disparate senses of its predicate. Like the interpenetrating vocables of syllabic sequence, this is a cross-limbed syntax at once tandem and composite, dovetailed, terraced, you name it—where one line of thought is superimposed upon another without the possibility of being entirely correlated.

And if we want to think of this effect as enhanced and varied from midcareer forward because of Dickens's traveling engagement with his portable Shakespeare while beginning, in America, to conceive the plot of *Chuzzlewit*, that thought can only sharpen the focus of our attention. For many Dickensian phrasings wheel into the orbit of this hypothesis. In returning, for instance, to certain forking or handcuffed effects—one's figurative terms dependent on the gravitational pull sensed in a given case—let it first be noted that the above comic aside about feet versus legs isn't the only allusion to Shakespeare in the novel under development by Dickens while journeying with his plays. We can look to another such explicit mention, considerably more suggestive, before returning to the potential Shakespearean resonance per se of any such splayed grammar—and its often accompanying sound play.

I refer to a passage that indirectly anticipates later psychoanalytic thought about the relation of dreamwork to the verbal unconscious—including the composite formations that Freud saw shared by conflationary portmanteau puns and the melded associations of unphrased desire. Tacitly foreshadowing this, Dickens's evocative sense of verbal dream sounds, rather than just dreamwork, makes this next passage as central to the enriched texture of Dickensian Writing from here out as it is digressive in this particular plot. Martin has asked Mark to read to him, and, accepting Shakespeare as a suggestion—"He'll do"—adds that "there's no greater luxury in the world, I think, than being read to sleep. You won't mind my going to sleep, if I can?" One more revealing proviso follows: "You needn't leave off when you see me getting drowsy (unless you feel tired), for it's pleasant to wake gradually to the sounds again." Steerforth may have felt the same way when being narrated to by David, as I surely did when my babysitter sent me under—and brought me back—with the rhythms of their story. But there's more at issue in this seeming digression about hearing Shakespeare intoned, for what rouses audition from drowsiness has already brushed the threshold of a verbal unconscious.

Concerning the portmanteau terms that model the transformation of waking impressions into oneiric form, Freud gave as example such a pun as "alcoholidays," not slurred on the lips of the celebrant but figured in the slippages of the written syllable. Or "famillionaire."[3] Think again of Esther's tentative approach to "portlimportant." Dickens indulges in such a conflationary logic, of course, in the overlapping of single words as well as in the cross-wiring of their syntactic expectations—so that both syntax and lexicon can momentarily be sparked into short circuits at different scales of conflation. The latter mode of overlap is rarely as crisp, obvious, and semantically charged as "alcoholidays." The reader, like Martin with his Shakespeare, wakes more often to dreamier skids and backslidings between syllabic boundaries: those border aids to further semantic fallout. When not rippling the text with an elusive undertow of phonetic energy, these effects may well be totally candid and rhetorical, as when, in a mockery of prosecutorial bombast in the first of the trial scenes in *A Tale of Two Cities*, we're treated to a checklist of adduced villainies in Darnay's recent past. In this, we are to believe that his consorting with the French enemy was done, not just by seditious premeditation, but "wickedly, falsely, traitorously, and otherwise evil-adverbiously": the last hyphenate suggesting, beyond the *v*-alliteration, a mock-composite of "adverbially" and "verbosely." Such is an induced internal fusion within this one novel's broader disjunctions, where the frayed grain of semantic abrasions—or, again, the sprung valves of demarcation—operate in a broader rending of syntactic sense.

Further, "adverbiously" can help remind us that Dickens, adept at grammatical terminology and often wielding it with aplomb in comic circumstances, is never slyer with it than in this same novel, when describing the overseas shopping practices of the feisty and combative Miss Pross. Refusing to learn any French, but bargaining with Parisian grocers nonetheless, her "manner of marketing was to plump a noun-substantive at the head of a shopkeeper without any introduction in the nature of an article," where we might at first expect the last word to be part of the grammatical template. After all, nothing has been "plumped down," just thrown out for response. But it isn't a question of *orange*, for instance, sans "introduction" as *une orange*. The "article" in question, as referred to by Miss Pross in cahoots with the Other Dickens, is the item itself, waiting on the other side of a defiant illiteracy of designation. The self-styled grammarians among us have thus been tripped up, even while the devotees of syntactic ingenuity are almost immediately rewarded when the modus operandi of Miss Pross is now fully explained. At such times "her manner was," following out the sentence structure again, "if it happened not to be the name of the thing she wanted, to look round for that thing, lay *hold of* it, and *hold on by it* until the bargain was concluded." Even that unwavering "hold"—when switched to the pertinacity of "hold on," the latter verb being more metaphoric than the first—straddles two divergent idioms in just the mode to which we're becoming accustomed. Not only when it arises in connection with actual linguistic terminology like "noun-substantive," we might well wish to designate any such vernacular pivot a case of metagrammatical comedy.

And the mode is a multifarious one, as variable as the facets of both syntax and syllabification. Many effects that intrude upon meaning like unconscious slippages can seem less lulling and "dreamy," to say the least, than Martin's wish for the soporific of literary recitation. We're more likely to have the rug of utterance pulled straight out from under us, as in the case of Miss Pross's hard bargaining in the economy of reference itself. Yet varying Martin's terms for the half-aware audition of Shakespearean word sounds, one notes that certain grammatical couplings, not just sound clusters, can wake from dormancy a second sense of their own predication—and thus, one might say, find themselves turning a phrase and a corner at once. After all, it is the connection between sound play and wordplay—up and down the scale of effect, as well as across the spectrum of its variety and potential thematic impact—that each chapter so far has been demonstrating. That alone is a way to phrase the Shakespearean legacy in Dickensian prose. And the effect, of course, can be as much nightmarish as sleepy. Recall, as Dickens may well have done in his capitalizing on such effects from here out in his writing—and soonest of all with the toxic wordplay of Carker the Manager in the next novel, *Dombey and Son*—the venomous punning by Iago in just that forking mode to which we now return. For his suggesting that Cassio has either "lied with" or "lied on" Desdemona—the latter if only in the sense of "fibbing upon" rather than topping her—is enough to inflame a homicidal chaos of further association. And eventually to trigger Othello's final tragic repetition of "put out the light" in both its senses, literal and lethal: snuffing his candle and his bride at once.

Dickens has, in fact, unleashed a tamer version of two different kinds of "lying" in *Martin Chuzzlewit*, by stating that Mrs. Gamp, disreputable funeral assistant as well as midwife, once "setting aside her natural predilections as a woman," certainly "went to a lying-in or a laying-out with equal zest and relish"—as if even the sibilant redundancy of "zest and relish" was somehow assigned, one each, to birthing and burial respectively. The Shakespearean variant of such a phrasal cleft (again hendiadys, a "twinning" in the A and B of C mode) would materialize in something more like *the zest and relish of an equal hour*. Further to compare the ridiculous with the sublime, who can rule out entirely some connection between Sairey Gamp's duplicities, as marked by split syntax, and the three-pronged lament by Hamlet's father's ghost—in an inverted grammar capturing in final downbeat the swiftness of his triple deprivation: "Thus was I, sleeping, by a brother's hand / Of life, of crown, of queen, at once dispatch'd"? Again "at once," like "simultaneously" in Dickens (when Pickwick "fell into the barrow, and fast asleep, simultaneously"), flags a temporal convergence not quite matched at the logical level. This is because life, even in Shakespeare, is not snatched away in the same sense (or gesture) that a crown is. Normalizing this to a more familiar joke form in modern nightclub comedy: *Take my wife—please!—before my hat or life*. In its sidestepping of anything like tragic anguish, stand-up comedy, as much as Dickensian phrasal slapstick, may often seem to have several legs to stand on at once, made apparent in the unexpected dropkicks of grammar.

But how, more specifically, does Dickens on the subject of Sairey Gamp seem to take on a motley version of the Shakespearean mantle? In her being said to bestow her enthusiasm equally on a "lying in" and a "laying out," Mrs. Gamp's spur to the narrative's verbal invention is stationed at some halfway point between Shakespeare's royal rhetoric and some funereal punning out Joyce's *Wake*. But it's her more radically divided (rather than selfishly egalitarian) motives that bring the prose to its fullest two-faced life. Funerals aside, certainly Mrs. Gamp's relish for the birthing moment is strikingly misplaced in a later passage of forking grammar not just generally invested in wordplay but hewing to that punning doubleness of prepositions (and hewn apart by them) on which so many of those strained shackling phrases depend, in Dickens even more often than in Shakespeare. Approaching the newly wed but bitterly mismatched Mercy (Merry) Pecksniff and her loathsome mate, Jonas Chuzzlewit, Mrs. Gamp addresses them silently, not as people but as business prospects, "with a leer of mingled sweetness and slyness; with one eye on the future, one on the bride, and an arch expression in her face, partly spiritual, partly spirituous, and wholly professional and peculiar to her art." As if to enforce the preceding wordplay whose split reference emerges from the initial alliterative dichotomy of "sweet" and "sly," the Other Dickens goes so far as to avoid the more idiomatic *expression on her face*, substituting the chosen "in" it, so that the riven idiom of the preceding "on" sequence will speak more openly for itself. You don't, that is, keep the same eye on the future as on the bride. One is a metaphorical vision, the other literal. In reading Dickens, we are frequently asked to keep grammar's own sort of binocular perception in mind.

Punning iterations of any sort, including phrasal off-echoes of either aural or grammatical cast, illustrate only that broader straddling of linguistic gaps whose narrower variants can be forded as well by single truant phonemes. Such divisive phrasing at the sublexical level can thus be thought, but first of all sensed, to resonate with all the other split ends of stylistic advance and unravelment in Dickens. At each stratum of notice, continuities are fissured, their cognitive nodules—and recognized semantic modules—obliquely redistributed. Flux, ordered by recurrence, is the shared condition vexed by such syllabic, dictional, and phrasal splayings. To appreciate this is further to sense the potential diffusion of any Shakespearean influence, filtering up as it might from the level of single syllables to complex syntactic armatures in a scalar contagion that is almost at times fractal in its proliferation. In the spirit of this imbibed influence from his long attachment to the Bard, it's not hard to imagine—hard *not* to imagine—Dickens responding equally, in uptake, to both the grammatical doublets of Shakespeare and his lexical dovetailings, the handcuff grammar and the cross-word threadwork, as if they were part of the same stressed webworld of human speech in inspired mediation. In the matter of two-for-one grammar in a comic vein, there is, for instance, Mistress Quickly in *The Merry Wives of Windsor* fearing a row that will result in "an old abusing of God's patience and the king's English," where the reader (or even faster, the listener in performance) needs to think—yes, quickly—to get the joke. Why should this be dissociated from the quickened ear needed, later in the canon, to hear a slur on Cressida in the famous sound pun "Trojan's trumpet"? Lubriciousness is only one facet of a lubricated vocabular arsenal that fuels Shakespearean wordplay from the level of the least sibilant of sexual innuendo ("*s* trumpet") to that toxic pun about "lying upon" the body of Desdemona—and to which Dickens and his Other have equal access.

Forkings and Skewerings: Slips of Syntax and Tongue

Moreover, aside from double *entendres* (intentions) of this manipulative and character-driven kind, there is another sense of double "hearings" (understandings) implied by the received French phrase. And where else but in Shakespeare could Dickens have found a kind of higher license for the syllabic punning that would enrich and diversify what could otherwise seem merely his derivative lifting from the logic of Cockney jokes in the popular Victorian magazine *Punch*? But make no mistake. There's nothing credibly Shakespearean to be found in the delirious blunt punning deployed so brazenly at the start of *Martin Chuzzlewit* in connection with that least witty of families and their desiccated ancestral tree, descendant from "The Lord No Zoo." But *Chuzzlewit* boasts quieter deposits of suspected influence, with the Other Dickens on hand to manifest and ramify them—as do the other and far greater novels coming, where the rebound from stenography, on the one hand, and the simultaneous grounding in Shakespeare at the start of Dickens's career, on the other, keep maturing each other in continuous cross-fertilization.

For the sake of argument—my own so far, that is—I have no wish to overtax a thesis that is barely one to begin with, but more like a considered inkling. Yet I promised to come back, and I am doing so now, to a curious way in which the stenographic approach to the programmatic blank-ing out of preformulated phrasing, at what chapter 1 called "dash speed"—in other words, that accelerated address to the rhetoric of recurrence by mere horizontal strokes—might have some light to shed forward on later inveterate habits of Dickensian phrasing and its alternate, pattern-breaking wit. This is the suspected case regardless of whether such effects are occasionally woven in with subliminal phonetic linkages—and whether or not the broader syntactic spans may seem as convincingly derived (like reinjected vowels) from shorthand's constraints: as the purposeful obverse of brachygraphic economies. In any event, these broken grammatical spans are too rich for most writers' blood—and it seems at least worth entertaining them here, often entertaining as they are, in their speculative role as a Dickensian reaction-formation to the routinization of series in stenographic ellipses.

If much of the declamatory rhetoric transcribed by the young Dickens had a fill-in-the-blank cast and cadence, lulled by expectation and availed in the pace of transcription by iterative dashes, why not later—in his coming of age as a comic maestro of phrase—try making hay of this dullness by deviant variation? Why not, for instance, make the blandest of conjunctions in shorthand's own version of *&*—rather than the adversative and redirective *but*—come newly alive as the lever of an unpredictable contrast after all: by rendering the pace of conjunction (in syllepsis) suddenly disjoint? Where the equivalent of blah, blah, blah would once have communicated a predictable parliamentary anaphora to the stenographer, now—in vocabular slapstick—the ampersand can mark a grammatical quicksand, where any steady footing is impossible. In Dickensian phrasal farce, that is, borrowed even for noncomic disjunctions, the relation of collective grammatical objects to a given verb is not, for instance, a comfortable matter of A and B and, yes, inevitably C (or, in other coding, derived from the ellipses of brachygraphy, a formulaic A, and —, — —), but instead, breaching the serial grammar, a destabilizing move from x through y to see-this-instead. Such are the handcuffed disjunctions not just of Dickensian syntactic farce but sometimes of a more telling conceptual straddle. In any case, what is involved, again in the sense of phrasal tensility, is a test of pretension and retention at the grammatical level.

Often, of course, the series is rendered all the crisper by being tightened to a syntactic doublet ("went home in a flood of tears and a sedan-chair"), but elsewhere, by contrast, it is so drawn out as to make a separate point in itself, as emphasized in the following case by an ancillary phonetic nexus coming on the heels of a distended series. Quoting the echoic wrap-up momentarily out of context: "But the last item was long, long, long, in linking itself to the rest." In brachygraphic series, code it "long, —, —," while in the actual phrase's vocalic elongation, what we hear evinced is the gradually activated link between the tripled **lng** and the arriving **lnk**. But the sentence that precedes and precipitates this minor phonetic fitness has also maximized the lexical, the metatextual, irony of "item" in its reference not to an entity (except verbal) but to a condition.

Here, then, is the full broken parallelism, the preceding sylleptic slipknot, that levels material and psychological provision in the prison life of *Little Dorrit*—this, on the occasion of the hero's being accidently locked up overnight in the incommodious snuggery: "The two tables put together in a corner, were, at length, converted into a very fair bed; and the stranger was left to the Windsor chairs, the presidential tribune, the beery atmosphere, sawdust, pipe-lights, spittoons and repose." Yet it is precisely that "last item"—in the plosive decline from "spittoons" to "repose"—whose "linking," not just descriptively but *grammatically*, has been so "long, long, long" (and no doubt unexpected) in coming.

And if we may wish to think of this elongated phrasing as itself mimetically drowsy in its fading out into grammatical dissociation on the way down into unconsciousness, we may sense a yet more poetic variant of somnolent phonemes, rather than grammar, in a later description of the dream state that follows its own oneiric logic of syllabification. One level down from the bowlegged grammar of syllepsis, this involves the straddling, instead, of a vowel nucleus by a variable consonant bracket—in a mode of "concertina" play that may just as soon have recalled Gurney to Dickens's scribing novelistic mind as it does to our reading ear. It is certainly among the finest single phrases in his noncomic prose, exquisite in the unusual simplicity of its registered desperation. Dickens is here portraying the emaciated and dehumanized peasants on the Marquis's estate in *A Tale of Two Cities*: "Dreaming, perhaps, of banquets, as the starved usually do, and of ease and rest, as the driven slave and the yoked ox may," they are left to consume only their own dreams. Paraphrase aside, this we learn in a vocally "yoked" effect, between alliterative past participles, that comes in compensation when the syntax of this same sentence completes itself with its delayed plural subject and consequent predication: "its lean inhabitants slept soundly, and were fed and freed." Not just separately and expansively **fd** and **frd**, the wish fulfillment is spread wide before our eyes (and ears) in the long double *e* sound released from within the triggered fantasy. Such is the language of the unconscious springing a momentary utopian respite in the immediate fueling of revolt: anticipating, in deflected cliché, the very *taste* of freedom—in the form of revenge—to come.

Other straddlings, of conjunctive syntax rather than paired lexical frames, are certainly more common. I've several times written lately—gone into enthusiasm and print, that is—about the effect of lexical cross-coupling (or handcuffing) in Dickensian fiction, most recently in *The Deed of Reading*, with scores of examples amassed in various treatments (and convened under the loose rhetorical rubric of syllepsis, related debatably to zeugma in the ranks of professional rhetoricians).[4] Allow me to think, without rehearsing this litany of instances from previous cullings, that my point here about its ingrained fascination for Boz from his *Sketches* forward—or say, its inveterate temptation for the Inimitable and his Other—is rendered all the more convincing by my not needing to recruit previous examples. A considerable batch of new evidence seems sufficient in itself to trace a pattern and cement a tendency. Further, the fact that the derivation of the term *syl-lepsis* from the Greek for "taking together" is closely related to the etymology of the word *syl-lable* encourages the conceptual link between sublexical clusters and syntactic jointures.

As early as *Nicholas Nickleby*, in fact, we have two models for this cleft reference, this straddling of grammar and phonetics alike, in the quick-change artistry of narrative discourse. Here, in a minor comic passage from *Nickleby*, the joke of arbitrary yoking is expanded in a move beyond two predicates splintered from the roots up, in the initial pair of verb phrases, to the more common form of a single predication with two discrepant objects grafted onto it. First: "Poor Madame Mantalini wrung her hands for grief, and rung the bell for her husband"—a false parallelism that sacrifices standard grammar ("rang the bell" rather than "rung" it) to the homophonic pun. This preposition-hinged twist then gives way in the same sentence, as if by the inertial force of sliding association, to the crisper doublet already tested in *Pickwick Papers* with the same phrasal verb "fell into." For immediately following those swiftly rung grammatical changes, we get this after a semicolon: "which done, she fell into a chair and a fainting fit *simultaneously*" (as with the lack of lag time in Pickwick's own double "fall"). The Other Dickens must relish that repeated adverb "simultaneously" at least as much in reference to the near instantaneity of prose's own spliced, coterminous wordings as to the precipitous events under depiction. Then, too, as far from this comic tonality as Dickens gets, in the bloody retribution of *A Tale of Two Cities*, the idea of armed women drawn to Madame Defarge's side is captured not just by the elliptical grammar of their swarming response, but by the leashed final abstractions, further eliding cause into effect across very different modes of fortified fury: "And to her, with a shrill thirsty cry, trooping women variously armed"—as the sentence fragment goes, swallowing up the verb-free distance closed by fury's magnetism—"but all armed alike in *hunger and revenge*." As if to say the hunger *for* it—by which, once more, they might be "fed and freed" in their dream of reparation.

That's one model, then, with discourse taking its own syntactic aim at characterization. But, elsewhere, a given plot agent can take similar matters in hand against another. Sometimes an entirely likable character, as in the case of Mr. George in *Bleak House*, can deliver up such cleft phrasings in a satire all his own. At one point he is mocking Smallweed's greed over hearing that one of his debtors is presumed dead. Grilled aggressively on the subject by the obsessive skinflint, George replies: "Don't lose your temper as well as your money." Even as a light jab, this catches exactly the idiomatic mismatch of subjective and objective referents—and hence the leveled difference, in the case of this exacerbated money grubber—between spirit and matter, temperament and legal tender. The wit is not so extreme as to be "out of character," nor does Smallweed have the least rejoinder. Though falling short of any real sparring match, the dialogic version of this verbal doubling, however, is often triggered by the word of one character in uptake by another. In an interpolated tale within *Nicholas Nickleby*, orders are given to a servant: " 'Leave the lamp,' said the Baron." The rejoinder is pro forma: " 'Anything else, my lord,' inquired the domestic." And in delayed uptick across this displaced "portmanteau" grammar: "The room." We'd be forgiven, I think, for assuming the Other Dickens as the Baron's invisible teleprompter at this neat turn.

This planting of a phrase on uniquely separate feet, even if on the same interrupted lips, can therefore be seen, and sometimes even more imperiously, to rope two distinct characters together in a directed speech act—rather than marking a simple grammatical gap in discourse alone. In such aggressive use, such stark abusage, the forked compounds can immediately convert the fleeting cognitive static of sheer narrational wordplay into the stance of a narrated power play—especially when deployed in phrasings peremptory and contemptuous like that from *Nickleby*'s inset tale. Or worse. In *Dombey and Son*, the reptilian Carker the Manager indulges in a mild skewing of phrase as a deliberately cruel skewering of his interlocutor when asking Captain Cuttle to remove himself and his nautical metaphors from the premises, or in other words: "To have the goodness to walk off, if you please . . . and to carry your jargon somewhere else." Later in the novel, when the squalid Mrs. Brown is expecting Dombey to succumb to her intrigue and accept her offer of secret information in the pursuit of Carker, the interlock of dialogue with her daughter in the wait for his uncertain arrival, given the locked horns of their exchange, twice splits their verb phrases down a contested middle—until Alice's attempt at a trumping punch line amounts to the apocalyptic equivalent of "not till hell freezes over." The fact that she's wrong, and that Dombey is soon to show, as of course Dickens knows he will, only foregrounds the importance of this time-filling exchange as strictly a symptom of emotional divisiveness, not of narrative uncertainty.

"He will come here."
"We shall see," said Alice.
"We shall see him," returned her mother.
"And doomsday," said the daughter.

Beyond Shakespeare, there's an echo of Greek drama in the stichomythia of such cross-laced dialogue—as later when David Copperfield throws back in Uriah Heep's slapped face the idiomatic question (about David's having "taken leave of your senses") with the compressed and contemptuous "taken leave of you" instead. In the above scene between the embittered Alice and her neglectful crone of a mother, two harpies gnaw at each other across a bipolar predication that might elsewhere have been telescoped by internal grammar rather than quotation into a discursive nexus like *They must wait to see what comes—him, if he does, and the doom that in any case lies waiting*. (The fact that what does happen when he arrives, in the full byzantine shape of its word-centered peripety and linguistic reductionism, should deserve most of the next and last chapter for explication can only lend premonitory weight to the mere bantering interplay of words in this scene of melodramatic buildup.)

Over against a testy waiting game like that scene from *Dombey and Son*, couched (or shackled) in such bipartite grammar, the act of parting rather than arrival can certainly be far from sweet sorrow, as Captain Cuttle well knows from being *thrown off* as fast as Carker's own turn of phrase. In a more dilatory and torturing fashion yet, this happens again, as late as Dickens's last novel, in the snarky wit of Eugene Wrayburn in *Our Mutual Friend*, who can't resist browbeating the slow-spoken Bradley Headstone with his spry contempt. Promising to defend the honor of his student Charley Hexam, who has just now vacated Wrayburn's quarters, against any toying with his sister's reputation on Eugene's part, Headstone's "I am his friend, and you shall find me so" gets batted back, in waving the threat off, by "And you will find HIM on the stairs." The "shifty evasions" that Bradley "scorns" on exit include just such slippery verbal put-downs—as followed next, in the face of his insistence that both his "hand and heart" are "open" to the boy, by Eugene's contemptuous chiming: "And—quite a coincidence—the door is open." In more conjunct and grammatically disruptive form, and without those pauses in dialogue that spark inspiration, a more ponderous Eugene might further have economized as follows: *Your moral support could be no more open to him than the door is to you, beyond which you'll find him, not just bravely befriended, but on the stairs*. This is a sideswiping snideness one doesn't associate with mild-mannered David Copperfield, but we've heard how the infuriations of Uriah can nonetheless draw it out of the hero's verbal repertoire when losing, not his mind, but all patience with that sycophant.

A pattern is clear, then, in the social register of such phrasing. The second shoe falling in this particular brand of straddled grammar, when manifested in dialogue, constitutes its effect as a wry punch line in the mode of one-upsmanship. A passing barb by the interpolated Baron of tangential comedy in *Nicholas Nickleby* is one thing, but a symptomatic thing. When activated by, and between, characters posited in the main story rather than just brandished in prose by narrative discourse—and showing the hand of the Other Dickens in either case—the idiomatically rarefied wit of a cloven vernacular phrasing is often directed downward along the rungs of a class or filial ladder toward the unsuspecting butt of its slick joke. Yet on rarer occasions, with no trace of comedy remaining, the contemptuous throwing of words back in the teeth of the speaker evokes an intensified stichomythia that aspires almost to the status of tragedy—Victorian rather than Greek—as in the mad fury of Rosa Dartle in the House of Steerforth at the news of his drowning. Hers is a rage, a dialogue-rending frenzy, that remains hyperarticulate at just the point where the mother's grief goes wordless. Not only that, but Rosa's ferocity incorporates the waver of alphabetic sounds and syllables back into the broader slippage of grammatical structure, evincing two scales of the same rabid derailment. The mute "moan and groan" of the nearly catatonic older woman, first rendered in discourse, is picked up by Rosa's own echoic dialogue, where a figure of sound is pounded out under further pressure from metaphoric cliché: "She has s*own* this. Let her *moan* for the harvest she reaps today" (her emphasis on the redirected trope)—an echo of agonized recrimination later sounded out further in the mother's depiction as "*Motionless*, rigid, staring; *moan*ing in the same dumb way . . . with the same helpless *motion* of the head." Phonetic iteration folds back on itself as cataleptic symptom, with "moaning" the inner force of all deadened movement.

David tries to abate Rosa's cruelty to this suffering woman, thinking that her resentment against Steerforth has motivated her, yet is cut off with a declaration, instead, of her undimmed passion for David's dead friend: " 'But if his faults,' I began." Immediately she explodes in objection: "Faults!" After extenuating remarks, but still sensing her resentment toward the deceased, David struggles again to suggest, across a gnarled phonetic counterpoint, that "If his faults—you have been bitter on them—" until she interrupts him in a fury: " 'It's false,' she cried, tearing her black hair; 'I loved him!' " In an almost perfect phonetic anagram and etymological convergence, the phrase "his faults" is contravened to "it's false" in the fault lines of interlocution and its vocalisms alike, as if almost by sheer—fierce and fixated, hardly free—association on Rosa's part. Not grammar here, so much as alphabetic substructure, seems operating astraddle in respect to an unsaid common core, banding together antithetical homophones around a dead center of rhetorical contradiction. It is this abyss into which we hear her denial slipping.

The norm for such jolting phrasal variants, however, whether phonetic or merely semantic, is more tongue-in-cheek than heart-in-hand.

Certainly that is the case in *Martin Chuzzlewit*. Even without being vol-
leyed back and forth across shifts in dialogue, there can be something
intrinsically haughty, as suggested, in a character's way with words in this
vein. The spoiled young Martin, for instance, in his presumed superiority,
slurs together a loose run of prospects manifestly beneath his station, if
not his diction. These foreseen but refused indignities are collateral fates
that couple economy and unglamorous passion in the very mode of their
indifferent dismissal: "It would never do, you know, for me to be plunging myself into poverty and shabbiness and love in one room up three
pair of stairs, and all that sort of thing"—where even the dead metaphor
of "plunging" is rendered further inert and trivial in illogical connection
with that up-stairs hovel of love. At the other extreme from a grammar of
blanketing discrepancies in real speech—in itself less common than narrative wordplay, and here incriminating at that—there is the kind of ajar (if
not quite jarring) parallelism that at one point gets lifted even above the
line of narrative discourse to pride of place in a chapter title. As the mar-
quee phrase for the forty-sixth chapter of *Chuzzlewit*, Dickens has seized,
to be sure, on a highly flexible verb in "make," but the result doesn't settle
for any such crisply handcuffed syntax as, for instance, *the prisoner made
both apologies and bail, simultaneously*. Here, rather, the effect may be
even more comic than usual, or certainly more flamboyant—if only for
the way in which the Other Dickens has arranged that the braided and
overlapped idioms don't quite mesh. For this is a grab-bag chapter "In
which Miss Pecksniff makes Love, Mr Jonas makes Wrath, Mrs Gamp
makes Tea, and Mr Chuffey makes Business." What is being made here
are phrases alone, not dramatic progress.

But these same grammatical straddlings between one verb usage and its
alternate or surrogate, even when less categorically bedraggled than in that
title, can have a risible poignancy all their own. This is especially apparent, two novels later, in the softened style of *David Copperfield*—where
such effects tend to congregate around the seriocomic disaster of the
newlywed Copperfield housekeeping. Two honest idioms part company
in order to make space between them for a middle and nonvernacular
third term at exactly the moment, in David's reported married life, when,
by hopeless domestic economy, comfort is being squandered along with
the very different sense of surrendered funds and tempers. It is here that
David tries patiently to explain to Dora how marital niceties as well as
savings are forfeited when "we lose money and comfort, and even temper
sometimes, by not learning to be more careful." (The low-keyed tweaking of idiom in "lose money . . . and even temper" later finds its way, as
we heard above, into the mouth of George in *Bleak House*; at this point,
for all the efficacy such crisp wit entails, it might as well be the Other
Dickens rather than David lecturing Dora from the wings of discourse.)

What is "lost" in all this domestic mess, rather than "kept," is spelled out shortly—before being splintered into different constituents of a noun back-formed from the "keeping of a house." Certainly any vernacular oddity like that is likely to get the Other Dickens going—and send him forward in the same vein. "After several varieties of experiment," writes a resigned David, "we had given up the housekeeping as a bad job. The house kept itself, and"—in bifurcated idiom—"we kept a page." But even this equilibrium is short-lived, since they can neither keep order at all nor servants for long. And so it goes.

We saw in the last chapter how Pip's "I'm for London, and greatness"—off for and bound for, destination and destiny in the same attempted deep breath—was tainted by just enough trace of comic forking to backfire against his pretensions. Yet there is surely some measure of self-mockery in his reporting, as previously alluded to, how he "formed a plan in outline for bestowing a dinner of roast-beef and plum-pudding, a pint of ale, and a gallon of condescension, upon everybody in the village." The cleaving of idiom opens a wound in his own vanity. Elsewhere, he's in fuller command of his grammar in these twin-pronged usages. Constables down from London after the bludgeoning of Mrs. Joe "had a mysterious manner of taking their drink, that was almost as good as taking the culprit." Later and elsewhere, Pip can be negligibly "busy with my books and Mr. Pocket" (258) after marking the more profound difference, in the ill-starred production of *Hamlet*, between inconveniences of staging and the tragic pitfalls of the portrayed world, with Mr. Wopsle's plight doubly precarious "on the brink of the orchestra and the grave." Sometimes, as we've seen before, this branching but roughly tethered grammar can be strung on a trellis of dialogue. Asking about the father of Herbert's fiancée—"What does he live on?"—Pip is surprised by the rejoinder "on the second floor." Latent here, however mild-mannered in this case, is the preemptive one-upsmanship of more scornful characters, like Carker or Wrayburn, throwing words back in the interlocutor's face.

Such tucking of phrase back upon itself in the umbrella-like folds of association is a tendency, as suggested above, that could well have been inculcated first, or at least incubated, and then later fortified, by Dickens's bouts with the Bard. It certainly may be that the renewed horizons of Shakespearean cadence to which Dickens's American reading opened him have found an immediate use in his own parody of these New World vistas in *Chuzzlewit*. For one can readily sniff out a Shakespearean hendiadys (again phrasal "twinning," rather than the splittings just exemplified) in a sentence marking the verge of the long American digression in *Martin Chuzzlewit*. This is a many-chaptered episode launched amid just that trivial hubbub so characteristic, in Boz's treatment, of the American shores—and where the Other Dickens is certainly quick off the boat as well: "Some trifling excitement prevailed upon the very *brink and margin* of the land of liberty." And, like everything else there, this noisy American land tends—in perhaps a further fallout from the unlabored circumlocution—to "prevail upon" (in the more common transitive sense of this verb phrase) one's limited tolerance for the raucous, the raw, and the grossly self-promoting. Then, too, a whiff of satire wafts across that "brink and margin" in its actual semantic measure—as if the approached border were indeed a social and spiritual precipice, especially given the experiences to come in Eden as a terrible falling off in the immigrant hopes of Martin and his friend Mark. But the main point at issue here, in Shakespearean derivation or otherwise, is the lexically padded border zone of the phrase itself, where two words stake out a coterminous terrain in a kind of decorative (mock-honorific) redundancy. In the mode of melodrama rather than satire, a redoubled version of this unsorted substantive crush occurs later, in *Great Expectations*, when Pip must make his anxious way in London through "the stir and motion of the commoner streets; through the roar and jar of many vehicles, many feet, many voices." Any logical distinction between "stir" and "motion" is itself a cognitive blur. Once again we find the Shakespearean overtones of an oversegmented A and B of C format—even while "motion of the commoner" calls up, on the fly, the very *commotion* that is again redundantly expanded with "roar and jar" (rather than "jarring roar" or "roaring jar"): in each paired phrasing a "concertina" of dissonance, involving in the latter case another faux assonance in the internal sight rhyme of "r*oar* and j*ar*."

As often in such wavering compounds, the discrepant tread of grammar finds itself syncopated with such phonetic quirks. In returning to *Martin Chuzzlewit*, we see how the most visible and tempting—if lackluster—of everyday anagrams can come to the surface with some additional phonetic force. After a fainting fit on the part of old Anthony Chuzzlewit, it "was past midnight when they got him—*quiet now, but quite* unconscious and exhausted—into bed," with the fact of quiescence taken up in the very intensifier of its designation. Then, too, at a certain level of perked notice, the wordiness that fosters a general spreading-out of phrase can be marshaled, in the same passages, alongside certain actual yokings and cross-shacklings of syntax. When effects of this sort are mated, for instance, with a complacent and expansive alliteration, we may at any point encounter as well the passing stumbles of straddling grammar limping between metaphor and literal inference. Look no further—for it awaits in this same novel's last chapter, as if summing an entire lexical motif on exit—than to Charity Pecksniff's vain triumph just before her jilting at the altar. Riding for a fall at the wedding breakfast, she is not just "full" of a merely alliterative "clemency and conciliation" but thus in a "frame of mind" to be recognized as "equally becoming to herself and the occasion," both flattering and festive in a conjoint haughty formality. All this before she is left in a lurch that might have been predicted from an earlier and miniscule wobble, if not lurch, between syllables—to which, in its ludicrous prenuptial clue, we return toward the end of this chapter.

Beyond a slant echo like *quiet/quite*, when the grammar of *Martin Chuzzlewit* snaps almost tight, but not quite, around a splayed predication, the effects can be even more suggestive. At its best, and almost at its most inveterate, the cross-braided or yoked syntax operates in league, one notch down in scale, with the cross-stitching of vocables. At that level, for instance, Mrs. Prig is said to be "bonneted and shawled and all impatience to be gone," where bracketed between the *b* and *p* of the overarching alliteration waits the vowel-heavy flip from state of dress to state of mind across the pivotal phonetic regroupings at "sh*awl*ed a*nd a*ll." Only the prose is all dolled up for our lingering notice. In such proliferating examples of *wordsplay* in this and later novels, in either mere vowel sounds or whole grammatical arcs—and whether anchored in a continuous passage of description, assigned to a single speaking voice, or divided in dialogue across the exchanged salvos of banter or the savage backstrokes of contemptuous dismissal—evidence suggests a common core of malleable phrasing, compressed or expandable at linguistic will. Or say, "encrypted" by script and syntax and then read back by oscillating sonority and a wavering semantics of phrase. With Gurney's stenographic grind undergoing an ultimate recuperation from *Chuzzlewit* on—after passing through, so to say, a year's therapeutic reprogramming by Shakespearean assonance and phrasal dilation alike—the Other Dickens is primed for the great second half of the Inimitable's career. It's up to the reader to hear along, to keep and listen up.

How else, in *Dombey and Son*, to register the echo, whether timely and clipped or intentionally awkward—and whether or not, in the closer chiming of British pronunciation, involving the pervasive overtone of "gain" in the Dombey emotional ledger—when his lost and otherwise devalued daughter is returned by Walter? As the phrasing has it: "In good time Mr Dombey's mansion was *gain*ed a*gain*, and a*gain*"—breaking stride with the latent idiom "again and again"—"there was a noise of tongues in the library." There's no little tongued noise in that sentence itself. It is, indeed, this next full-length novel after *Chuzzlewit* that will also maximize the byplay of phrasal alternatives as never before (especially in a familiar bifold mode), in everything from the negligible mention of Dombey in typical emotional retreat ("withdrew to his hotel and dinner," with the uncertain parallelism of an implied second "his") through the passing deflation, on his son's funeral day, concerning the lachrymose Cook, "who struggles about equally between her feelings and the onions," to the sliding prepositional twist in a description of Miss Nipper, "with her hair *in* papers and herself asleep *in* some uncomfortable attitude," to the unwitting play on words (with another preposition: the "for" of intent versus procurement) delegated earlier to the sickly but quizzical Paul Dombey himself, who, hearing that the rigorous Miss Blimber, even in bad weather, "was going out for a constitutional," wondered why, whatever "that" was, "she didn't send the footman out to get it." Out of the mouths of babes—including here, in Paul's precocious fragility, a hypersensitivity to wording itself. Whether one thinks of such plunges into the mysteries of idiom as compacted or unpacked, with straddling verbal options suddenly abutted or pulled asunder, the exploratory linguistic instincts engaged in these grammatical turns are hard to deny—and the shimmer of their phrasal farce (one manifestation of a deeper lingual force) hard to overlook.

As we had begun to see in the last chapter, the nuclear vowels suppressed by the Gurney discipline can come to the aid of the antiparliamentary false parallels doled out by Dickens's syntactic banana peels and their induced pratfalls. Syllable and syllepsis, again, in their own kind of "secret prose," are found operating a cabal of vowelization and grammatical divisiveness alike. In *Little Dorrit*, amid the mimetic sonorities and dubious euphonies already listed, the predominance of inherited family pride over legal tender in the person of Tite Barnacle comes packaged by a three-tiered assonance (available only to the ear, not eye) in skewering a bureaucratic parasite "more fl*u*sh of bl*oo*d than of m*o*ney." Not surprisingly, this is an effect less sustained and colorful in the mouth of a villain than of the narrator in this same novel, as when Rigaud later mocks the imprisoned hero for having "shown yourself more fr*ee* of sp*ee*ch than body, sir." There, of course, the sucker-punch body blow is meant not to sustain, but to break from, the assonant coupling ("free of speech") that precedes. And the effect can be darker and more complex yet in Dickens's late writing, splayed even beyond compounding in *Our Mutual Friend*, bleeding over into the syntactic wake of the structuring doublet. When Headstone chooses masochistically to inflame his murderous will by taking every chance to discover a liaison between Lizzie and the hated Wrayburn, his purpose, phonetically flagged at first, is to "*incense* himself with the sight of the det*es*ted figure"—but the sight of him, more specifically, "in her company and favor, in her place of retirement." The third "in" seems almost absorbed into the syllepsis in a further estrangement of prepositional norms. With a similar mordant tone, an antonymic preposition, "out" rather than "in," does comparable work in this novel when Mrs. Lammle warns Tremlow against her own effect on the Podsnap daughter, insisting that the girl is "best out of my house and my company."

Packing the Portmanteau

As must have been obvious, I've many times jumped the (historical) gun in anachronistically assigning a tempting name to more of the preceding verbal effects than are usually compassed by the term—but whose elasticity is properly invoked by it. Victorian popular philology saw Lewis Carroll coin the term "portmanteau word" in 1871—in dubbing such conflations, common enough today, as *brunch* or *smog* or *hangry*. As later theorized by Freud at the turn of the next century (without mention of *Through the Looking Glass*), such interpenetrating word blurs, as noted, operate like the condensations and displacements of the unconscious. Earlier, Humpty Dumpty, as if to make up for the *incompressible* jingle of his own name, recommends that a well-balanced mind, undecided whether to fume or to be furious, should identify itself as "fruminous." But this intertwine of lettering is less common than the mutually truncating collapse that adjoins whole intact syllables in such hybrids while squeezing out others—as in the more recent and self-designating neologism, and lexical pastiche, of *frankenword*: designating the kind of new term artificially birthed from a surgical graft of found vocabulary.

Although the less pejorative designation "portmanteau" was waiting beyond the horizon in Dickens's day, coined only a year after his death, the Other Dickens was walking the walk before there was a terminological talk to talk. The variably *brief*-but-decisive-*case*, if I may, for this malleability of speech forms—an expandable lexical valise or grip or briefcase—was part of Dickens's flexible travel kit in navigating the deliberately expansive but irregular terrain of his prose. As such, it operates at times directly alongside his ironies of lexically cross-straddled names—and even when a character is shown to be explicitly oblivious to the joke. As if in revisiting career-long habits of nomenclature in the summa of his last completed novel, *Our Mutual Friend*, and with undertones still from the truncated nuclear vowels of stenography, Dickens has his unimaginative man of one leg, when asked his name, append to his answer—in a disclaimer that may even put the "less" (less one leg) back in "Silas" as well as the n/omen into the inescapable portmanteau of "w[ooden l]eg": "I don't know why Silas, and I don't know why Wegg." Only the Other Dickens could fully inform him.

When glimpsed even further back in the rearview mirror of Humpty Dumpty's coinage, there is in *Martin Chuzzlewit* an irresistible, if entirely accidental, irony in the fact that at one point Dickens deploys one of his dialogic updendings, this time with a full semantic ambiguity, in connection with none other than just such a namesake valise or portmanteau. Irresistible, that is, for a chapter like this that finds in such compressions a broader principle of Dickensian stylistic comedy, from phonetic to grammatical. The reflexive moment in question occurs when such a common mode of actual suit-casing is found carried—almost by prescient terminological parable—between two denigrated figures in the plot. It's a passage that begins, typically enough, floated on a strained vocalic byplay in communicating a surplus of spirit under depiction. For here we find the ordinarily snarly and introverted Jonas Chuzzlewit becoming in his contemplated amours "so very buoyant—it may be said, boisterous—that Mr. Pecksniff had some difficulty in keeping pace with him." Kept from redundancy by stressed escalation, the slide from buoyancy to boisterousness only gains from a surreptitious continuity and build of sound—almost with a stenographic encryption all its own—across the non-eye echo of *uoy* and *oi*. The "pace" of effusion, figurative at first, soon becomes literal, as the men's physical stamina is taxed by a shared burden. As it happens, the conversation grows suddenly testy during the time when they have found it convenient to carry none other than a single portmanteau between them as they walk. Jonas has suddenly shrunken into himself and wants no more prodding about his sexual fantasies and schemes, leaving his servile companion—when assaulted with the unexpected command "Drop that, Pecksniff"—caught out "not exactly knowing whether allusion was made to the subject or the portmanteau." (Get a grip, Pecksniff.) If we ourselves weren't quick to assume the former in shelving any ambivalence attending the joke, chalking it up instead merely to Pecksniff's momentary discomfiture, here would be a marked, parsed, and rapidly unpacked portmanteau of grammar rather than lexicon—turned not to extraneous wordplay but to diagnosed narrative confusion.

Even when the "give" of Dickensian enunciation is broken open from within cited dialogue like this, there is still nothing here like the morbid spectral brilliance of the anagrammatic "his faults"/"it's false" in *David Copperfield*. But there is much that can be felt preparing for it. Such is the flexible capacity of the language game in this one early and transitional novel—as if deliberately brandished across the full spectrum of its linguistic manifestations: not just in the logical and vocalic domino effects of narrative treatment ("bonneted and shawled and all impatience") but even in dialogue itself, from subpunning doubleness ("Drop that") on down to miniscule equivocation of a single lone (and long) *o(h)* sound slung meaninglessly between interlocutors. The accordion form of a portmanteau logic enfolds multitudes—and often in the irrepressible voice of the Other Dickens: whether speaking, as it were, in or out of character. Varying Freud's use of the portmanteau model, we might well want to generalize, as hinted earlier, that this verbal Other to fictional narrative has a way of tapping the condensations and displacements—phonemic, syllabic, semantic—of prose's own unconscious.

We can stay with *Martin Chuzzlewit* a moment longer in this regard, without giving Pecksniff's confusion the last word, but rather turning—as promised several paragraphs back—to the fate of his spawn and victim, his spoiled daughter Charity, deserted at the altar as the novel draws to a close. Discussion has waited until the "secret" typifying force of the moment's syllabic accordion would be more fully heard to access the broader comedy of Dickensian naming in those extra phonetic ironies so often injected by the Other Dickens. Having earlier cajoled the grieving Mr. Moddle into becoming her reluctant lover, although his irremediably broken heart is pledged to her more attractive sister Mercy, we can only react to this coerced suitor's silly name as wedged somewhere in onomastic logic between *muddle* and the *model* fiancée he certainly isn't. But then Charity has nothing to lose by marriage in this regard, when surrendering the infelicitous name of her hated father. Even for his part, the ground-feeding abjection implicit in the pecking and sniffing of the patriarch can hardly be compensated for by the hypocritical rhetorician's own "Christian" name Seth—especially when so often punned on by the Other Dickens when flagging his arrant flights of hypocrisy with the verbal inversion of "saith Pecksniff." One generation down in the pecking order of selfishness, it might still fall to Charity to utter an equivalent lament to that of Georgiana Podsnap in *Our Mutual Friend*, as if in celebratory valediction to Dickens's own nailing of characters with the ironic slurs of nomination. How luminous a truism: "It's awful enough to *be* Miss Podsnap, without being called so."

Everything, then, points to a Pecksniff daughter happy to give her hand and name away in marriage, not least as she might become the cynosure of all gaze in her new status as Charity Moddle, the very paradigm of said virtue. Few readers could miss the blatant phonetic play between "blighted" and "plighted" at the splendid apex of the couple's forced rapprochement. Certainly the best man at this betrothal scene is the Other Dickens—when, that is, phrasing is hinged around an almost legalistic circumlocution: "Moddle was goaded on to ask whether she could be contented with a *blighted heart*; and it appearing on further examination that she could be, *plighted his dismal troth*, which was accepted and returned." Yet, just in advance of this, the foredoom of his eventual weakening and flight on the wedding morn is captured when the Other Dickens, with a vocalic extra flourish, reveals what could well be the true associational origin, if not etymology, of the sad man's goofy tag-name. "Moddle . . . had by this time become in the last degree maudlin." The last narrative degree, and the first syllabic degree as well: moddl(e)in. The involuntary suitor's name has revealed its true inference, cross-grained, in an enunciation that turns to a diphthong the soft *o* at its squishy center, then lengthens the liquid (*l*) sound to allow for a fuller second syllable.

The double take involved here may seem again like a poststenographic message from the inner creases of muteness itself, bringing the silent final vowel back to signifying life from the dribbling "le" of the man's surname. Such are the animating mechanics of the Dickensian vocabular apparatus all told: an infectiously flexible portmanteau system, by any other name, in a "concertina" of letters, lexemes, and idioms in retractable and expandable patterns—where what Writing stands astraddle of can be either the differential minims of word formation or the whole infrastructure of a sentence.

Extrapolated well beyond the low comedy of Pecksniff and Chuzzlewit trudging along athwart their shared portmanteau, the current chapter title in itself tilts both ways, like the textual effects it is meant to evoke across the whole gamut of Dickensian prose invention. While a story by Boz rolls along, its words keep to their own inner pace and beat in the march and frequent phrasal sidesteps of letters, syllables, and whole linked word sequences. Always in passing, in the continuous progressive tense of textual encounter, legible effect and generative cause are in this way not quite fused at a certain pitch of verbal attention, still twofold in their unfurling. Really reading is where—is when—one intuits this: intuits by producing it on the silent tongue. And many a local rift can contribute to this double recognition of Dickensian storytelling and its motoring prose. Along the reeled-off track of cellular wording, the signs of phrasing astraddle—flanking the very difference such prose is there to materialize and mark, and sometimes momentarily addling cognition in the process—are often what the intensive reader finds to transact with. In those same moments, at any scale of reception, phrasing astraddle is what the Other Dickens does.

Does, and is still doing even amid the audible tailing-off of stylistic inspiration in the unfinished *The Mystery of Edwin Drood* (1870). An early lament that the "cramped monotony" of a character's existence "grinds me away by the grain" may offer a less than riveting, however typical, lexical pulverization—and granular mimesis. Yet in describing the "portentous and dull" auctioneer and self-styled rhetorician Thomas Sapsea, an attenuated Dickensian wordplay—vestigially alive and still gamely (or at least recognizably) kicking—stresses in addition (via loosened syllepsis) the pompous local celebrity "having a roll in his speech, and another roll in his gait." As an alternative to the blowhard's own prose, though slowed a bit in mockery of its self-patience, phrasing here induces a tiny cross-word version of the alveolar trill (or "rolled r" itself) within the broad forking prongs of the satiric lampoon. It does so by further bringing to bear, in slant rhyme with "an*d d*ull" just before, an extra "ull/oll" of pulsation—through the elision of "anothe*r r*oll"—as if to confirm again, by phonic association, the dullard's lulling drone. Such is the longevity of the Other Dickens even within the waning powers of the Inimitable.

Comedy, as evidence has shown, is the usual stomping ground for the reciprocal sidesteps of such straddling grammar, but split syntax also has its darker, sardonic variation, as noted as well. This we see again in an almost morbid form in late Dickens: less a matter of semantic breakaway, in this climactic instance from a novel's famous sacrificial closure, than of narrative lockdown. At the guillotine finale of *A Tale of Two Cities*, the trope of "the Farmer, Death" introduced in the novel's first paragraph, even while dodging there the biblical formula "As you sow, so shall you reap," has come home to roost—along the destined route of execution. As the death carts part the mob in carrying Carton on to the guillotine, the agricultural figure (though no longer in personified form) has returned in the present tense when, in a clausal sequence thickened by a driven wedge of prepositions, "the furrow ploughed among the populace is turning round, to come on into the place of execution, and end." Any momentary sense of "ploughed" as the main verb is instantly corrected to "being plowed," in its purpose "to *come on into* the place of execution, and end." As observed earlier, the Other Dickens is a master of the extra preposition, so that, in this case, the sheer momentum of "come on" is impelled further, if paradoxically, by the rapidly elided result of all onwardness in the stoppage of "come into." And if this registers as a compressed and precipitous lexical enjambment, even a directional portmanteau, the thought is only confirmed by the straddling shift of phrasal weight at "and end": a terminus figured as both event and impasse, compound of the infinitive verb and a noun of finitude. With handcuff grammar in a variation as far from comic as anywhere in Dickens, the grammatical death grip of such phrasing is as anomalous as it is quintessential. So prodigal is the Other Dickens's tacit latitude in this vein, this variety of internal syntactic variation, that exemplification could go on for twice again as many pages. It is only this tragic rather than comic outlier from Carton's martyrdom that allows this single chapter to highlight, by such a final contrast, the prevailing norm, in its typically lighter-hearted loose ends, and end.

But not without helping, in conclusion, to sound a last elucidating note. With its depicted progress through the streets, that sentence about the ultimately halted tumbril enacts not just its own terminus ad quem but the general conversion of *textual space into recognition time*. This much about syntactic decoding should have been evident at every turn, yet certainly deserves "spelling out"—itself an idiom that speaks of alphabetic s/pacing as not just an ortho-graphic function but a cognitive prolongation. It is the latter aspect that needs stressing here—and overall. When this chapter isolates phrasings caught "astride" of linked transitional letters or compounded grammatical possibilities, or packed into a stretched "portmanteau" form of variable width, it is thinking in metaphors, using figures of stance or array or breadth for what is in fact a temporal (because in part aural) recognition across the lines of prose. Same when I speak at one point of a "binocular" notice. The time frame for such double vision is entirely the reader's, not that of visible script.

The rein of accelerated code has been displaced by spaciousness itself in operation. Sensing that each of the effects in this chapter may be felt (at least speculatively) to descend from Gurney, by aversion and reversal, is one response to their energetically refused logic of raced compression. Whether just in syllabic stretching or in whole phrasal chains expanded beyond expected semantic limits, what either mode of dilation can be thought to represent is a new and unruly dynamization of the brachy-graphic scribble. In what they both do and undo in the manner of phrasal linkages, the deep connection between cross-word slippages and the syn-tactic sidlings of syllepsis is that each tendency maximizes the temporality of reading by adjusting its recognition speed in process. That gear change is often the work of the Other from within the fabled flow of Dicken-sian narrative. One phrasal element magnetizes its successor too fast for the simple typographic logic of either gap or ampersand, break or series. We're still reading some of the last word when we should have cut loose into the next; we're still processing one predicate while being made to attach it to a further object in an unanticipated sense of the verb phrase. This is wordplay at two different scales, yes, syllabic and syntactic. But it is, first of all, the reader who is being played, played upon, across the partially unstrung pace of wording.

That the cross-weave of such effects lends itself to widely variable up-endings, rather than any clear taxonomy, may need, by now, no further justification. But might benefit from one last double example, veering from the miniscule to the rhetorical (and broadly comical—broad in both senses) in a single expansive verb phrase. As usual, the tiniest skids of indi-cation can operate in tandem with open schematic parallelism. The miser-able withered Smallweed in *Bleak House,* consoled in his impotent rages only by jaculating cushions at his detested wife, is manhandled in disgust by Mr. George at one point, who "appears in two minds whether or no to shake all future power of cushioning out of him and shake him into his grave." In a novel that alternates in its idiom between "whether or no" and "whether or not," with several instances of each across its length—used, it would seem, interchangeably—this time they seem, instead, used all but *overlappingly.* Then, too, as launch for the infinitive—at a different scale of straddling syntax rather than blurred word borders—the variant British idiom for the American "of two minds" installs its "in" ("ap-pears in two minds") as a closer prepositional setup for the relaxed (and faintly sylleptic) chiastic switch at "shake all . . . *out of him* and shake *him into.*" If Mr. George stops short, that is, of relieving this villain both of his vestigial bitter strength and his existence per se, the two being indistinguishable in his characterization, the ambivalence of the decision may seem hinged from within at first, by the Other Dickens, on the orthographics of "whether or *no to*." Hinged on contingency itself, that is: intuitive counterpart to comic ingenuity, whose phrasings are themselves often "in two minds." Not least, certainly, in the prepositional pivot that collapses a seeming dichotomy between "out of" and "into" toward a center of gravity in the victim's inert body (for whose death "the grave" is, of course, only a metonym): the limp body as seat of removed ire and life at once. The specter of agitation, we may say, is already phrasal before fatal. And its deliberation spun out across the elastic span of prose's own temporality.

In the slippery grips of all such verbal discomfitures, the difficulty of noting what exactly is astraddle of what, at more than one level of attention, is really the point of this chapter's titular formulation in the first place: its phrasing of both lexical and syntactic matter as it comes under distribution, in part, by the Other Dickens. This is what I meant above in suggesting that the structures of such wording approach almost a kind of fractalization. Phonic and syntactic alike, straddlings at more than one scale operate astride their counterparts, piggybacking on the other's kinetic energy in the very shift between registers. Undue phonetic latches and untoward syntactic bucklings operate athwart each other, in this way, not to thwart coherence but to suffuse narrative discourse with the ongoing temporal subplots of its own turbulence, marginal uncertainty, and productive suspense. Pacing, again, unstrung—and readjusted on the run. Engaging the linear and the temporal, prose line and its timing, a reading keyed up enough cannot help notice how many sentences in the novels come across to us—as we move across them—like a distended fuse set to detonate just out of phase with expectation. Hence the need to be absolutely clear. Spacing is only the girder for what is activated in and across time; straddling, for what is in fact serially stepped off through the choreography of phrasing and the inner musculature of its phonemes, syllables, and syntax in readerly production. It is only through such a somatics of enunciation, after all, that reading the One, Other, and Only Dickens really kicks in. The next and final chapter now moves toward—and then through—a narrative passage that imagines this whole process slowed almost beyond recognition, diminished to its mere alienated rudiments.

4

READING LESSENS

Reading—when one is really reading—lessens all intensities but its own, which it teaches anew from within. This is the lesson of the Other Dickens preeminently. With incomparable characters to wonder at, and ingenious plots to track and unravel, and with those bursts of extravagant comic phrasing throughout, what this kind of reading must go up against in Dickens—in slowing over its own verbal recognitions—might seem, at first blush, as propulsive a deterrent to any lingering stylistic attention as we have in our literature. Who would ordinarily wish to put brakes on the fun so as to study its fundamentals, to excavate in action the underground springs of linguistic inspiration? Such famously unhampered narrative flow as we find in Dickens's novels is, however, answered by a "compensatory" texture entirely up to the task of an intrinsic stylistic distraction from phrase to phrase, with all its heightened overlays of sound, syllable, and idiom. Here is the Other Dickens as the very bonus of the ongoing: the genius of such Writing always taking shape (like that of later vocal comedians) as a matter of timing—in both delivery and induced uptake.

So, in fact, the idea of compensation isn't quite right there, seeming as it does to put the cart before the horse—or, rather, the passengers and destinations of the story's course before the accentuating vehicle of its words, its discourse. There is no covert fictional bargain struck in such cases, where pockets of style, intensively submitted to in reading, would be part of a system of checks and balances, whether serving to relieve the tension of narrative or, alternately, to rev it up again. Nor are there stylistic intensities regularly "secreted" from all novelistic impulse. One may say, instead, that Writing in Dickens is the everywhere unsuccessfully repressed truth about narrative event: the other to its every thrust. And it is in the key of immediate appreciation, rather than in some later sterile analysis, that we may still find the "ha!" weighted down with the "huh?"—the rhetorical howler by the how of its achievement.

One result of such Writing is that, even in a concluding chapter like this, one is not ready simply to glance back—but only to look and listen harder across new narrative terrain. Closing in on *Dombey and Son*, as the breakthrough novel in Dickens's career, offers a review of the elasticity of phrase that has, more than once, invited an accordion analogy for the variable pleatings of both sound and syntax, whether across dialogue exchange or at the fragile interface of single syllables. The appreciative attention that results thus puts us in mind, once again, of the "concertina" model (Douglas-Fairhurst) in the decompressions of stenographic recovery. At one late point, the prose of *Dombey and Son* bears down even more radically than before on the individual disappearing acts of word production: the vanishing of one letter into the next that constitutes the reading act. It is an act slowed in this case to a node of suspense both melodramatic in plot and microstylistic on the re-enunciated page of unvoiced reading. Emblematically, we encounter this episode, within plot, as it is (paradoxically enough) read out in silence—yet even under this constraint, revealing certain otherwise repressed processes in the energetics of word formation.

Never functionally repressed—yet nonetheless readily minimized in the grip of wider-angle (and, for many readers, more commanding) fascinations. Examples so far have been meant to maximize the fact of such Writing even against the onward drift of novelistic adventure. Examples are everywhere. To say that you can't miss them is necessarily to acknowledge that they do involve a certain pausing over, after all—even if only for a split second. This is partly because, time and again, they are the nub of a portrayed moral upheaval, the pressure point of an inference, the lid lifted from an absurdity. But not necessarily. Internal structure precedes (and undergirds) function. For all the circumlocution and hyperbole—the extended flourish and inflation—of Dickensian rhetoric, most of the compact, and thus manageably quotable, effects we've been concentrating on have been linguistic concentrates in their own right: here a factoring down of syntax to a tension of phrasal discrepancies, there a strategic logjam of phonemes, now the ghost of a pun or cliché not explicitly spelled out, now an inward fault line of grammar induced by competing idioms. On and on—and always onward at the same time, hurtling to the beat of plot and its descriptive interludes that these stylistic flash points have been sparked to punctuate.

At every level, the protocols of narrative may be broken up, open, and down by pressures verbal at base and unstable at that. Yet these more curtailed fillips and tremors of localized phonetic or lexical effect follow the broader stylistic paradigm of exaggeration in its altogether ungrudging collaboration with story. With plot taking in stride these compressed spikes of invention—just as it does all that alternate rampant grammar in the complex "wordy" dance of subordination and amplification—story pulls us through. That is how Dickens remains so sublimely "readable" in the unrepentant thick of things. But not *effortlessly* readable in the prose's forward drive. This is why, as well, any teaching of the novels to a craft-oriented student body in a creative writing track, as mentioned in the introduction about my own recent experience, is all the more inclined to take note, along with the rhetorical mastery and finesse, of a certain aberrant craftiness to boot—not quite harnessed to narrative drive. With Dickens tirelessly at work in his storytelling, the Other Dickens, as we've seen, is often at play—and counterplay. And playing upon us in the process.

It is in this way that reading—*really* reading—lessens that story-driven impetus in tarrying over the extraneous uprush of wording, where the prose takes turns of phrase more often than of plot, with these being frequently turned back on themselves in microdramas of discrimination, wit, and linguistic syncopation. Such pockets of wording are readily extractable for exemplification in a study like this, for the good reason that they are, in one sense, expendable to momentum at the level of storytelling. They offer, in short, the manifestation in pure form of the Other Dickens: exaggerated prose per se, operating in blithe defiance of sheer speed and in variable syncopation with those other "frequencies" of plotting on which expectation tunes in. When thus timed to Writing in its inner rhythms rather than to the strict pace of story, that is how reading lessens. It dials down plots and their populations, crisis and character, to the ventures of prose's own phrasing. It reduces narrative movement to the motors of word forms and sentence formations. And that reduction, or call it distillation—through whose showy if minor intricacies one grows hopelessly attached to the Other Dickens—is the headiest elixir of all from page to page. Unique in English fictional prose at least before Conrad, in all the writerly density of its articulations, is exactly this incessant delivery of the medium within the message—fostering in the reader the often awed awareness of *wording* in the work of what is said.

But that would never be Dickens's way of putting it. Medium is our word. Writing is his word, as well as his way with words. Yet his middle novel *Dombey and Son* (1846–48) skirts as close as mid-Victorian writing comes to inferring the concept of a communicative medium, among other contemporaneous definitions of the term. That sense of a technological "medium" (including writing) is not as yet received vocabulary, but its pending usage tends to analyze what we've already encountered. As amply recognized so far, reading Dickens—when entering the crevices of his enunciation—can slow reported story to a grammatical, even syllabic, snail's pace: lessening its sheer narrative service, instructing us otherwise in the propellant force of Writing. We've seen evidence of this wherever we've looked. But *Dombey and Son* restages it for us in one strained, weirdly eccentric, fiercely unlikely, and yet deliberately pivotal dramatic turn. It is a moment concerned exclusively with the written word—a single compromising word that precipitates the climax of the novel's revenge plot. In tabling that climactic examination of a chalked tabletop script, in which lettering and enunciation are held in serial abeyance in a bizarre scene of slow-motion (because letter-by-letter) disclosure (of the incriminating place-name "Dijon"), we are only preparing for its unique autopsy of Dickensian style.

From first to last in Boz's career, from *Pickwick Papers* to *Our Mutual Friend*, we of course find ourselves laughing *with* the wry asides of everyone from Sam Weller to Jenny Wren; and whether in genial empathy or contempt, laughing *at* Pickwick and *at* Podsnap alike. What's so unusual about the texture of descriptive Writing in this fiction, however, apart from dialogue, is that we are invited all the while to be laughing both *at* and *with* the style itself, reveling in an excess as risible in its own deadpan exactions as it is discriminating about the hilarities of character or setting. But the laughter itself darkens over time, and yields place increasingly to deeper-dredged satiric targets—and to a prose syntax less strictly festive at its most ambitious. Certainly this is the case from *Dombey and Son* on—and in ways no one could have quite predicted from even the most spirited writing in the novels down through *Martin Chuzzlewit*.

From *Dombey* forward, and not just in the matter of style, nothing is ever the same again. As if overnight, the miracle has happened: Dickensian people have become real. Not all *that* real, most of them, and certainly not too real for the prose—but nonetheless, and suddenly: characters contoured and shadowed, curved, furrowed, and warped, like recognizable modern psyches, even when, in many cases, still swollen out of shape by caricature. With *Dombey*, even casual readers—those wanting more a page-turner than a phrase-turning display—can sense motive and desire and denial at a whole new register of credible intensity. We actually now feel what the Dickensian people are feeling, whether in sympathy or recoil. Victimage and abjection, as much as dominance and pomposity, share a new inner desperation, and villainy has stepped from the melodramatic stage to become genuinely novelistic. The wizened churlish misers and gross lechers of the earlier novels, the vile thieves and homicidal sadists, have matured into the wielders of a cruelty as neurotic and self-poisoning—and a class *ressentiment* as raw, merciless, and often defeating—as one could, if that's the word, wish.

In all this, Dickens's women are not the least of those who have come of age. Some of them, at least. There is no one like Edith Dombey before now, her psychosocial diagnosis extended to the equally unprecedented reprobate mothering, the virtual pimping, of Mrs. Skewton (for all the raucous comedy attending the latter); no one like Dombey himself in his fossilized joyless egocentrism; and still less like that coiled spring of serpentine malignity—more power-hungry than greedy or libidinal—represented by his absconding Manager Carker. Not *motiveless* malignity, as Coleridge said of Iago. In Dickens, as in Shakespeare as well, sheer envy can run deep—yet never before, in Dickensian plots, so deep and festered as here. Still, even Iago aside, the Shakespearean influence, after its incubation during the writing of *Chuzzlewit*, is vivid everywhere, especially in the continuous risk that Dickensian fiction—turned more tightly analytic and psychological from within its signature traffic in satiric laughter—has by this point developed not just a melodramatic but a potentially tragic cast. With only five major novels, and *A Christmas Carol*, to his name, Dickens would already have indelibly secured his literary-historical fame as both an original and a perennial. He is the Immortal, however, because of what happens from *Dombey* on. For, as if to prove that the Shakespearean catalyst is now fully operational, it is the work of the Other Dickens to carry the aural density of the prose, and its histrionic extravagances, to new "stagey" heights in themselves.

Over the course of *Dombey and Son*, the reader has been well acclimated to these new demands on—and rewards for—our verbal attention, even long before the point where plot slows, all but stalls, over the late forensic scenario of subsyllabic verbal production in that slow-motion textual encounter with the lone word "Dijon." Once we have arrived at this intensity of textual decipherment degree zero, this ad hoc and improbably exacerbated reading lesson in the processing of a single word, it cannot simply be that a major plot destination is revealed—in the villain Carker's secret decampment to France. Something more fundamental about that action is being made manifest. At just this tightly wrought melodramatic turn in a revenge plot whose aftermath will find Dombey in utter isolation at a quasi-tragic and nearly suicidal dead end, it would appear that some primal instinct of Dickensian Writing means to remind us that all of this new (Shakespearean) power in his prose stills depends on the tireless calibrations of one word at a time, even one letter.

The acute pressure exerted upon wording at that point of feverishly parsed syllabic aggregation is demonstrably unprecedented. Yet it is detached neither from the specifically linguistic profile of the villain nor from the strain under which even the most neutral grammar of everyday pronouns and their antecedents is then further submitted in the moral retribution subsequently directed at Mr. Dombey himself. Prose undergoes at that later point, so we are to find, the nearest thing to its own mental breakdown. At that stage of intensity, *reading lessens* the very distance between the deviances of discourse and the violence of event. We thus move here from a chapter canvassing the straddling and interpenetration of phrasal grammar and lexical phonetics—at various levels of advance and overlap—to one in which we watch these and other such sustaining relays of sense and sound, tested to unusual limits, driven almost into the ground.

"Oily of Tongue": A "Medium" Degree Zero

In the mincing out of the "Dijon" phonemes, certainly that labored sabotage to come of the villain's dastardly schemes, if by a roundabout logic, gets Carker just where he lives: punishing exactly the surreptitious manipulations of a suave verbal hypocrisy, a rhetorical will to power, suggested by the formulaic epithet by which he is typically designated: "Mr. Carker the Manager." Under the thin disguise of distinguishing him from his spurned brother and mere clerk (the alternative Mr. Carker), and thus symptomatic in its own right, this managerial monomania is exposed for just what it is by an iterated formula that spills over at one point, along the initial runnel of alliteration, into attributes so stiffly and inextricably couched that the phrasing seems as calculating as the man himself. So it is that "Mr. Carker the Manager, sly of manner, sharp of tooth, soft of foot" (all of a piece in everything, as logged by each new metrical onset), "watchful of eye, oily of tongue, cruel of *heart*, nice of *habit*"—with that final alliterative bracket capping the contrast between inner and outer man—"sat with a dainty steadfastness and patience at his work, as if he were waiting at a mouse's hole."

Mixing metaphors as Dickens repeatedly does in capturing the multiple repulsions of the man, Carker's full battery of serpent's teeth (those "teeth" mentioned more than two dozen times in the novel) operate as gleaming, indeed beaming, antennae for his every deceptive or contemptuous inference. "Oily of tongue," as we've seen, he is also sharp at times with this organ: the *arch*-villain in every sense, mordantly sarcastic as well as extreme in his meanness. Yet, to be sure, his pervasive falsity is usually exerted by swallowed speech and sinister feline grins, rather than outright barbed words. He is, in fact, so slippery "of tongue" that this fleshy appendage speaks for itself even when not forming his otherwise deceitful words. In a prevaricating exchange with Captain Cuttle, for example, Carker's acquiescences are entirely "mute" even in their anatomical articulation: "Mr Carker, with his mouth from ear to ear, repeated, 'Time enough.' Not articulating the words, but bowing his head affably, and forming them with his tongue and lips."

This isn't just a bizarre yet intuitive idea on Dickens's part: letting a dupe put words in a villain's not-quite-confirming mouth. It is that, for sure—but then some. What we realize soon enough, from a term deployed later at a moment of crisis by Mr. Dombey, is that Carker at his most essential and insinuating, being already a servile go-between or "medium" (Dombey's word) in his own person, doesn't need in fact to speak, just to channel, his messages. And almost more remarkable yet, he doesn't just (in an idiomatic sense) *lie through his teeth*, but instead *reads* with them, so that a "postscript" in a note of instruction from Dombey "attracted his attention and his teeth." There, alliteration aside, is the familiar split syntax of verb and ill-sorted objects in Dickensian comic grammar, whose effect, icier than usual in this case, makes dentition seem coextensive with consciousness for this predatory stalker and his clenched ferocity. Rather than a man of words, a "medium" like Carker needs neither to speak nor to read; he simply materializes in his own person the transfer of signals—via an "attention" (in its etymological sense as "stretching") that is both grasping and retentive at once.

One of the great imagined moral voids in Dickens—a sociopath hyperbolically smaller than life—Carker is so thoroughgoing a villain, and so insistently described by the grotesque double synecdoche of his slippery phallic tongue and castrating teeth, that his fate certainly deserves sealing in the very terms of his surreptitious plotting and its grinning vindictiveness. Dickens wasn't likely to have missed this chance. Having been tricked by Edith into a supposedly amorous elopement, the toothy feline Manager meets his comeuppance in the precise terms of predation balked—since from now on, as Edith soon snidely dismisses him, he will, beneath the pretense of sexual conquest, "go forth and boast of me, and gnash your teeth, for once, to know that you are lying!" The teeth once eloquent in themselves are to be gritted in rage—should Carker ever "go forth" in other than fatal flight.

One link between Dombey and his Manager lies in the way that the rigidity of the former's speech can seem like the obverse of the latter's insinuating venom. First there is this: " 'Mr Dombey will forgive the partiality of a wife,' said Mrs Blimber, with an engaging smile." And at once: "Mr Dombey answered 'Not at all:' applying those words, it is to be presumed, to the partiality, and not to the forgiveness." The presumption may be unduly generous. If, in fact, Dombey's words were as cruel as they are curt, one would certainly note their match in an equivalent rhetorical idiom—and virtual moral syndrome—further on. For like Master, like Man(ager)—with the result that the hypocritical Carker's similar (if privately couched) haughtiness in conversation with Captain Cuttle needs no authorial gloss in its refused sympathy: " 'You'll excuse me if I've been at all intruding, will you?' said the Captain." Nothing pro forma about Carker's answer: " 'Not at all,' returned the other,"—as if, in the process, his narrative demotion to unnamed interlocutor ("the other") is less for variety's sake than to register Carker's distance from normal social response. The Manager, this ethically dissevered "other," is, however, elsewhere quite capable, in a related vein, of the snippy dismissive segues that are part of dialogue's contrapuntal comedy in many Dickens novels. Deploying another variant of the snide "astraddle" grammar we saw him wield in chapter 3 when contemptuously dismissing Captain Cuttle, he is even more openly sarcastic with his ostracized brother, a disgraced menial in the firm, with the Manager in this case picking up the man's tentative dialogue by sarcastic discontinuity and redirection. "'May I go on?' said John Carker, mildly." And as if grinning maliciously at his own word-play: "'On your way?' replied his smiling brother. 'If you will have the goodness.'"

Phrasal Turns Mis-Taken

Words never stay put for long in Dickens, as we well know, and their manipulation is no less potent when delegated to an ingenious villain. More often, however, even in *Dombey and Son*, it is the narrator who takes credit, rather than his delegated ironist, for the branchings of sense and iterations of sound that color the prose. A passing Shakespearean allusion can get contorted by a double negative (litotes) and the rush of alliteration, as in the very picture of consternation in a character like Rob the Grinder, "whose withers were not unwrung"—a nod to *Hamlet* as odd as if Dickens were to say of some other character, for instance, that *he was on his own petard not unhoist*. As with *withers/wrung*, however, alliteration or assonance is the most replenishable stock-in-trade of such local wordiness—or *wordness*—in Dickens. Think of the euphonically motivated redundancy of Captain Cuttle's being "indifferent to br*uises* and cont*usions*"—as if the narrator were pouring verbal balm on the very thought of such injuries (incurred in his precipitous flight from the widow MacStinger). It is a phrasing that finds its internalized equivalent in the voice of the woman herself, who rails against him, when cornered, for "his guzzlings and his muzzlings," in which burst of fury she "used the last word for the joint sake"—reenacted on the spot by discourse—"of alliteration and aggravation, rather than for the expression of any idea."

Though this sounds like a marginal gloss from the precincts of the Other Dickens, it remains the case that, in the prose's typical deployment (and delegation) of such verbal effects, a sense of aggravation would be ferried on alliteration—not irrelevant to it in a mere conjuncture of sound. This we note, for instance, even in a canceled passage in which the busybody Miss Tox—to whose lexical seedbed of a name we must soon return—dances attendance on the young Dombey heir, making his official nurse seem "superinten*ded* to *death*."[1] It is a case of an aggravating intervention getting syllabically manifested. Yet again, too, the multiplied verbal force of alliteration in its many retained versions (those that survive manuscript revisions, that is), as of other chiming sound patterns, connects in the stylistic register with larger-scale bifurcations of phrase—as well as with the tiniest extrusions of sound play, of the sort most strangely engaged, so we'll find, when young Paul Dombey nears his death. In Dickens at large, these phonic effects range from the farcical Cockney wordplay we saw at the opening of *Martin Chuzzlewit,* with the accidental Mandarin ancestry hinted in the mishearing of a dismissive "the Lord No Zoo," to related phonetic slippages that can, in *Dombey and Son,* be either more genially comic or downright plangent.

Such delight in the cascades, pitfalls, and slipups of sibilance, in particular, has been so wholly ingrained by the time of *Dombey* that a passing description like "the bold Toot*s t*umbled staggering out into the street" — in its jumble of past and present-progressive tenses — catches Toots stumbling as if over the narrative phrasing of his own tumble. Alternately, in the lyric rather than comic register, prose seems to occupy the mindscape of the dying Paul in one of his bouts of semiconscious metaphor verging on delirium. Beginning with the bald redundancy of "swift and rapid" for the river-of-no-return — coruscating in imaginary reflected light upon the wall of his sickroom — all this transpires in a "dream" reported afterward to his sister Florence in the ripple of an unconscious condensation and displacement (to borrow again the terms of Freudian dreamwork) at the phonetic level itself: "His only trouble was, the swift *and* rapid river. He felt forced, sometimes, to try to stop it — to stem it with his childi*sh hands* — or choke it*s way* with *sand* — *and* when he saw it coming on, re-sistless, he cried out!" The straddling syllabic effects discussed in the last chapter seem to be losing their own footing in the forward rush of fate. As the river claims its "sway" over him, captured by the very surge of the off-rhymed and cross-word echoism there and elsewhere in this impacted phrasing, the "and" of the initial redundancy (slipped in by the Other Dickens under cover of sheer padding?) has its vestigial returns after all. Its undertow shapes a triple echo just barely avoiding, in its final iteration as "with sand," what goes unsaid (and undoable) in all that the dying boy cannot *withstand.* Further, Paul's is an ultimate capitulation distilled in the double grammar of the modifier "resistless" when the adjective is recognized to apply at once — in the same rhetorical as well as dramatic instant — to the unopposable force of destiny and to the surrendered defenses of its (also all but said) *listless* victim. One is certainly tempted to audit, in all this sibilant granularity of phrase, a subterranean emblem of word formation's own shifting sands in the flux of a molecular disintegration timed to the dissolution of consciousness itself in mortal fade-out.

Just as frequently in this novel, however, it is the larger modular pattern of the lexicon that won't quite cohere for certain characters. So back to the provocative nomination of Miss Tox. Any long-term reader of Dickens sees trouble coming, good verbal trouble, even before she is entangled with the insincere manipulations of Mrs. Chick. Given that there is nothing "toxic" in her dithering manner, what, we begin to wonder, will Miss Tox *mistake?* Indeed, there's been a dry run for the later explosion concerning this character early on. We've just met the ferocious but lovable Spitfire three chapters in, "whose real name was Susan Nipper" (we shortly learn), with readers thereby readied for the further fun: first an oblique and defiant double play on her nickname (a cognomen, Spitfire, bestowed in discourse only, not by any character in the story) after a gruff remonstrance to Florence—who acts "in *spite* of being thus adjured, and in *spite* of some hauling on the part of Susan Nipper." Then, after this initial etymological pressure on her nickname, we come upon the sibilant sound play that kicks in with the narrator's tongue-in-cheek descent to a bland honorific title for the heroically snippy "Mis*s Nip*per." Shades of the snag, if you will, in the nagging Mrs Snagsby. Names, in the flexions of the Other Dickens, are not just symbolic but plastic, not just allegorical but glutinous in their sticking—rather than simply staying—power. Later, a new retainer in the same Dombey household, when quoted as objecting to the vicious Mrs. Pipchin in Brighton, is castigated with the natural first epithet that comes to a mind on automatic pilot: " 'Wickham,' retorted Mrs. Pipchin, 'is a wicked, impudent, bold-faced hussy.' " All of this can only fuel our unfocused expectation of some nominal comeuppance for poor mistaken Miss Tox. We don't wait long.

For the pattern can be sensed building soon enough in the willfulness of her supposed patron and friend, Mrs. Chick. That voluble and preachy woman is often found at a loss for words, and only on the rebound, at one point, do we hear her "recovering her voice—which was synonymous with her presence of mind, indeed they were one and the same thing." Is that last clause a case of pure wordiness, snuck in under cover of the joke? Or is Dickens somehow, even if obscurely, out to distinguish mere "synonymy," as a verbal effect of speech or voice, from the more radical *equivalence* of utterance and self-presence in the hectoring yammer of this know-it-all? In any event, Mrs. Chick('s) is a speech vortex by no means typically infallible, nor guaranteed in quickness, since she frequently patronizes Miss Tox in using her as an implausible mnemonic device. At one point the fulsome Chick, lecturing her bereaved niece Florence on the virtues of bucking up, turns to her satellite Tox to provide, as if by telepathy, a word she is fumbling for. In the upshot, she seems overly repulsed by the wrong guess, as if it were a Freudian slip from the used and soon to be abused hanger-on: " 'If any—my dear,' turning to Miss Tox, 'I want a word. Mis—Mis—.' " Despite the calculated stuttering of the Other Dickens, the word sought has nothing to do with the "Miss" of "Miss Tox," certainly, and the friend herself is quite at a loss:

"Demeanour?" suggested Miss Tox.
"No, no, no," said Mrs Chick. "How can you! Goodness me, it's on, [with the comma suggesting that she has no instant recall even of the coming idiom] the end of my tongue. Mis—"

"Placed affection?" suggested Miss Tox, timidly.

"Good gracious, Lucretia!" returned Mrs Chick. "How very monstrous!"

Monstrous indeed, as in Mrs. Chick's imminent cruel rejection of the fellow sycophant smitten with Dombey, whom until now Mrs. Chick has, as it were, egged on. "Misanthrope, is the word I want. The idea! Misplaced affection!" Out of the mouths of babes again—or their spinstered counterparts.

Such dissevered syllabic comedy, including its parsing of potential negative prefixes like "mis," is thus only a premonition of the open explosion coming, as seeded from the first in nomenclature itself. Neither crime nor misdemeanor, "misplaced affection"—as it would seem that Mrs. Chick half realizes—is exactly the aptest word for Miss Tox's relation to her. Their pairing has been fraught with instability from the start, of course, as if the unhappy bond of Chick-and-Tox might be spelled out phonetically in a bizarre rhyme with *chickenpox*. The game is up when, with Dombey's new marriage in the offing, Mrs. Chick finds it expedient to cut all ties with Tox in a salvo of false accusations, the gist of which—as if the misplaced affection had been all on her side, not on Miss Tox's—is that "I have been mistaken in you, Lucretia," followed by a haughty punch line that rather smacks of Carker. "I wish you well, and I shall ever wish you well," but given the situation, "I can wish you nothing else but good morning." If the route of separation were reversed, the dismissal couldn't have been more blighting, with Chick sending Tox from Dombey's door (rather than storming from Tox's own) with something like *I wish you good day and gone*. More to the point, it is as if the kiss-off line should indeed have been not "I have been mistaken in you, Lucretia!" but rather *I have mistaken my Miss Tox*. In the same spirit, we may be encouraged to hear in *Little Dorrit* later, concerning one Miss Wade, not just how this creature of sadomasochistic paranoia is everywhere mired—wading neck-deep—in her own projected sense of demeaning patronage, but how, in her deliberate inflammation of Tattycoram's comparable resentments, she has poisonously *missuaded—which is also to say misswayed*—this young alter ego. Miss Wade is, by name, of Mrs. Nagsby's and Miss Snipper's, even Mrs. Scamp's, party without knowing it—her name a fossilized or freeze-frame pun. Once more we find the Other Dickens caught, as if under arrest, within the most rudimentary ingredient of the Inimitable's cast of characters.

In any case, the latent phrasal play shadowing the name Miss Tox only exacerbates to the point of parody a certain tendency in the earlier novel, at this maturing turn in the Dickensian style. The prefix that can find no stem; the syllable that lingers beyond its utility into another word; the phrase that divides against itself (or its interlocutor) to punish the expectations of grammatical continuity—these recur with determined frequency, if in no special pattern. And then there is the oscillating monosyllable that is two parts of speech at once, and not always in the mode of comic double take—as in the instantaneously *close/d* gap at the death of Carker under the wheels of the locomotive engine of death: its glaring headlights figured as animate and vindictive, its approach now adjectival, now verbal, when he "saw the red eyes, bleared and dim, in the daylight, *close upon him*—was beaten down, caught up, and whirled away upon a jagged mill, that spun him round and round, and struck him limb from limb, and licked his stream of life up with its fiery heat, and cast his mutilated fragments in the air." As far from the lyricism of "secret prose" as one can get, here in Carker's fate is instead a sequestered deviance in which we may intuit the Other Dickens voicing ambiguously for us the difference in sibilance between the soft *s* of "close" as adjective and its elongated *z* sound in "close" as verb, thus narrowing the infinitesimal gap of the death moment. And doing so with that extra deforming twist we may recognize here. For the logic of the prose at this violent turn departs from the fact that limbs aren't ordinarily struck "*from* limbs," but instead from the bodily trunk—in all but the most radical dispersions, that is, of human anatomy. Not since "resistless" was pivoted between the river-of-no-return, on the one hand, and the giving out of Paul's dying energy, on the other, has a single (partly adjectival) duality in this novel offered so striking a fulcrum in the mortal trajectories of plot.

But I jump the gun. Our villain's time is not quite up. In building toward the scene of reading that betrays him and his perverted role as "medium," and sends him eventually to this dismembering destiny (prose's fragmentation along with it), we need to keep two loops of phrasal recycling in mind together. On the one hand—as compressed, for instance, by "clos/ze upon" in a single syntactic double entendre—there are the local creases and folds of lexical sequencing. On the other hand, there are whole orchestrated refrains that appear in this novel as never before, their iterations operating in one case across vast swaths of narrative material. Yet the next thing to note about these different scales of effect is that the impact, in the latter case, is also linguistic before descriptive: the wording exposed as such, rendered utterly opaque, by repeated (as much as by overlapping or off-rhymed) utterance. Suddenly, with the emergence of such refrains in Dickensian rhetoric (of the sort later perfected, and perverted, with the "echoing footsteps" of those "headlong" feet in *A Tale of Two Cities*), the plot is not just tacitly propelled by words, as usual, but for a moment manifestly advanced by just so many words—and in just this order. Such an advance, being not a thrust of narrative but a recursion to its own rhetoric, thus resembles what happens at a narrower scale whenever descriptive efficacy seems, however slightly, impeded by phrasing per se. As we've seen across a broad spread of examples, this can occur whenever the smoothness of sense is phonetically inconvenienced, lexically thickened, syntactically self-enmeshed, or in any case slowed by wording alone. No passage makes this intertwine of refrain and refractory phrasing more apparent than the most incontestable symbolic tour de force, or at least the most arduous and elusively phrased set piece, in Dickens's career so far. In eliciting what is at stylistic stake in this marathon threnody and near-miss suicide at the climax of the Dombey plot—which means in submitting to its own reading lesson (after the more obvious and reductive one centered on the five letters of "Dijon")—its prolonged challenge to descriptive cohesion should return us with fuller recognition to the pivotal and explicit "scene of reading" that, in facilitating the disposal of Carker, clears the way for Dombey's climactic ordeal.

So we work backward here to see narrative preparation at work in the very grain of its Writing—while pausing, first, for another point of comparative stylistics. Two particular tendencies repeatedly intersect in Dickens at a stylistic scale beneath the level of normal scholarly notice. Or say two compactions converge: phonetic and syntactic. One is contextualized by actual philological history, the other an ad hoc invention of compounding and splitting. Consider, in the former case, the implicit linguistic genealogy in *Dombey and Son* by which the uncrippled if gradually senescent Mrs. Skewton takes to a "wheeled chair" only so as to strike a recumbent pose reminiscent of her early portrait in a horse-drawn barouche. That contemporary wording, strictly descriptive, anticipates one of those shaky border-crossings in lexical collocation by which the dental (*d/t*) sound of a past participle is gradually absorbed over historical time, as previously noted in passing, by the opening diphthong of the next word so as to reformat itself, in this case, as the contemporary forward roll of enunciation in "wheel chair" (*wheel tchair*). The same instinct leads students to speak of "advance degrees," though the dictionary hasn't caught up with them to legalize it. Earlier historical compactions of this phonetically dovetailed sort include the classic place-name elision by which North Thriding became North Riding. Other examples: the nonbiological evolution by which, through the two-way vagaries of the indefinite article, *an ewt* became *a newt, a nadder an adder*, as well as the renaming by which *an ekename* ("also"-name) become *a nickname*.

And, as we well know, what can thus be lexically cross-stitched in this fashion can also be semantically imbricated across a split grammar that grafts one sense onto (or into) another, often accompanied by extra phonetic links to seal the deal—as is the case, with Mrs. Skewton again, where time itself seems to fork between the passage of the carriage in something like horizontal duration and that of her beauty in another kind of disappearance. Here grammar, we might say, is found straddling the essential narrative a prioris of time and space at once: "The beauty and the barouche had both passed away, but she still preserved the attitude," with the phonetic residue of that first assonant pair being all that survives—and across three different orthographic manifestations of the phoneme, at that—in the falling cadence of "attitude," complete with its almost chiastic chiming of "-itu-" against "eauty." As if answering later to these tiny vanishing acts in intransitive grammar, there is a ghastly syntactic dismantling in Mrs. Skewton's case—when all that's left of her charms are the trinkets with which she bedecks herself, and where the unsaid phrase *putting on airs* (conjured in our minds by the Other Dickens) seems to lie behind the antithetical spectacle of divestment: "She appeared to have taken off her manner with her charms, and to have put on paralysis with her flannel gown." The blur between literal and figural, material and characterological, is strikingly complete in this implosion of categories as well as confected display. And yet again the subordination of taxonomy to surprise—itemized stylistic feature to experienced twist—in the phonetic, syntactic, and rhetorical intertwine of the prose encounter, phrase by phrase.

The Crisis of Antecedence: Micro to Macro

Again, though, for a fully comparative sense of structuring parallels at different narrative scales, we need to look past such local armatures of recurrence to broader refrains and their governing rhetoric. In the fifty-ninth chapter, called "Retribution," the "ruin" of the Dombey mansion, after disgrace and bankruptcy, is three times accompanied, at intervals, by news that "the rats fly from it," figurative more than literal. Yet it is in this very chapter that we encounter the final soundings of another originally threefold and much-distended refrain. This has taken the form of an urgent apostrophe to no one in particular (as if to the very condition of narrative attention)—"Let him remember it"—very different from the closing address in the preceding novel: the "Ah, Tom, old friend!" of the coda to *Martin Chuzzlewit*—friend there of the writer and the reader alike. In *Dombey*, however, the apostrophic subsumption of story to discourse in "Let him remember it" emerges in the mode of a flash-forward in pure rhetorical prognosis—to be confirmed, only much later, by explicit self-citation. This time, as opposed to the apotheosis of Tom Pinch, it is neither the reader nor even the character who is buttonholed. It is as if the narrator were addressing himself in auto-instruction—somewhere between the optative mood ("May he remember it") and the imperative ("Make sure he remembers it"). What we read in this manner, early on, at least if it weren't shaped into a triadic chiming pattern returning across a great leap of chapters, would seem more like a brief notation in one of Dickens's laconic number plans: namely, *Don't forget to have him remember it!* It is as if some authorial paratext has invaded story as its own metatext, distending through iteration an early searing moment in the anticipated traces, and scars, it *will have left*. If "secret prose" is the "music of memory," spoken to itself, according to Greene, "with no one there to listen," the overt iterations here are more like memory's curse. Yet, even across a forty-one-chapter mnemonic interval, the contorted arc of authorial intrusion also feels as quintessential as uncanny. Voices speaking out of and into the blue, cued by duration and suspense but remaining disembodied across it. What else is new? What else is (a) novel?

More like memory's curse, did I say? I suspect something more specific as well: a perhaps unconscious allusion. With Shakespeare recently on Dickens's mind, there is something here, in the monitory grammar, that may well recall—in prolonged and distended form, in this Merchant of London novel—the concentrated threefold repetition in a single speech of Shylock's: "Let him look to his bond." In any case, the notorious apostrophe in *Dombey and Son*, the original "Let him remember it" twice replayed, comes across as the reverse of a more common convention fundamental to Dickensian writing—and perfected for satire in this novel. Here I refer again to the bread and butter of every narratology conference: free indirect discourse, where telling converges with and co-opts the told, or in other words where authors speak for their character—sidewise, since without dialogue markers (quotation marks)—in the latter's own words. Quite different here, then, is a rhetorical "aside" injecting itself into an emotionally inoculated consciousness—and this only for a later flare-up of recognition—in words to this effect: *Let him one day realize the blind pride that will have led to his downfall!* Such is a future-perfect bond or binding (one day he *will have seen the light!*) under wraps as a subjunctive rather than a command.

It is in just this way that such an apostrophe inverts a process of free indirect discourse that has reached its apogee in the lampoons of Dombey's leading sycophant, Major Bagstock, whose fetid deference operates in direct league with his exuded auto-gratulation. It is an effect oozing from his every pore—and even into zones of discourse ventilated by his absence. A bizarre example—and a remarkably strained one on the narrative's part—shows how far Dickensian prose can go in taking the pulse of the character's all-absorbing egocentrism. Worried about her brotherly friend and eventual lover, Walter Gay, Florence is too preoccupied to read and thus "puts down her book," thinking in part, without quotation marks, of that "poor wandering shipwrecked boy, oh, where is he?" Jump-cut across this montage of paragraphs—for a close-up now on a nonexistent response surfaced under negation from unspoken and unconsidered thoughts of the Major, far across town. The transition is too showstopping to be smooth: Where might poor Walter be now? "The Major don't know; that's for certain; and don't care." We find the latter poised between his own jaded grammar and a direct first-person citation ruled out by the fact that the whole question is the furthest thing from his mind. Nowhere near the scene to be appealed to in Florence's mental rhetoric, still the self-interest that radiates from his person seems uncontainable by plot. This abrupt scene change—nothing like it before or since in Dickens, or in other English fiction of my acquaintance—is achieved by a strange ellipsis in cognition (and narrative continuity) so forced as to be funny in itself. With this strident exception proving the very rule of seamlessness in the normal management of story, we are again, under guidance from the Other Dickens, laughing *at* as well as with the style.

Still, the intrusive apostrophe to Dombey we have begun to consider—putting ideas by indirection into a character's head, and this only for future fruition, rather than extracting present thoughts by rhetorical osmosis—is something quite different, though equally a violation of narrative protocols. "Let him remember it." Unlike the semitransparent thought bubbles of free indirect discourse, here is a stage direction whispered, as it were, from the wings of destiny—and of novelistic schema. It is thus worth noting, or in fact impossible to ignore, how a further measure of this discourse/story split obscures the question of antecedence in the very rhetoric so mobilized. "Let him remember it"—but what, exactly? In an effect that must be partly intentional, as a closer look will disclose, we can't say precisely; the latent portent of this trauma will emerge only in retrospect. From here out in the Dombey plot, that single neuter pronoun, the "it" of inescapable recognition as well as memory, is the repeated agonistic flash point, its referent lost for dozens of chapters at a time in the obscurities of repression itself.

At this early crisis point in the eighteenth chapter, with its flatly balanced but radically disjunctive title, "Father and Daughter," Florence herself has recognized all too clearly what the father's more than unfeeling look bespeaks, if not the full narrative shape of what it portends. Beyond the recurrence (and internal echo) of "old indifference and cold constraint," we hear that these rigidities "had given place to something: *what*, she never thought and did not dare to think, and yet she felt *it* in *its* force, and knew *it* well without a name: that as *it* looked upon her, seemed to cast a shadow on her head." The "it," extracted from the whole image of paternal frigidity, obscurely reified here in this tortured syntax, is then re-personified as an "it" coterminous with the gaze of his icy looks. The shadow cast on the moment is the fleshed abstraction of festering hate itself. Reverse shot in a tentative free indirect discourse: "Did he see before him the successful rival of his son, in health and life? Did he look upon his own successful rival in that son's affection?" Two more sentences of hovering interrogation of this sort, with his "looking" its focal point, and then the speculation-disbanding countershot: "Florence had no such thoughts. But love is quick to know when it is spurned and hopeless: and hope died out of hers, as she stood looking in her father's face." Brilliant, that pivot at "out of hers," with the antecedent of the possessive pronoun being "love" until the nearby noun overtakes it with the parallel sense of "her (face)" (as opposed to her father's)—as fully drained of hope as is her inner devotion. Yet, as we've seen, that "something," the unthinkable "it," the lovelessness that dare not speak its name, has not been entirely absorbed into his visage per se, but remains lurking there in his look rather than his looks, an inference by which the reader is (protocinematic intercutting yet again) automatically sutured in.

The subjunctive format of anticipation in "Let him remember it," cast into a kind of narratological imperative, soon triggers a sharp break into present tense for the return to scenic rendering. Discourse is locked tight now—as if flash-frozen, in wait for memory's bitter thaw—by a congealing internal (and cross-lexical) rhyme between "the air" and its more rushed enunciation as the circumambient "there." The sentence as unfolded: "It has faded from *the air*"—"it," the recognized meaning behind the look—"before he breaks the silence. It may pass as quickly from his brain, as he believes, but it is *there*. Let him remember it in that room, years to come!" It is, indeed, the very air, the atmosphere, of his lethal freeze of feeling that will return on narrative demand. It is as if, in promise of this, the passage has itself broken from the narrative past tense of this episode into present report—so that what once hung, still hangs: in and as the very gloom of foreboding. And where the slipped phonetic sprockets, if you will, that spin "the air" round again in "there" exhibit once again those incremental differentials that I've been proposing as the granular filmic equivalent of a more obviously cinematic Dickens.

What surfaces here is the present tense of premonition itself, cutting the grooves of its own later retrieval even in its current iteration—and even after another curt exchange sends the daughter away to bed. By a remarkable internal economy, the pending and long-deferred remembrance will, when the moment comes round to haunt him, effect a comparable wrench of tense—precipitating a stylistically heightened present, as we will note, back into a contained narrative past of charted emotional conversion. Here, though, with dozens of chapters about to intervene, the idiomatic wailing of the wind after Florence's exit from paternal space is further animated as a keening grief, followed once more by the proleptic refrain "*Let him remember it in that room, years to come. The rain that falls upon the roof: the wind that mourns outside the door*"—personifying the dead metaphor *moans*—"may have foreknowledge in their melancholy sound. *Let him remember it* in that room, years to come!" The "it" has become the free-floating sign of antecedence per se, the very pressure of past upon present—as modeled and rehearsed in passing by the pressure of one word upon another in the emphatic serial displacement of "the air" by an ambient "there." At this point of deliberately vitiated precision, the "it"—in the atrophy of all incarnate feeling—could refer simply to the mise-en-scène itself, the house evacuated of all home values, as emblem of Dombey's resident desolation. Yet that earlier grammatical ambiguity and refused admission—the "it" of hate written across the features of rejection—shadows both the present space and the time to come. We might say that antecedence itself has become the sequestered poetics of a prose apostrophe secret not to us but only to Dombey, for whom memory is to have no music (Greene's phrasing again) when the time comes. For it is then that the shift noted from a past tense into the hovering and eventually retrievable future present of this intruded injunction will be embedded once more in the normative narrative past. This is to happen at just the point when, as anticipated, the "let him remember" is let through again, displacing Dombey from a treadmill of "Retribution" (chapter 59) into a narrative of reparation.

As planted ambivalently at the earlier stage just examined, the underdefined "it" is to return with the force of a repressed remorse so severe in its previous denials that it will eventually erode Dombey's very identity, as before it had effaced his daughter's whole filial subjectivity. The buildup, once the appointed time has arrived forty-one chapters later, is swift and decisive. Even before the neutering "it" has begun its further corrosive work, we come upon the following unabashed return, not to free indirect discourse, but to what we can only call an aggressively shackled *direct discourse* of recovered and executive apostrophe, this time in self-citing quotes. " 'Let him remember it in that room, years to come! The rain that falls upon the roof, the wind that mourns outside the door, may have foreknowledge in their melancholy sound. Let him remember it in that room, years to come!' " At which point one follows Peter Brooks's *Reading for the Plot* in not knowing whether such signal recurrences in fiction (though of a less strictly discursive, more plot-based, sort; his example being from the subsequent story line of *Great Expectations*) constitute the return *of* or the return *to*: a point only exaggerated by the authorial anomaly of quotation marks around the text's own recursive apostrophe in this case.[2] The narrative is here quoting itself not just at the expense of character but at the risk of vaporizing the story world altogether, unabashedly hollowing out the narrational time between setup and downfall. By prose's eliding the very thread of plot, any productive tension between the telling and the told has been snagged into a loop and a noose at once. Here is a flashback to rhetoric itself, not to the scene it once inflected. The effect would be overheated and threadbare at once if it weren't also densely entangled with that attenuated neuter pronoun.

And more. For the optative "Let him" is followed by the confirmatory "He did remember it," thus having, again, the odd extra effect of displacing the very grammatical framework of a chapter until now dispatched in the present perpetual tense of destitution, sustained as such for dozens of paragraphs after the opening sentence: "Changes have come again upon the great house in the long dull street." What we might thus have expected to follow the chapter's pivotal rhetorical question in the narrative present—"And the ruined man. How does he pass the hours, alone?"—is the avowed fact that he "does," does indeed, here and now, "remember it." Yet this consequential turn has been shifted into the more traditional past tense, as if the convention of retrospect has intersected the future-binding subjunctive in the cross-wired space, not of an ongoing present-tense limbo, but of a determinant (narratable) event—leading to a full cathartic reversal.

Twice again now: "*He did remember it.* In the miserable night he thought of it; in the dreary day, the wretched dawn, the ghostly, memory-haunted twilight. *He did remember it.* In agony, in sorrow, in remorse, in despair!" And a fourth time, with a textual as much as an emotional recursion, word for word: "Oh! He did remember it! The rain that fell upon the roof, the wind that mourned outside the door that night, had had"— rather than the less hammering and perfectly grammatical "had"—"had had foreknowledge in their melancholy sound." Dickens is to be recognized in all this at a glance, even as his unleashed rhetorical powers are at a new stretch in this transitional novel. And he continues to bring his Other in tow as well. After three repetitions (at the head of three separate sentences) of "he knew, now," diction is phonetically released to a new figurative version of both the *known* and the "now" in the replacement of mourning rain with icy recognition. This occurs "when every loving blossom he had withered in his innocent daughter's heart"—as the phrasing continues in a kind of jumpy frame-advance derivation from the opening adverbial "now" of immediate impact—"was *snowing* down in ashes on him." In the hyperattuned inflections of this phrase, *knowing* is by now its own kind of inundation. All that remains is the fierce backshadowing of his blindness in the return—and further internalization—of that neutered *it*.

Which prose gives us as follows, focalized through an adjacent mirror: "A spectral, haggard, wasted likeness of himself, brooded and brooded over the empty fireplace. Now *it* lifted up its head, examining the lines and hollows in *its* face; now [it] hung *it* down again, and brooded afresh." A cliché like "pale shadow of his former self" has been deferred, though of course not entirely, to the fact of optical capture. Even as the deadening thud of the *it* is partly relieved by the elliptical license of syntax itself, still the sentence is left filling in the blank of ontological blankness per se with this flatly awkward *it*-eration. Agency and face are equally alien, the "it" pitched between identified self and the features of its own despised head. In almost a textbook case of what psychoanalysis calls "melancholic introversion"—where the suddenly recognized loss (as in the death of a loved one) cannot be tolerated as such, but is instead internalized as the subject's own harbored death, with mourning thereby becoming suicidal—the "it" he intends thinking about tomorrow has swallowed *him* up entirely.

It is the essence of things Dickensian that comic style has itself strewn the path toward this melodramatic impasse, beginning with the first two forking predicates of the novel. Laid low near the end is the man whose designation as a clichéd *stuffed shirt* is originally averted, even while otherwise asserted, by the literal/metaphoric yoke of "stiff with starch and arrogance." His was the false front of pride that once required an unbroken continuity between fortified personality and social surround, so that his very speech was enunciated with "a lofty gallantry adapted to his dignity and the occasion": a fitness of inner to outer that has by this later point suffered so extreme an externalization of his psyche that, in the indignity of collapse, it—only an "it" now—is strictly an image outside, and beyond, himself. As the hopeless man contemplates the likely flow of blood from a foreseen knife wound, the so-far checked hand of suicidal intent seems as removed from him as the agency of a second self. It is the mirror face, now, that is sick unto death with the image of itself it sees: "When it had thought of this a long while, it got up again, and walked to and fro with its hand in its breast. He glanced at it occasionally, very curious to watch its motions, and he marked how wicked and murderous that hand looked." Off-loaded onto the optical ("looked") is a motive only subjectivity, even on its way out, could confirm: another variant of free indirect discourse in displaced self-recognition. Only momentarily is the "he" twice retrieved from the "it" as a marker of reflective (rather than just reflected) self-consciousness, but the reverse shot again embeds us in the secondary optical plane, where unflinching objectivity is screened off, in recess, from tortured acknowledgment: "Now it was thinking again! What was it thinking?" It is the mirror image that is alone still cognizant, as the prose would have it—until a shifted focus restores POV to the man himself across a more secure grammatical shift from "it" to "he."[3] The wrench is the shock cut of redemption itself: "Suddenly it rose, with a terrible face, and that guilty hand grasping what was in its breast. Then it was arrested by a cry"—as if the root syllable of "(ar)rest" were wrested redemptively (preventatively) from "breast" itself, with the reading ear never being too nervous for its own good at such uncanny moments. It was, in any event, "a wild, loud, piercing, loving, rapturous cry—and he only saw his own reflection in the glass, and at his knees, his daughter!" An overarching mor(t)al logic of the plot is here complete. Live by the "it" of an inarticulate hatred, die by a related "it"—unless the remembered murder of love can be reversed.

Intermedial reprise: I should perhaps stress again that, for all the hints of a protocinematic Dickens drawn out by such analogies as the POV shot—the same Dickens who, according to Sergei Eisenstein, would famously teach early American screen master D. W. Griffith everything he needed to know—nonetheless the articulatory mechanisms of the suturing reverse shots and deflected lines of sight in this mirror-inset nightmare remain intrinsically linguistic.[4] That is their true volatile power, their real kinesis. As before in the face-off of "Father and Daughter," the narrative charge rests with such microshifts in grammatical advance as when "he" drifts to "it," as well as when inference emerges by phonic overlap in effects as different as "the air . . . there" and the later triplex iteration of "knew now" in the void of the never before *known*—until it finally *snows* down on him. Or, most recently, in the countering force of "arresting" in regard to the "breast"-hidden blade. To peg these devices as producing linguistic even before narrative effects is another version of the analogic film/cinema divide, where cellular units of the syntactic strip are overlapped in motion to generate higher-order materializations and their scenic shifts. So it is that such oscillations delineate a filmic, even before a cinematic, narrative force, serial and self-revising: call it the flickering phrasal impetus of the Other Dickens within the melodramatic shot-changes of Boz's narrative apparatus. One needn't care here about this distinction as a "theoretical" point, however, since in this context any allusions to the audiovisual dynamic of cinema are simply in the service of a stricter description of what goes on, forward, under, and around again in the spoolings of Dickensian prose. Enough said, in the abstract, on this head. Examples are everything.

And concerning them, a further clarification. In its abrading of an obvious stretch of Dickensian melodrama in that pivotal phrasing previously discussed, one might wish to say that the grammatical glitch serving to rewrite the antecedent in "died out of hers"—from "her love" to "her face," in the retro-anticipation of "his face"—is a telltale fillip of the Other Dickens. Yet for this final and summary chapter, attention to the more suffused antecedence of the evolving "it" refrain, together with the disorienting shifts of tense that convey it, has deliberately broadened the frame of consideration. Made evident by these longer-span verbal disturbances are not so much the local disruptions of some vagabond linguistic Other as the pervasive formative *alterity* that constitutes language itself in operation: on whose elemental rudiments we'll ultimately zero in via *Dombey*'s own narrative parable of linguistic production in the decoding of "Dijon." With every voiced choice functioning only in light of its differential other, this is precisely the conditioning thickness of linguistic possibility into which the Other Dickens is, of course, likely to tap—beneath the surface of any vacillation, lurch, or turn—but that is elsewhere manifest in less pointed, let alone less comic, ways. So that this broader-gauge chapter, though punctuated with several testimonial moments from the Other Dickens in their quirky salience, continues to be, in casting back over the preceding three, more about what makes such blithe deviance possible in the whole spectrum of linguistic options.

So in all this, where were we? And was "he," Mr. Dombey, there at all any longer? The impersonal discursive "Let him remember" seems repaid at this turning point, rhetorically rather than just dramaturgically, by the implicit free indirect discourse of the man coming into new recognition of his rebuffed daughter in present-tense space: "Yes. His daughter! Look at her! Look here!" The despoiling "it" of recoil and rejection, all that once lingered in *the air there,* is rectified even phonetically by the *her here* of fortuitous return. Anticipating this texture of amelioration even at the phonetic level, we have in fact—by stark contrast—recently passed through the kind of cross-word slurring, as with the slower shift from *her* to *here,* that has set up the half-hallucinatory mirror passage in the first place. This happens in a stunning turn, earlier in the chapter, where, amid the still present-tense nightmare of degradation, with Dombey's domestic holdings rifled for auction, the Other Dickens is the very voice of misery's encroaching delirium. Amid a phantasmagoria of mortification, the footprints of Dombey's marauding confiscators, when gutting the household furnishings, seem personified in their own right as a jostling greedy mob. "He looked at their number, and their hurry, and contention—foot *tread*-ing foot out, and upward track and downward jostling one another . . . with absolu*te dread* and wonder." Cause and effect are collapsed into a not-unfamiliar syllabic lapse between words, with stenography again a potential spur in the compressed *t*/*dread* matrix of l\rd. As the very "medium" of his humiliation, in fact, prose has its own dread tread.

This impacted node of verbalized irony takes us again to the deepest linguistic principles at stake in any reading of such prose fiction, with its own internal frictions and skids. Here, what gets lessened in its pace with such attention is not the hurry of desertion in the plundered mansion but only the phrasal timer-belt of its representation. The point isn't that Style is somehow privileged to delve character at this extra depth of panic. What happens, instead, is that the Other Dickens, in synchronizing a "contention" of footprints to the slippery pace of the description's own Writing, uncovers yet again the transformational energy of language: language *in action,* its workings shown forth in what it moves forward, even when, we may say, stepping on its own lines, its own serial syllables. Leave it to the Other Dickens to effect a later withdrawal, an ironic cash-out, from this same phonetic memory bank. Though without the cross-passage confirmation of the skewed echo in the *Dombey* deployment ("foot treading"/"absolute dread"), the same inferred phonic ingredients are even more fully thematized as an ominous whisper when they converge later at the opening of *A Tale of Two Cities*. There "the Woodman, Fate," together with "the Farmer, Death" discussed in our previous chapter, is said to "work unceasingly, work silently," with only the shiver of sibilance, so far, to bind the verb phrases. The premonitory reverb of such allegorical labor is again lent an ear only by prose—when otherwise "no one heard them as they went about with muffled tread." Though it is only a graphic, not a phonic, shift from "heard" to "tread," the actual epithet attached to the latter noun—whether or not the "they" is deemed momentarily ambiguous in the description of the populace or the fated personification—summons in undertone precisely the muted aural forecast of a "muffle*d tread*." This is the same dread to recur later in the novel, of course, when figured by those undefeatable echoing feet of the Revolution marching on.

The earlier *Dombey and Son* makes its own metanarrative use of this dread tread of destiny as well. For such is the tacit story of its whole long arc of plot. Antecedence, recurrence, convergence: just as "treading" returns as "absolute dread," Dombey's own act in having once trodden underfoot his only chance of affection comes back not just to taunt but to haunt and eviscerate him: the mercantile subject reduced to an illusory "it" in the looking glass. Only at the last minute, as grammar as well as melodrama has it, is he rehumanized, re-personified. Not only do such variable linguistic effects, congregated as never before in Dickens around a sustained psychological diagnosis, offer the narrowest scaffold for a defining dialectal tension in the Other Dickens between Writing and its reading, but they do so, as promised, in a novel that stages (and does so in the immediately preceding phase of the plot) a most curious emblematic scene concerning just this inherent fact of prose in process. That episode's time has come for discussion, since a passage like the surgical probe of Dombey's self-image, as we've just negotiated it, makes several tightly exercised demands on linguistic cognition—both grammatical and phonetic—of the sort we might well come to think the earlier and pivotal passage has been positioned, by its oblique and baroque means, to anticipate, channel, and more closely delineate. Or think of it this way: if one feels—and who wouldn't?—that *Dombey*'s unprecedented stylistic reach has put a new premium on verbal attention in response to his fiction, especially in that climax of "Retribution," so that the novel constitutes a kind of enhanced reading lesson in his own right, then one might intuitively look for its tutor episode, its primer, somewhere in the thick—or thin—of the preceding story. And one might find it, for that very reason, not entirely threaded or webbed into the needs of plot, but operating in a separate register as well—and this in a chapter on the scent of a "retribution" (Dombey's against Carker) very different from the one that eventually befalls the cruel father. The elusive density of antecedence—emotional, syntactic, phonetic—that clots and complicates the prose of Dombey's ordeal has been submitted in this earlier scene to a litmus test of "slow" hearing in the very enunciation of word forms.

Mediated Plays of Power

Among the domestic scenes of paired or collective reading in *Dombey and Son*, the first two are paradigmatic in their oral format, the last (on which we are to concentrate) operating in pantomime and parody. Maybe other characters, besides Florence in the passage examined earlier, are too nervous to read, and let their books fall away. In any case, the least surprising early scene involves a simple and brief (because already prototypical) description, mentioned without further ado or detail. Carker the Junior sits alongside his devoted sister Harriet: "It was quite late at night, and the brother was reading aloud while the sister plied her needle": a domestic ecology of literary circulation familiar to any Victorian with a Dickens monthly number in hand or in earshot. We don't know what is being read in this scene from *Dombey and Son*. It might as well be the Dickens novel we are falling asleep over, or listening to on headphones, or paging through in our backlit Nook. But short of such anachronism, the domestic division of labor at the Carker hearth is already an icon—a locus classicus of tandem bodies—in the Victorian painting of reading: unraveling a text and knitting or sewing a fabric, two heads bent, two pair of eyes cast down in concentration, with the further inference at times, though often ambiguous, that we have entered upon the time of a presumed reading aloud: the unheard voice in audible (if invisible) transmission within the framed scene. As pictured in the novel's frontispiece, we also have Rob the Grinder, Carker's infiltrated spy, reading out the marriage service from the Bible, in his sloppy English, to Captain Cuttle, to prepare the Captain for the Dombey wedding: the very Grinder who will later efface, grind out, his complicity in helping the supposedly cuckolded husband (and former bridegroom) in his revenge plot—but only under the ban of sounding-out alphabetic characters from his self-produced text.

Far from conventional in this respect, though almost *requiring* an illustrative plate of its own (which it gets, fig. 2) to gloss its embodied sight-lines, that late scene of transmissive reading involves four pair of eyes, three reading, and the third not bent in knitwork but in plying the alphabet, one character at a time, in spelling out a most incriminating word. Transmission, yes, but no familiar reading aloud. Where domestic recitation in Dickens ordinarily works to restage the Victorian scene of family reception for circulated serial fiction, involving thereby the tangible aural quotient of his own prose, here not just the company of two but a crowd of four is arranged to dismantle and analyze the standard act, not of recitation exactly, but of privatized silent reading—typically fortified against distraction rather than, as here, against surveillance and retribution. The normative condition: letters passed over as swiftly as possible, in syllabic clusters, while eyes register them, inhibited muscular enunciation executes their phonemic function, and recognition accrues to them by rapidly noted lexical segmentation. More inhibitions apply to this scene of group decoding in *Dombey and Son*, however. Disinterested reading is entirely distorted by clandestine intent.

How so? The feckless and craven Rob the Grinder, now inadvertent "medium" of disclosure, has been privy to the passing of a message to Edith Dombey by Carker the Manager, that previous connubial "medium" (suddenly addressing her on his own blatant behalf, no longer in the name of his Master, about the intended foreign site of their adulterous rendezvous). Half in due clandestine diligence, perhaps, half in contempt, she immediately tears up the note and tosses its "mutilated fragments," as it were (like those of Carker's body later, under the train wheels), out of her carriage window. Only one shard remains behind for Rob's accidental discovery—and only one word on it, as it happens, the unlikely be-all and end-all of the mystery: the place-name "Dijon." Regarding all that laboriously ensues under needling interrogation by the greedy Mrs. Brown, there is only the frailest of narrative justification. When Rob objects that he can't "pronounce the names of foreign places," Mrs. Brown's assumption that "you have heard it said . . . and know what it sounded like" is met with "I never heard it said." He thus can only rewrite, not enunciate, it. No polyglot Rob—hardly boasting the well-oiled polylingual tongue of his Manager, who reads all of the Firm's correspondence "in various languages," and "almost at a glance," magically. Carker's schemes for the eventual ruin of the business have all along been tacitly facilitated whenever he "made combinations of one letter with another"—sheet by collated sheet, that is. It is only later, in the episode before us, scaled down from the sorting of whole epistolary pages to the linking of single foreign letters in combination, that fate takes its overdetermined toll.

Everything in the scene builds toward this, but indirectly, obliquely. Even the idiom "heard it said"—as in the case, say, of a rumor—seems implicitly skewed by the more specific "it" of the place-name itself in the above exchange with Mrs. Brown. Before Rob's appearance in her dwelling with, of all things, Carker's parrot—the Grinder's subhuman vocal contrast, able to sound out speech without understanding what it says—there has been a preternatural emphasis on audition. Dombey's arrival is recognized by his footfall, a broad and implicitly *well-heeled* tread not familiar in their neighborhood—even though Mrs. Brown is said to be, in another bent idiom as they await Rob's subsequent arrival, "slow of hearing" rather than "hard" (concerning such telltale approaches). A related slowness will retard the entire scene of silent "eavesdropping" by a first spatial association with that unsaid architectural dead metaphor, Dombey being poised on the threshold of her "hovel"—as if under its eaves—warning her, by no doubt unwitting metonymy, to pause on the "threshold of your scheme" if she intends him no good. She convinces him otherwise. And there at the actual threshold he lurks, in effect, for the duration, hiding beyond the squalid parlor as the scene unfolds—but not before Carker's sworn enemy, Alice Marwood, insulted by Dombey for her presumptuous speech, promises in present rather than future tense that "My saucy tongue says no more." True enough, in the developing scene, though her tongue and lips, in a necessity unrealized by her as yet, will be required to form the one word that can't be said—but must be shaped for somatic recognition. The scene's preparation, via perceptual idiom, continues unabated. Alice's mother knows that Dombey would not trust her information secondhand, so she wants him there as she extracts it from Rob, herself not knowing that her own formulaic phrasing to Dombey, that he "shall see with your own eyes and hear with your own ears," is not quite accurate either. Dickens is putting words in their mouths in ironic anticipation of the coming word that won't in fact be enunciated, even as Dombey almost growls to find out what she knows, saying "Go on" in "a deeper voice than was usual with him" (changed from the more vulnerable "hoarser" in the manuscript).[5] So, too, does Mrs. Brown's cackling gabble deepen as she tries wheedling the secret out of Rob, her voice "choked with the effort to be coaxing." Beyond its assonance, the slippery consonance of that very phrase takes a minor turn—before the major one coming—into the usually unnoticed tension between alphabetic and phonetic indication in Dickens, here *k* rhyming with hard *c* and *ch* nearer to the hiss of the *x*. But even for a reader not keyed to, or cued by, such subliminal nuances, the graphonic bilingual tension of "Dijon"—when mouthed out phonetically later in this scene—is likely to hit home in its emblematic match with Dickensian word processing.

From Somatic to Semantic

Writing and reading, graphemes and phonemes, meet only on the common, and sometimes syncopated, ground soon to be materialized in the *somatic* mediation of Alice's silent "lip reading"—a reading *with* rather than *of* the lips. And so a bit more context in the One and the Other Dickens for this knowing somatization of speech. Several novels down the road, *Great Expectations* will bring certain aspects of the sound of language, apart from its signifiers, into a convergence that reflects back on this agon of the embodied word in *Dombey*. Ironically, there is the scene—inverted microcosm, yet again, of a novel's own familial reception in Victorian households—where Magwitch wants Pip to read to him in a language he doesn't understand (perhaps a French novel set in Dijon?), so as to bask in the gentlemanly learning he has funded. In a quite different mood about the force of discourse, Magwitch, in the oral narrative previously delivered of his own life, has been determined to narrate it, not as in a "story-book," but in a quick "mouthful of English." The alien tongue he later insists on is the proof only of "proficiency," not of communication—just as a "mouthful" of speech operates in service to an earful of understanding only when the labor of mediation has a shared linguistic platform. This is clear enough. But if, in a Dickens novel particularly, "a mouthful of English" is a notable somatic metonymy for spoken language, so all the more striking is the link between lips and speech in the macabre scene in which the dying Miss Havisham takes Pip's gesture of parting as the conduit of her own somatic messaging: "I leaned over her and touched her lips with mine, just as *they* said, not stopping for being touched, 'Take the pencil and write under my name, "I forgive her."'" In a fitting perversity, the import is physiologically rather than semantically delivered. Lips don't "say" in themselves, without the rest of the mouth being full of aired speech. It is almost as if Pip, symbolically, is made to physically internalize one last—and uncannily literal—time, after years of submission, the overweaning force of her will, even in contrition.

In any case, when lips and tongue are requisitioned in the enunciation, not of "Foreign language, dear boy!'" (as Magwitch demands of Pip), but, in *Dombey*, of two not quite English syllables, *di* and *jon*, the function of continuous speech undergoes a further reduction to gesture rather than discourse. And with further ramifications in turn, looking ahead still to *Great Expectations*, for the accidents to which a more normal mouthing of word sounds is prone—not just in Pip's secret prose, as we've seen, but even in Magwitch's oral delivery. Taught to read, as Magwitch was, by a deserting soldier in hiding at a tramp's shelter ("a Traveller's rest"), Pip's benefactor in polyglot literacy was himself the beneficiary of another itinerant as well, complementing his reading skills, when "a travelling Giant wot signed his name at a penny a time learnt me to write." Indeed, as derived from the recurrent signature effects of a Giant among stylists once paid by the word, who but the Other Dickens could have taught Magwitch to narrate his story with such snappy byplay as we come upon just before? For there "warn't a soul that see young Abel Magwitch, with as little *on* him as *in* him, but wot caught fright *at* him, and either drove him *off* or took him *up*"—with this fivefold ingenuity sounding to Dickens, perhaps, more credibly inventive in the third person of a more self-conscious narrative act on his character's part. In a phrasing that distances his own physical body as that of another and beleaguered itinerant (a third party in third-person grammar), Magwitch's prose has shown him not only keenly aware of the world's antipathy but keyed to the prepositional wit of just the kind of written narrative within which his oral performance is showcased. The result of this described vagrancy and repeated apprehension is that, in a return to standard autobiographical grammar, "I reg'larly grow'd up took up"—the most tongue-twisting mouthful of all.

In its dogged inferences about literacy, *Dombey*'s scene is sparer by far than this intuitive flourish of Magwitch's storytelling—yet not without its peripheral wit. With somatic metonymies like "saucy tongue" in preparation, we return now to the actual work of the curtailed mouth in that silent reading scene. The building tension of the plot itself does nothing to prevent not just such loosely pertinent alphabetic play concerning the voice as we've noted in that "choking"/"coaxing" slide, but even the digressive Dickensian comedy of circumlocution, as when Rob tries conciliating Mrs. Brown with "much constrained sweetness of countenance, combating very expressive physiognomical revelations of an opposite character," where "character" almost implies a second, vindictive self struggling to escape her smothering clutch. And physiognomy turns phonetical in the next anagrammatic roll of the syllabic dice when Rob, answering whether he is "out of place" with Carker gone (Carker's death scene eventually climaxing a chapter under no less a title, and with no more inferred regret, than "Rob the Grinder Loses His Place"), echoes back that he is still "in pay," adding "to—keep my eyes open," with the narrative itself then adding, in a no longer figurative sense, "rolling them in a forlorn way." With ears as well as eyes open, the reader may note the "rol" revolved to "orl," but Rob's mind's eye is fixed on the one and only word his present audience cares about in order to intercept his employer's treachery. That is the word he is willing to offer up only on the promise that "you'll never tell anybody." Again idiom gets ahead of the characters in its misfit with what's coming. The promise is "readily" given by Mrs. Brown, "being naturally Jesuitical; and having no other intention in the matter than that her concealed visitor should hear for himself." Little does she know that there will be nothing for the hidden auditor, in his off-stage site of reception, to hear: that Rob's paranoia will, in short, prevent vocalization, even while the Other Dickens is crisscrossing the passage with continuing phonic undercurrents, as in the implied third term of

Secret intelligence

Figure 2. "Secret Intelligence" from *Dealings with the Firm of Dombey and Son: Wholesale, Retail and for Exportation,* by Charles Dickens (1848).

Illustration by Hablot Knight Browne. Source: Project Gutenberg.

"sulking" between Rob's "skulking" in a "sullen" manner on the verge of the coveted word's slow disclosure.

Fearing Carker's demonic omniscience, as if the very walls have ears, the Grinder insists on neither writing the foreign place-name plainly nor letting it be sounded out for overhearing. He thus, in effect, further shreds the already torn note, constituting its own incriminating "letter" of intent, into separate sublexical letters with the cautious action of chalk on a tabletop, and then *obliterates* them in the full etymological sense, their function literalized and eclipsed cipher by rubbed-away cipher. It is as if Rob comes most fully into his nickname, the Grinder, by this act of serial abrasion. In the meantime, Mr. Dombey, in hiding, is peering in on this covert inscription, enacted in hyperbolic slow-motion—looking over Mrs. Brown's shoulder as she looks over Rob's. All the while, the equally vengeful Alice Marwood, once brutally wronged by Carker, is offering up the letters for his enemy as she deciphers them upside down from across the table in an attenuated lipreading of chalked symbols leaving no incriminating trail. So extreme is Rob's erasure that he is "not content with smearing it out," but is seen instead "rubbing and planing all trace of it away . . . until the very color of the chalk was gone from the table." So exacting is this commentary on scriptive transmission that it puts exaggerated somatic pressure on the disappearance of all alphabetic "trace," all cause, in the effect of comprehension. In any case, the chapter title, attached as well to the illustration, names a "Secret Intelligence" doubly surreptitious: both occulted in production and covertly intercepted.

All internal rhythm nullified, this process of accumulated erasures offers the clear deformation of a norm. In straddle mode as well as in a more kinetic overdrive, so the last chapter made plain in closing, the Other Dickens is the covert grammarian of a parsing inseparable from tempo—but reduced ad absurdum here to the scratching out (both senses) of one letter in retarded isolation from the next. So it is that "Rob, having nothing more to say, began to chalk, slowly and laboriously, on the table": with the verb "to chalk" operating by back-formation from the material of signification. After Mrs. Brown deciphers the first letter *D*—as if by association with Death or Destiny, as we might imagine, or Dombey, for that matter—and blurts it out, Rob begs her to "keep quiet please," after first exploding with the more anatomical, and also translingual, dead metaphor "Hold your tongue." Indeed, English must be held in abeyance for the French orthography to pass through shaped pronunciation into decipherment. Rob resumes in the same peevish, quailing manner, "muttering to himself"—but in grunts of disgruntlement rather than enunciation. Thus, "returning to his work with an ill will, Rob went on with the word," not knowing that Dombey, from the doorway, "looked eagerly towards the creeping track"—the better to be *keeping track*, a dodged idiom in twisted mutation—"towards the creeping track," that is, of Rob's "hand upon the table." Surely we have none but the Other Dickens to credit with the lexical and cognitive slink of that "creeping." Moreover, we have the illustrator Phiz (Hablot K. Browne) to thank—as if he couldn't quite believe the scene either—for handling the ajar door's perspective so badly that Dombey's vantage point seems to be from *behind* the door, with no possible access but audial to the silence inside.

In the prose itself, how much longer can this improbable scenario be prolonged? Every detail is as meticulously spelled out as are the five letters of Rob's secret. As if the invaded privacy of this scribal cabal weren't enough: "At the same time, Alice, from her opposite chair, watched it ['the creeping track'] narrowly as it shaped the letters, and repeated each one on her lips as he made it, without articulating it aloud." The track of chalk, rather than talk, requires the tracing out of phonemes on the lips—an effort to produce, in a perversely optical way, what structural linguistics (in the influential terms of Ferdinand de Saussure) calls the "acoustic image" of the letter forms (unique to any one language) that can then, in the aggregate, trigger a "concept," or otherwise a referential image. Actually, Alice's role here is to supplement unseen inscription with something more like the viseme, rather than phoneme, of speech production: that physical shaping of sound forms with lips, tongue, and teeth with which the hearing impaired are trained to "read faces" in the act of vocal production. In contrast, the standard reading of a text, we are hereby reminded, entails the decoding of both systems together: script and phonetics, and not least in translation (however modest the French challenge in this case). "At the end of every letter her eyes and Mr Dombey's met, as if each of them sought to be confirmed by the other; and thus they both spelt, D.I.J.O.N." Not really—and certainly not in Dombey's case. The verb choice marks another reversion from effect to cause, comprehension to alphabetic impression. Rather than spelling it, they both read the name Dijon, a place-name made out in tardy recognition. Only Rob and his graphemes *spell* it—and do so only in this uniquely double sense of writing it *out*.

And how, one might wonder, in a mood for historical reconstruction, would the second-degree transcription of his orthography be read aloud at the family hearth? The graphic periods that suggest the fragmentary dispensing of subsyllabic matter would go unpronounced, of course, as they do at the end of whole sentences. Incurring a further conceptual pull between the scribing and sounding of linguistic markers, here the punctuated summary of staggered graphemes operates, in fact, more as a miniature reenactment of the scene as a whole than as the authentic transcription of its decisive reveal. On this understanding, the piecemeal lexeme D.I.J.O.N., as a parody of phonemic sequencing, is visualized in something like the prose equivalent—to invoke such subcinematic elements one more time—of a jammed and dragging filmstrip caught in the misaligned sprocket claws of projected frame advance. In any case, what the conspiratorial human characters have been doing in the narrative past, the alphabetic characters now do, as with all lettered text, in the spelt present of the novel's reading: they indicate, here and right now, what in present tense they *spell* ("spelt, *D.I.J.O.N.*"). In the closed circuit of this episode, spelling and reading, scribing and its acoustic imaging, have been rendered radically distinct but ultimately inseparable in the prolonged, though ordinarily all but simultaneous, labor of recognition. In the process, the normal work of Dickensian inscription—in this chapter on "secret intelligence"—has been surveilled from within by its Other in drawing forth yet again the deep audiovisual collaboration, the founding graphonic bond, that is the open secret of such prose.

Between Mark and Message

A secret open, in this aberrant instance, to the novel's audience alone, however. For in this markedly strange moment, and yet typically as well in another sense, it is Dickens's reader only, none of the characters in the scene itself, who is invited to see the marks of what's really going on—going forward textually—on the page of their encounter: in this case, those arbitrary full stops of "D.I.J.O.N." as indicators (in recap), via discourse alone, of halt and erasure in the prevented flow of a phonemic stream within the narrative episode. The norm of unpronounced graphic indicators, like commas and periods, is reversed into new visibility. But only so as to remind us of the general condition of fictional prose: that characters live in ignorance of the writing that transmits (or artificially reinterprets) even their verbal doings. Such puncture wounds of the lexeme represent a borrowing from the syntactic code of sentence making to inscribe, one level down, the abrupt ruptures of a character's timorous word-formation. A standard aspect of linguistic operation at another scale thus enters through the backdoor of its own lexical exclusion. And it does so with a further medial overtone as well. In a novel published at the end of telegraphy's first decade, those full stops imposed by narration may well evoke the telegraphic style of "stop" between words or word clusters, diverted in this aberrant case to the breathers between unspoken, unbreathed, phonemes. By discursive prose alone, not the scribal action it depicts, are other formats of communicative language thus summoned and undone at once.

But these may seem just curious associative wrinkles of a pressurized inscription, negligible in context, within the overall fracture of narrative logic that this turn of plot imposes. There is no overstating how improbable the whole episode is. Could either the One or the Other Dickens have put these narrative characters through such labored paces if it weren't good trouble: good for something, that is, beyond itself? Or beneath? The play between letter sounds and letter names, as between independent alphabetic characters in one language and all but silent diphthong markers in another—the thicket of this densely complex transmission, if we really imagine our way into its relay system—is as intense as the whole setup is either silly or sensationalist, or both. If only by default, then, the entire tableau comes across as more a parable than a plausibility.

And any resulting sense of the episode as emblematic rather than credibly dramatic certainly carries through to its abrupt conclusion. For just as the tabletop words disappear in the artificial rigor of their production, so does their uncomprehending amanuensis—in the person of the Grinder—drop away from agency. He is fitly ushered out of consciousness altogether—after a linguistic cognition denied him in progress—by way of a more than ordinarily disjunctive and splayed syntax, as if faint-headed in its own right. We find Rob stretching his spent presence, that is, across a triadic register declined from emotional to physical attribution as we read. For the miserable creature is "overcome," thrice over, "with mortification, cross-examination," and the nameless booze he has been plied with: namely, and generically, "liquor."

Never would the term *handcuff grammar* better apply, perhaps, than to this aftermath of his coerced and discrepant instrumentality. Early in the scene, the Grinder, "between his sense of injury, his sense of liquor, and his sense of being on the rack, had become so lachrymose" that the internal sound rhyme of "rack" with "lach"—even against the alphabetic look of the script—has tightened the normal rhythm of cause in succession to effect across the three normatively parallel phrases. Much later now, after he himself has more fully dissevered the optical from the aural in language production, it is up to a variant threefold syntax—putting the further consumption of liquor last, by juggled parallel—to put his labors to rest. Prose does so by straddling separate "senses," this time, of the participial "overcome" itself, now emotional, now physical—as if to say both overwhelmed by the aggressions of this grueling event and drenched in its lubricant. And no sooner, that is, does the commandeered go-between, this second-order "medium," find himself "overcome with mortification, cross-examination, and liquor" than the tabula rasa reasserts itself against his previous and involuntary writing. This happens when, straightforwardly enough, Rob "folded his arms on the table, laid his head upon them, and fell asleep." So do all mediums virtually disappear in the delivery of a given message. And so it is that we sense the open-weave mesh of disjuncture across the entire linguistic infrastructure activated by Dickensian prose. This recognition traverses not just, as often noted, the fused interstices of enchained phonemes in single alphabetic clusters but, one level up, as equilibrated with each other repeatedly in chapter 3, those syntactic latches, those *and*-cuffings, that conjoin divergent mind-body registers like "mortification" and "liquor" according to the ironic deep structure of narrative grammar itself.

All told, the precautions on Rob's part have been so addle-brained, elaborate, and protracted that if they fascinate Dickens with something about the nature of writing in relation to retinal and subvocal uptake—fascinate him enough to have concocted and executed this whole dilatory scene—its linguistic curiosity may well have had some relevant preparation in the hundreds of pages leading up to its pivot point in *Dombey*. What (one therefore ultimately asks) do the chalked machinations of Rob the Grinder—now the cajoled scrivener, copyist under duress, grinding out, then rubbing out, one letter after another—have perhaps to suggest about Dickensian writing practice more generally, beyond this particular default of eye-ear coordination? This question would take us outside that local circuit of irony by which the punishment involved here is suited to the crime, or at least to the criminal. For Carker, that man of "attention and teeth," of dentition and penetration—who must often be lip-read rather than listened to in his swallowed, deceptive speech—gets tripped up, for once, by the pantomime of that rare paper trail he has, in his lust, allowed himself to leave. Beyond this, however, there must be something more at stake and at play—something the Other Dickens would more fully infuse with a network of stray verbal enthusiasms and thus, so to speak, more characteristically underwrite.

And what there "must be" in Dickens, certainly in stylistic matters, there always is: the prose reliably exhausting all of its myriad possibilities in the spaciousness of its invention. So there is a curious precedent for those capital letters end-stopped five times over in the chalked performance of D.I.J.O.N. (with the periods, intended by Dickens, gone missing only in the most recent Penguin edition, though there in earlier imprints from that publisher and in other scholarly editions). With their punctuated resemblance to a more fully encrypted acronym, these periods have in fact been anticipated by a conjured but never completed version of the heroine F.L.O.R.E.N.C.E. ceremonialized by verse orthography. And not just once but twice—in what we might call rival failed acrostics, unknown to each other and both truncated: one proffered by Captain Cuttle on behalf of the heroine's destined husband, as if elicited by Carker himself; one, in close sequence (and tacit association) with it, from the pen of Florence's disappointed suitor Toots. The tactically worst first. In a scene of perversely misled hopes, Carker—having his own scheming eye on the nubile Florence before the idea of Edith arrives for a more vindictive triangulation with Dombey, and a sweeter revenge—lets Captain Cuttle maunder on when seeking assurance that Walter, once sent to sea by Carker precisely to separate him from Florence's sphere, has thereby been vouchsafed a token of the Firm's confidence as an omen of his rising star. Carker answers ambiguously, as usual, mostly by exposing his sharpened teeth, so that the scheme of exile and convenient imperilment is turned from seas-wide-enough-to-drown-in to horizons so bright and unlimited as to be cause for buoyant hopes. Young Gay " 'has brilliant prospects,' observed Mr Carker, stretching his mouth wider yet: 'all the world before him' " (if only in the matter of nautical expanse, not in the full idiomatic sense). In spontaneous enthusiasm, mistaking the shared nature of the sentiment, the Captain overflows with an irrelevant idiom ("All the world and his wife") and then, unguardedly, begins to free-associate on the idea, the trope, of "the world's wife," with Carker leading him on. With the Captain guessing that he knows what Carker is "smiling at," the result is an added lure: "Mr Carker took his cue, and smiled the more." After a further volley of deception, so begins the Captain's euphemistic scrabble-game of conspiratorial name-dropping, a game which he's lost from the start without knowing it:

> "You're thinking of a capital F perhaps?" said the Captain.
> Mr Carker didn't deny it.
> "Anything about a L," said the Captain, "or a O?"
> Mr Carker still smiled.

Carker wouldn't be smiling if he knew—in the later evolution of his revenge plot—how much of its imploded hopes even a mere D.I.J. would begin to trigger in exposing his intended secret hideaway.

And though Walter's prospects are bad enough at this point in regard to the waiting F.L.O.(rence), there is, more hopeless yet, the terminally disappointed Mr. Toots. Three chapters later, before we have forgotten the snaky deception on Carker's part in his manipulation of Cuttle, the lovelorn Toots tries to work his own kind of magic with "a capital F," as well as "a L" and "a O," and so forth. Not for want of passion are his compositional ambitions balked almost at once: "He had made a desperate attempt . . . to write an acrostic on Florence, which affected him to tears in the conception. But he never proceeded in the execution further than the words 'For when I gaze,'—the flow of imagination in which he had previously written down the initial letters of the other seven lines, deserting him at that point." Verse isn't everyone's strong suit, to be sure. "For when I gaze" is followed by nothing—nothing, for instance, like *Lovingly*

upon her/Open eyes so bright . . . , etc. The only spelling out is that of
the Other Dickens, we may say, in coming to the syllabic rescue with that
punning phrase "flow of imagination," a quality noted in its very exhaustion. Florence thus remains unenshrined in meter—for Toots, an unten-
able "Flo of the imagination" only—not a plausible fantasy capable of
verse capture. Only the prose poetry of the Other Dickens has plunged us
at this point into the eddies and depths of word formation itself.

Certainly the self-conscious linguistic energy behind such phonetic punning as "flow" for "Flo" may seem to anticipate the later alphabetic charade (*D* pronounced "dee" in advance assimilation of the waiting syllabic
"I") by which Carker is bested in absentia by a taste of his own medicine
in the confidential transfer of a coded name, this time of place rather than
person. With the Manager once deviously acquiescent in the alphabetic
insinuations of Captain Cuttle, now it is the dashing of Carker's own
"brilliant prospects" in the courting of a female Dombey, the imperious
bride of Empire, that is enacted in the same manner of tactically throttled
and decrypted speech. But any such sublexical symmetry would operate,
again, only within a single ironic circuit of the plot. The verbal insistence
on Dickens's part seems more broadly encompassing—or undergirding. It
reaches to a matter of literary, and hence textual, bases, where, as always,
one is trained to encounter such structuring lingual momentum as the
everyday disappearance of f-l-o into "flow"—precisely in the serial facili-
tation of all sense as well as sonority.

As if staged in pointed reprisal against a man who often communicated without producing sound, and who absorbed foreign writing almost
without individual lexical recognition, Carker's comeuppance is given the
most exhaustive treatment of these matters, this alphabetic materiality,
anywhere in Dickens—in all its studied declension from emplotment to
phonetic sequence. Across the minimal filaments of buildup in that climactic scene, writing shrinks under duress in resistance even to rudimentary
linkage, let alone message. In that analytic breakdown of communicative
form, the former "medium" of expressive teeth and tongue is done in by
a run of unaired, unbreathed speech not his own: ultimately entrapped,
that is, by the work of language in production even before exchange. Yet
the arrival of this phonetic nemesis for Carker—answering to the previous episodes of acrostic risk and fizzle—is staged not just tactically, but
strategically, for the theme of reading at large. It operates, in the long run,
as if to rehearse the whole linguistic enterprise of narrative reception. For
it is the scene not just of secretive spelling but of hyperinvested reading, a
reading both in embryo and in action.

One letter absorbed into the formative drive of the next—as, elsewhere,
"FLO" into "flow"—only for each accretion to vanish in turn into a
meaning never there whole and at once in the lexical signified: the deed of

reading in parable, absent, in Rob's rare case, only the book or page itself. Rob resembles some demoted Victorian typesetter executing one discrete letter at a time in material form; Alice, the overinvested reader taking upon her own formerly manhandled body the somatically registered phonemes of a soon-to-be-delegated revenge (until, in her later guilt, she thinks better of it); Dombey, the cognizant function intent on acting upon the text once it passes through grapho-phonemic shape into a meaning simultaneous with a geographical "concept" (or signified)—and thus offers a vector of destination in the revenge plot. In this ad hoc and claustrophobic scriptorium, those normative moments of synchronized (because inseparable) inscription and its phonetic enunciation—to be replayed only later at the remove of our own novel reading, being initially blocked for Rob in the form of a foreign and thus silenced word—are thus parsed into travesty and revaluation from within the labor of a word's self-consumed transmission. Here in miniature, realized one scrawled alphabetic character at a time, is the anatomized structure of textual generation, as so often tapped and maximized in Dickensian prose: material before emotive; somatic before cerebral; first printed, then (unless read aloud) sounded under muscular inhibition, and then projected into the named scene of imagined event—including, in this case, its foreseen violence.

Yet beyond such a tacit allegory of enunciated representation, it is the deepest rhetorical anomaly in all this that makes it perhaps most broadly revealing. When the lexical abyss of D.I.J.O.N. is recouped by the normalizing comic relief—and recovered syntactic verve—of "mortification, cross-examination, and liquor," a principle, honored here in the breach, is brought to unusual clarity regarding the normal balancing act of Dickensian prose. This exception only confirms the typical conservation of energy that puts the Other Dickens in recurrent, if often briefly disruptive, touch with an inimitable storytelling drive. The usual pattern or priority is strikingly inverted in this episode. With a privileged phonetic Writing approaching its own vortex of disintegration, it is the wit of a more familiar Style that comes to its immediate and reorienting rescue. Yet again the One, Other, and Only, even in extremis, are found to be not just inextricable but forcefully inmixed and mutually reinforcing. Still, if only by such a curious reverse route, this most ornate and ingrown of melodramatic episodes becomes yet another lesson in precisely that level of inherently alphabetic (before narrative) momentum—lessening one level of tension and suspense in momentary deference to another—where the Writing of the Other Dickens so intuitively drives its wedge and leverages its sequestered pleasures.

And even here, with this strange dilation of the phonemic trace in *Dombey and Son*, we can still comprehend the signifying Other on the model of portmanteau or concertina phrasing. One novel, *David Copperfield*, taught us where we might look for a prime mover in the aurality of Dickensian writing: showed us from the start in the conduct of its prose and then told us further in the content of its own retrospect. We were directed there, explicitly, to the coerced tactical abbreviations of stenography—deliriously alleviated ever afterward. All the novels teach us where to listen for this. And some of them revert to its original scene of alphabetic abuse and vocalic suppression. Where "In FX tion" in *Great Expectations* may well be meant to put illiteracy in the service of satire in an exposé of infectious upwardly mobile desire, the even more condensed *djn* (or *\jn*) undergoes its own laborious decontraction in something like a clinical performance of normal phonetic decoding. Nothing, in actual clock time, could be farther from Dickens's apprenticeship in a shorthand alacrity of transcript; Rob's ordeal has amounted, in contrast, to the longest hand imaginable. Enough to say that even if, escaping the Gallic paradigm for this concerted guesswork, the charaded word had called up the (beloved of Dickens) *Arabian Nights*'s origin of *djinn* for "genie" (**djn**), the sly and Gurney-haunted genius of this lexical challenge could scarcely have been more difficult to surmount in Mrs. Brown's crowded reading room.

What reading lessens in this episode, in the tension of plot's overall drive, involves, therefore, exactly what it loosens up for recognition. In a quite different sense from that nonidiomatic allusion to Mrs. Brown's debility, it is here that we are reminded of what it is to be productively "slow of hearing." With plot as catalyst, it is as if the inner shape of Writing is precipitated out, and crystallized, from the former's most out-of-the-way device. It is a hard claim to stake, and harder by far to make stick, but I would still want provisionally to say, in thinking back over all fourteen novels, that never in Dickensian fiction does the propulsive drive of the Inimitable's touted narrative suspense and the compulsive graphonic oscillations of his Other seem not so much to converge as to intercept each other at so sharp and self-conscious an angle as in the D.I.J.O.N. episode. Narrative dilation becomes linguistic magnification in this laboratory of the microtext. A stronger claim is nonetheless easier to lodge. Never in Victorian fiction, surely, could there be a more thorough probe into the materiality of the legible reading surface and its incurred discernment, from the manual labor of inscription to the bodily process of its phonetic decoding. The episode is almost as exhausting for us, as a grotesque staging of our standard attention, as it is for Rob. In putting the skids on plot in the very naming of its most dramatic scene change, Rob's s/crawling ("creeping") chalk exaggerates to the point of travesty a deep linguistic instinct of Dickensian prose. It is just this that we've tracked, over four chapters, whenever attention is invited to lessen—to shrink and yet quicken—the zone and focus of response.

AFTERWORD

"THAT VERY WORD, READING"

Nowhere more tangibly in the novels, not even in the passages of explicit political diatribe, does Dickens the socially observant magazine editor come closer to peeking from behind the narrative curtain than when, in his last finished book, he hands over to Eugene Wrayburn the following impromptu lampoon on the latest cliché of journalist reviewing. It's perfectly in character, and wonderfully out of place—interrupting Mortimer's urgent plea to hear more about his friend's risky sadistic behavior toward the dangerous Headstone:

> "You charm me, Mortimer, with your reading of my weaknesses. (By-the-by, that very word, Reading, in its critical use, always charms me. An actress's Reading of a chambermaid, a dancer's Reading of a hornpipe, a singer's Reading of a song, a marine painter's Reading of the sea, the kettle-drum's Reading of an instrumental passage, are phrases ever youthful and delightful.)"

The longtime editor in Dickens knows such knowingly phrased argot when he sees it, but needs a fictionalized spokesman to pillory the habit for him. Yet more seems at stake than topical comedy in this flagrant digression—very much "by-the-by," since, though he "had founded himself upon Eugene when they were yet boys at school," Mortimer is attempting to put some temperamental and moral distance between them in just this dialogue.

In the novel's climax, however, Headstone's impersonation of Riderhood, by imitation of his lockkeeper's garb, is a motivated version of this Grub Street triviality: a "reading" of the water rat that allows Eugene in turn to *misread* his pending assailant when passing by him almost shoulder to shoulder. This nonrecognition transpires in a minor ruffle of free indirect discourse, in the subjunctive mood, when Eugene crosses paths with a man who "carried something over his shoulder, which might have been a broken *oar, or spar*, or *bar*, and took no notice of him, but passed on." The echo of *oar* with *or* and the off-rhymed release of "bar" from "spar" render almost a phonetic as well as an ocular prefiguration, in its thudding beat, of the bludgeoning to come. Shifting in its monosyllabic pace from Anglo-Saxon objects ("oar," "spar") to the more abstract geometry of the French-derived *barre* (of what material?), the initial uncertainty is only exacerbated before the human figures temporarily go their separate ways. As it happens, this test of Headstone's disguise exactly reverses the taunting logic by which Wrayburn, tailed by him back in London, has cruelly delighted in turning on him, after Headstone has followed him down many a deliberate blind alley, and then looking right through him—with no sign of recognition—on the reverse route. It is just this ruthless show of contempt that Eugene was about to disclose to a horrified Mortimer after stalling (via Dickensian interpolation) with his little ad-libbed squib on journalistic idiom.

Even before the extended joke may have come home to roost in this way, the satire was clearly that of a novelist with a major stake in the true work of textual engagement. Actresses who "read" rather than perform a character, dancers whose bodies "read" rather than enact their score, singers who "read" rather than sing a song, painters who "read" rather than represent their pictorial object, and, last but not least, in an almost Dickensian personification all its own, "a kettle-drum's Reading of an instrumental passage," make for a phantom horde of bibliophiles crowding the stage rather than the bookstore or lending library. An author who writes to be read must have found those other ways in which the vocabulary of reading has been vitiated, without actual script in sight, to be quite silly—and co-optive. It can scarcely have bothered Eugene much, but Dickens no doubt took sardonic umbrage.

Hence that standout passage at hand. The privilege accorded to textual prototypes in the matter of interpretation, however gratifying that might seem for a writer on the face of it, is spoiled by a routine, a trend, that no longer leaves actual Reading first among equals. A century and a half later, and in light of quite different if equally cliché-ridden grounds, this book has tried pushing back a bit. It has looked less to Dickens's "reading of his times" than to the time of reading his sentences, in all their alternately immaculate or slaphappy expansiveness and vocal charge. The hope has been to intercept this energy in its very writing-out before us, however the monosyllabic throb of a phrase like "oar, or spar, or bar" may be focalized by the author through a character's line of sight. But which author? Say, if you are so inclined by now, that the pulsing indecision of "oar, or spar, or bar," including the blur of orthographic and phonemic registers in the *o/a* matrix, is the Other Dickens recharging the batteries of narrative suspense. All you have thereby said, and it's no small thing, is to have named an alternating current in reception that renders *dialectical* the very act of Dickensian audition—for the author in the echo chamber of his own Writing, as later for us. The Other Dickens in these pages has never been otherwise:

strictly an inherent function of prose when taken up for reading, an othering of language itself from within the inscribed task of depiction.

In this novel of literacy for hire (where Wegg is paid by Boffin for his inept reading aloud), a more explicit critique of phonetic teaching when divorced from lexical understanding seems aimed at the very antithesis of Dickensian reading, whose syllables infiltrate and invigorate meaning. Such a glimpse into the imaginative inertia of disastrous pedagogy can only be corrected for, by loose association, through the reading lesson this novel puts us through. Under the vacuous regimen at Headstone's school, even the well-known Christian narrative is reduced to an explicit syllabic muddle, so that adults taught to read "out of the New Testament; and by dint of stumbling over the syllables and keeping their bewildered eyes on the particular syllables coming round to their turn, were as absolutely ignorant of the sublime history, as if they had never *seen or heard of it*" — let alone seen and therefore heard inwardly its recounting in print. Trained far better by the novel's own prose, in this very passage the Dickens reader has, in phonetic terms, seen the coming round of "stumble" through "syllable" to a spoiled "sublime" in a restored appreciation of these phonetic ingredients in their lucid satiric deployment. Certainly, the preceding chapter here has not done its work if it hasn't shown how keenly Dickensian narration wants us to be aware, even at the price of plot-slowing parable, of its own phonemic buildup, syllabic in the mouth in the very process of semantic recognition, from D.I.J. to F.L.O. In the seasoned ear's "Reading of" Dickens (the only cogent use of this gerund phrase, as implied by Eugene's mockery), the subliminal and the sublime answer to each other across just such cresting verbal increments, where the schooled syllabic "stumble," or phonemic tumble, rather than its useless variety in bad pedagogy, constitutes time and again a fortunate fall within an otherwise coherent lexical sequence: a felix culpa of syllabic errancy and recuperated verbal force.

We've encountered scores of examples, strung out and knotted off by assonance, alliteration, and the specialized effects of meter, sibilance, double entendre, and the rest, and not just compounded but "accordioned" from within. Yet one more instance can't hurt, especially if, even in its own context, it's too good to ignore in the uniquely mimetic prolongation of its bland *b* sounds and their unpunctuated adjectival buildup. In his parodying the elongated physiognomy of the droopy Lady Tippins in the second chapter of his last full novel, *Our Mutual Friend*, what Dickens delivers is a kind of syntactic similitude even before an explicit simile arrives. When speculating on the self-generative power of Dickensian writing, one guesses here at an immediate associational fallout: both from the mere table setting that she is another version of, on the one hand, and from the vast vanity mirror of the mansion, on the other, that installs her as a regular fixture at its joyless feasts. Among the famous fragmented litany of dinner guests at the stultifying Veneering table—all of whom are made numbly, spectrally manifest only in the mirror image of their superficial presence—appears a dowager no more prepossessing than one of the gilt utensils before her, and in whose polished surface she would, from the proper angle, though unmentioned (except by simile), be partially reflected. All we know for certain is that she is for us only a reflected reality to begin with, entirely subordinated to the mirror as grammatical subject in this present-tense chapter of perpetual social surface: "Reflects charming old Lady Tippins on Veneering's right; with *an immense obtuse drab oblong face, like a face in a tablespoon.*" I suppose there are no dozen words together in Dickens that I like any better than those, with the substantive anchor of all that adjectival bulk getting further extended, prolonged, squashed out, by the flat repetition of "face."

Yet this is scarcely the last of such syllabic fun provided by Tippins, whose cosmetized torpor seems vivified by prose alone. It is one thing for Dickens to string out his modifiers like this in imitation of elongated features. It is quite another thing—uncannier yet perhaps, and more frequent—when, one level up in grammar, an entire splayed predication works together with the spreading of sound play. With Tippins, this happens in what might be called a syllabic mimesis rather than phonetic onomatopoeia: the spacing out of sound in imitation of a spreading out of both flabby material shape and abstract attribution. The effect comes to immediate attention—in any actual Reading of her character in other than the "critical sense"—when one finds oneself caught up by, or tripping over, the hilarity of her "showing her entertaining powers and green fan to immense advantage." In an unbunching of semantic and syllabic association, at least one monosyllabic slat of "fan" is unfolded ("forked" apart, or made "to concertina")—and by yet another split predicate and an off-rhyme alike—into the syllabic spread of "ad*van*tage." So it is that Tippins is shown off but also *up* in the very fanning open of participial grammar and syllabic echo, the *and*-cuff of such grammar turned, along with its syllabic patterning, to a kind of preening peacock spread of accessorized senescent femininity. The prose seems as calculated a display as the camouflaging gesture it mocks: a display aural as well as graphically paced. In the study of Dickens, one ignores this sort of thing only at the peril of one's pleasure—and amazement.

It's important not to insist on more than this, for fear of losing the authentic weight of the claim. Well apparent by now, I trust, is the happy lack of any polemic edge to the rub of the Only against the interrupting Other of my title. This book has never meant to push the Other Dickens as the true and exclusive Boz, the one really worth studying, worth thinking, lecturing, and writing about. Far from it. The effort has been, beginning with the threefold title, simply to fold an enlivened sense of the linguistic uncanny in Dickens's prose into the more obvious thematic drives of the fiction—and thus to register the prose not just as storytelling but as Writing. Where to begin?—I had once asked. And now: Where in the world to leave off? It certainly shouldn't be by forgetting where we ultimately did begin, with the shortchanged vowels of Victorian shorthand. The point never ceases making itself even in the final stages of Dickens's career. Assonance is its typical sounding board, as we've often heard, whether smoothly probable or ludicrously overplayed. In *Our Mutual Friend*, there alongside Lady Tippins, an inability to tell "which is which" (regarding a pair of Veneering dinner party regulars) is phrased so as to exaggerate a leveling assonance with the chiastic "*fusion of Boots in Brewer and of Brewer in Boots.*" But the same novel can fuse sounds beyond the tolerance of any prose decorum. Describing the portly, boyish Mr. Wilfer with his typical metaphoric descriptor, Dickensian language waxes sing-song across, and beyond, an initial swivel on the noun "address" turned to past participle—this, when "during this short address, the *cherub* addressed had made *chubby* motion toward a *chair*." Still in payback mode, and with the framing assonance the least of it (*cher/chair*), the Gurney survivor in Dickens, the Other of his recovered syllabic fluency, can't help but indulge the generative chirp of **chrb chb chr** in the most overt and knowingly trivial of alliterations. Four decades after word sounds were first crunched, scrunched—rather than stretched—on the rack of brachygraphy, an unstinted lexical redress remains in play.

But a subsequent low-keyed assonance in the novel's closing sentence is certainly more tactical. In looking to the last (and one of the simplest) of all Dickens's own leavetakings, what would one be inclined to hear in the closing note of *Our Mutual Friend*? At the latest and last of the Veneering dinners, before the host's pending bankruptcy, we are told this: "When the company disperse—by which time Mr and Mrs Veneering have had quite as much as they want of the honour, and the guests have had quite as much as THEY want of the other honour"—this negative mutuality of social response is followed by a new fellow-feeling when "Mortimer sees Twemlow home, shakes hands with him cordially at parting, and fares to the Temple, gaily." What is evinced by the shift from bored social reciprocity to its cordial counterpart? Only the preceding scene can prepare us, justifying the simplicity of this closure.

Twemlow the timid has just risen to the gossipy occasion in defending the crippled Wrayburn's gentlemanly stance in marrying the bargeman's daughter who saved his life. It is a last-ditch effort, not just on Lizzie's part at the time but now on Twemlow's. Until then in this closing chapter, the choric Voice of Society has been in full satirized swing. Marriage beneath one's station? The very idea is bosh and nonsense: set the girl up instead with a boat and an annuity. That's one lucid suggestion. Another guest proposes more topical employment in one sector of a burgeoning female workforce, with an unconscious pun in his last phrase about this new communications industry: "If such a young woman as the young woman described, had saved his own life, he would have been very much obliged to her, wouldn't have married her, and would have got her a berth in an Electric Telegraph Office, where young women *answer very well*." Amid the welter and wealth of new scholarly material on exactly this aspect of Victorian media commerce and the gendering of its agency, here is the travestied case—by sequestered pun alone—of the marginalization and containment of women within just such a technological service sphere. As the transmitters of coded voice in this mercantile process, women answer the call only by not speaking for themselves. The message is received and transmitted only by their mediation, as that little twist from the Other Dickens telegraphs by its tweaking of an idiom.

Instead of these and other expedients volunteered by the canvassed guests, Twemlow insists that marriage for love is the only right course of action. Immediately Mortimer's spirits rise—along with the company for departure. At which point the present tense, wrested free of tedious communal iteration, holds open the hopefulness of this ending, the writing itself kept afloat on perhaps the most effortless and least assertive assonance anywhere in high-stakes Dickensian passages, the sound patterns first gingerly chiastic, then slant rhymed in the almost imperceptible "home . . . him" sequence, then spaced out adverbially: this, again, when Mortimer "sees Twe*m*low h*o*me, shakes hands with h*im* cordially at parting, and *f*ares to the Temple, g*ai*ly"—with as well, no doubt, the faintest closural undertone of fare*well*. Nothing could be simpler, more decisive, yet still provisional. Class inequity marches on, but the lighter tread of principled defiance dogs its heels across the course of social history and its fictional reports.

From my title forward, this hasn't been a book—deliberately not—about all the other Dickenses you may cotton to besides mine. Whichever they could be. Not just Another Dickens has been summoned up, but The Other: dialectically inherent. Notice has been aimed at that pervasive other dimension of his prose not just available to all readers, but unavoidable at a certain pitch of attention. This otherness marks a verbal impulse, an impulsion, inseparable from Dickensian narrative but not indelibly wedded to its increments at every turn—only legibly at play across them. It is a kind of wily verbal libido not wholly sublimated into narrative (so as to serve only its rhetorical armatures), but instead shadowing incident with a phrasal momentum sometimes contrapuntal to it. In laying myself open in reaction to this Other Dickens, the motive has of course been to open certain features and freaks of such prose to other willing readers. Leaving aside all talk of the Human Comedy and those characters so real they live a life of their own off the Victorian page, there is always to begin with—on that page itself—the curiously thickened double-talk (or underspeech) of phrasing, line by line. This includes sentences going two (or three) ways at once in their flexed grammar, extended metaphors freighted with extra similitudes of echo and half tone, more rhyme than needed by reason, clarities ground to a "huh?" if not a halt by odd clots of sound, syllabic inlays more mosaic than prosaic, and so forth: forth to the contingencies of recognition, its fortuities and lucky breaks.

Faced with the received edifice of "the Dickensian," with its monolithic Victorian profile, we may say that the Other Dickens is simply a way of reading otherwise. At its most free-form, preternaturally keyed to linguistic shimmer and static as it is, such a bandwidth of response operates within a long arc described, for instance, between that death-rattling wheeze of "The Lord No Zoo" in *Martin Chuzzlewit* and, a quarter of a century later in *Our Mutual Friend,* Boffin's mistaking Doctor/S Commons as a personal rather than a London place-name: as always in fiction, but more openly here, the generation of phantom people out of mere shuffled lettering. Just as the imagined Lord sticks in the throat of enunciated lexical juncture as well as the craw of a baffled Chuzzlewit genealogy, so does the elevation of Commons to proper name tickle the larynx of sibilance. Though less explicitly, the mistaken Miss Tox and the maudlin Moddle in flight are of this *nominal* human company as well (Mrs Scamp and Miss Suade into the bargain, along with Mrs. Nagsby and her antithesis in Miss Summer's Sun, all these lexical drifts lifted from the speed of sequence into the lockdown of ironic monikers, or celebratory in the last case). And the scale continues to be a sliding one, across the entire gamut of Dickensian vocalic and syntactic verve, where the festive swerve of wording operates with an abandon that never menaces narrative sense for long. The degree of calculation behind such wordplay, such splaying out of phonetic and semantic options, is anyone's guess at any one point. The very act of attention throws one off guard, makes one vulnerable to suspected waverings of phrase—and with no guarantee, from any moment to the next, that one is not in the proverbial sense hearing things rather than decoding some latent prose intent. We only know what grabs us, what gets our ear, what *takes.* To put it Other-wise, we can never say for sure what makes Dickens tick, but only what, for us, makes the prose stick.

Reading the Writing of this Other Dickens—in whatever degree of allegiance to the storytelling writer it may fitfully seem to owe—is (and has always been) an act of hard and close listening, however involuntary it often feels. In this way, at least, one recovers something of the original Victorian response, where such fictional transmission was most often an act of fully sonic as well as phonic audition in the family parlor. The cumulative result here, I trust: an ad hoc inventory of dispersed but gradually typifying features not regularly enrolled on the roster of Dickensian invention or sorted under any typical stylistics. For such is the assured and deeply warranted poetry (rather than intermittently harbored metrics) of Dickensian prose: a Writing porous enough even for bouts of vocabular slapstick within the panoply of its more sustained and compelling melodies—bringing forth in both ways what we've remarked on as the often sequestered poetics from which all such effects derive. Indeed, some of the best *bits* of this Other Dickens are just that: prose gone to pieces in the throes of its own shaping, shedding and sharing letter sounds in the fraying work—and indulgent worrying—of words. And who's to deny that by these bits, registered unbidden, one is often smitten? There is nothing precious about their notice except the glinting gems of conception they potentially exemplify. And nothing *lessened* in such reading (our previous chapter recalled) except—and crucially—the pace, and resulting inattention, by which we might miss them if merely hydroplaning across the pages of plot.

In contrast to a recent academic retrenchment against ideological critique and "symptomatic" analysis in the name of surface reading, I've identified the present book, instead, as a venture in immersive reading. You can't, in short, be immersed in a surface—certainly not just by scratching it. And verbally grasped, every surface feature of style is symptomatic of the variable linguistic options that both permit it and are implicitly probed by it. So let "immersive" stand—with only a minor alert about two competing usages. First of all, the emphasis here in using this term isn't, as in cognitive narrative theory, on how one gets caught up in the narrative world by way of submission to, and identification with, its constructed space-time events and agents. No denying this level of response, of course. However constructed in its own terms, discourse structures the occupied zones of narrative action. As becomes all the more obvious with the Other Dickens in mind, however, what one is most immediately awash in—or, paradoxically, absorbed by—is the language that conjures any such imagined world. That's the first and most obvious sense in which "immersion" needs clarification. As for the second: it was only when finishing up these chapters that I was made aware of the commercial variant of their pervasive disposition. In 2014, as it happens, Amazon introduced not immersive reading—that's always up to the reader in the inner reaches of response—but, rather, the technological prosthetics of "immersion reading." This multimedial affordance involves a direct link between the Kindle e-book and a recorded audio rendition of the same text, the two designed for simultaneous—and all the more engrossing—perusal. One warms to this multimedial idea, in the abstract if not in the rhythms of practice, because it can well be allegorized as the electronic destiny of Dickensian prose. As we've amply seen, this is a Writing that turns each novel into its own audiobook in the heat of silent reading. And does so with a resonance—of enunciation against script—the volume of whose echo chamber yields up the very definition of verbal depth, within which words are in frequent rebound against their own phantom doubles.

In offering certain soundings of such depth, it has always seemed too soon to say this, if never (I hope) quite too late. So here goes. Not because "Dickens is us" in his broad canvas of human foibles, still it may have slowly grown clear—if on altogether different verbal grounds—that the Other Dickens is, after all, only another name for the Reader. Or rather: for our (not just us) reading—an impersonal function of textual encounter. So that in speaking about the twin Dickenses I often *find myself reading*, the One and Only and his Other, I mean by this only *find myself to be reading*. Incurred here is no identificatory finding of my*self* in or when reading, through narrative involvement and recognition, ethical, psychological, or otherwise. Rather, in reading this thickly layered Dickens, not just reeled off in serviceable decoding but more deeply peeled away at, I *find myself a reader*, steeped in linguistic action, soaked through by the rippling surge of words, not bested by the madcap play of syllables but invested in it, embroiled—becoming now and then in my own right, to recall our opening hyperbole from *Martin Chuzzlewit*, and like such phrasing itself, "sanguine to insanity."

The thought in all this is not circular, tautological, but instead circulatory. The issue is a matter, material through and through, of Writing caught in the process of being delivered up and brought home. Like that Electric Telegraph operator alluded to at the end of *Our Mutual Friend*, though in a quite different sense, to the signals of this Other Dickens we do, when relaxing into them, "answer very well." They are nothing less than the welcomed Other of our own narrative attention. At this level of response, sender and message are dissolved in a medium whose felt texture reaches us only from within—from inside the immersive circuit of response—whenever, as the saying goes, we're really *into it*. Here, right here, where reading happens, is the true timelessness of such "immortal" prose. To borrow the false superlative form of the comparative degree from that same last novel, though applied there by a low-life villain to a character whose name he can't be bothered to use, the very idea of "T'Otherest" may best catch the intensifications at stake in the most extreme but exemplary wording we've come upon.

And so an optical technology (in addition to that quasi-acoustic, proto-telephonic one, the "Electric Telegraph") that we also owe, along with motion pictures, to Dickens's century—photography as well as telegraphy—can help sum up what we have all along, if I may put it this way, been seeing by hearing: hearing beneath and between the words, even the letters. I have, of course, frequently ventured a distinction between the shot plans of a cinematic Dickens and the frame-advance underside of his "filmic" microgrammar (comparable to the photogram chain), stressing the temporality even of syllabification, let alone syntax. But there is another way, in closing, to get a more fixed picture, in snap-shot form, of the prose differentials on which Dickens's temporal medium depends. The Other is in this sense less—and, yes, sometimes verging on the sense-less—less the flip side of the Immortal Dickens than the negative impress and origin or his more recognizable features and their manifestation: not photochemical of course, but often developing its own kind of phono-chemistry. The Other comes bearing the linguistic equivalent of that weird glow from within, that clarifying luminescence, one associates as well with radiography. But in registering this Other in the shapes of phrase, what one sees is not so much the skeleton of presentation laid bare; one finds, rather, the eerie inversion of tonal surface—of vowels, consonants, rhythm, and the rest—whose disclosure foregrounds, often unnervingly, those undergirding contrasts, as such, out of which the prose is composed. There is nothing ultimately "negative" about this generative obverse, its substrate bringing out only the intrinsic. By analogy with early Victorian photo-imprint, then, the divulged verbalism on the underside of narrative verve can recall in this way the daguerreotype double of the optical positive—bonded inextricably to it as both shadow laminate and counter-mold, throwing its more familiar contours both fractionally out of alignment and into definitive relief, however uncanny and unnerving the effect may seem: : :

ENDPIECE: THE ONE AND T'OTHEREST

NOTES

Foreword

1. A leitmotif in Chesterton's *Appreciations and Criticisms of the Works of Charles Dickens* (1911), Project Gutenberg e-text.

2. See John Bowen, *Other Dickens: Pickwick to Chuzzlewit* (Oxford: Oxford University Press, 2000).

3. A tactical decision is apparent here with this first citation from Dickens. Given the many paperback editions (and reprintings) in circulation, I have assumed that no reader, interested to see the wider context of a given prose snippet, would be inconvenienced by being invited to search the passage (verified here, and corrected for any rare slips in digital transcription) in the Gutenberg e-text version, where chapter and paragraph can be most readily located as well.

4. The full story of Dickens's early and abiding fascination, if not specifically his *verbal* engagement, with Shakespeare is readily gleaned from two among other helpful sources. Valerie L. Gager's *Shakespeare and Dickens: The Dynamics of Influence* (Cambridge: Cambridge University Press, 1996), though giving scant attention to the internal dynamics of phrase, appends an invaluable "Dickens-Shakespeare Chronology," 373–77, with mention of the early purchases of Shakespeare's collected works on 373. In a more compact form, there is Paul Schlicke's "Dickens and Shakespeare," *Japan Branch Bulletin of the Dickens Fellowship* 27 (2004): 84–98, with a thorough summary of Dickens's manifold Shakespearean commitments, especially in regard to stage productions, on the opening page of the article.

5. In addition to the tracking of Shakespearean intertexts for Dickens's novels in the critical works cited above, there is an intricate and intriguing use of the midcareer influence folded into Alexander Welsh's argument in *From Copyright to Copperfield: The Identity of Dickens* (Cambridge, MA: Harvard University Press, 1987).

6. See E Argo's first annotated appearance in *The Bill of Fare, O'Thello, & Other Early Works by Charles Dickens,* ed. Christine Alexander, with Donna Couto and Kate Sumner (Sydney: Juvenilia Press, 2012), 59. This *O'Thello* was a "travesty" written when Dickens was twenty-one as a private family theatrical, two years before the first of the *Sketches by Boz* began appearing in 1833.

7. See Gager, *Shakespeare and Dickens*, 373.

Introduction

1. A recent and parallel line of thought from another critic might help clarify, ahead of coming evidence. My sense of the filmic in Dickens, where each

rapid inching forward of phonemic advance happens by snatches—fleeting recognitions, that is, as well as subsyllabic sprocket grabs—is located one level down from Julien Murphet's model in *Faulkner's Media Romance* (New York: Oxford University Press, 2017), where Murphet concentrates on the genre tact of Faulkner, rather than the microtraction of his wording, in the narrator's way of inflecting a dated melodrama with technocultural invention. Including Faulkner's own allusion to the precinematic lantern slide, Murphet cites a passage from the 1935 novel *Pylon*, concerned with the literally instantaneous jumps of a clock's "second hand" that seem to elide each interval in an invisible shift of position—not unlike the way a child's "hand" (the actual appendage this time) might shift the slide in the magic lantern display of a train in motion (71). Only such an invisible sliding, as Faulkner stresses, induces the illusion of a visible one: the mirage of a continuous lateral motion. This is the ocular entrainment, one might say, that alone generates the picture of locomotion. Sensing the "Maltese cross" (71) thus implied here (in a cinematic extrapolation from this *Pylon* passage)—involving the rotary masking of the bar between spooling discrete frames—Murphet compares this to the deepest elisionary mechanism of Faulkner's modernism at the narratological (rather than stylistic) level, involving for Faulkner the suppression of melodramatic event in the chain of its consequential thresholds and afterimages. With no anxiety like Faulkner's about a "romance atavism," of course, Dickens may be said to screen his melodrama unimpeded, even while his prose in the process, syllable by syllable, can operate in the mode of discrete, sometimes intractable, increments not always completely veiled by the sweep of lexical progression and thus caught up in the not fully erased trace of graphonic segmentation across the roll of wording.

2. Murphet (*Faulkner's Media Romance*) is certainly in touch, by analogy, with this scale of staggered succession in Faulkner's own photographic imaginary, as when he notes how Joe Christmas, in *Light in August*, momentarily perceives the world "like a moving picture in slow motion." In Murphet's gloss, "the once-buried photogram is now discernible and a 'dreamy effect' of temporal pixellation steals over the naturalistic landscape" (438). To complement this variant of Murphet's paradigm with a previous suggestion of my own—also (as in note 1) in connection with the accelerated "lantern"-like slide of locomotion in a railway image from Dickens—consider the cinematic optic from a train window on which this single remarkable sentence of description in *Dombey and Son* is pivoted in a runaway adverbial fragment: "Away once more into the day, and through the day, with *a shrill yell of exultation*, roaring, rattling, tearing on, spurning everything with its dark breath, sometimes *pausing for a minute where a crowd of faces are, that in a minute more are not*." After the Doppler-like effect of vocalic decrescendo in the alliterative sequence *ill/ell/ul*, this stair-stepped phonetics yields to the serial—and protofilmic— disappearing act glimpsed in suspension between optics and ontology at "are . . . are not." See the appendix to Garrett Stewart, *Framed Time: Toward a Postfilmic Cinema* (Chicago: University of Chicago Press, 2007), 253–54, for a brief treatment of this passage within a fuller exploration of Dickensian "montage" in light of Sergei Eisenstein's dialectical theory of screen editing.

3. Oft quoted, never formally cited, this remark appears in the untranslated "Orthographe" entry in what is the otherwise variously abridged French as well as English version of Voltaire's dictionary. See *Dictionnaire philosophique*, in *Oeuvres complètes de Voltaire* (Paris: Garnier Frères, 1879), 4:157.

4. From chapter 2, "The Comic Element in Situations and the Comic Element in Words," in Henri Bergson, *Laughter: An Essay on the Meaning of Comedy*, Project Gutenberg e-text.

5. My emphasis differs from the genre-stretching claims of John R. Reed's *Dickens's Hyperrealism* (Columbus: Ohio State University Press, 2010) even where certain stylistic evidence overlaps, for what amounts to the linguistic hypomania of the Other Dickens is aural and grammatical, rather than, as in Reed's stress on hyperbolic form, more rhetorical and structural.

6. This is a term introduced in chapter 4 of my *Reading Voices: Literature and the Phonotext* (Berkeley, CA: University of California Press, 1990), as further developed in *The Deed of Reading: Literature • Writing • Language • Philosophy* (Cornell University Press, 2015), and meant to capture the dialectic between alphabetic and phonetic recognition in the lexical processing of prose and poetry. It is pursed in the present book, in part, to address the phonic core of scripted word forms once lost to Dickens in the graphic dominance of shorthand and its repressed vowel sounds—and then returned to a productive merger and interplay with lettering in his later prose. As a function of alphabetic (morphophonemic) writing, not speech, it is to be distinguished from any mystique of authorial Voice in an "undeconstructed" sense of literary communication.

7. Don DeLillo, "The Art of Fiction, No. 35," interview by Adam Begley, *Paris Review* 128 (Fall 1993), https://www.theparisreview.org/interviews/1887/don-delillo-the-art-of-fiction-no-135-d on-delillo.

8. Roland Barthes, *S/Z: An Essay*, trans. Richard Miller (New York: Hill and Wang, 1974), where Barthes's italicized stress on *slow motion* comes in apposition to its counterpart: "a *decomposition* (in the cinematographic sense) of the work of reading" (12), as related in turn to his complementary remarks on immediate "rereading" (16).

1. Shorthand Speech/Longhand Sounds

1. William H. Gass, "The Sentence Seeks Its Form," in *A Temple of Texts* (New York: Knopf, 2006), 275.

2. Robert Douglas-Fairhurst, "Dickens's Rhythms," in *Dickens's Style*, ed. Daniel Tyler (Cambridge: Cambridge University Press, 2013), 81.

3. William Empson, *Seven Types of Ambiguity* (New York: New Directions, 1947), 88–101.

4. Ivan Kreilkamp, "Speech on Paper: Charles Dickens, Victorian Phonography, and the Reform of Writing," chapter 3 in *Voice and the Victorian Storyteller* (Cambridge: Cambridge University Press, 2006), 69–88.

5. This is the primer for Dickens, in its raw challenge to his building fluencies, discussed most recently in Robert Douglas-Fairhurst, *Becoming Dickens: The Invention of a Novelist* (Cambridge, MA: Belknap Press of Harvard University Press, 2011), 60–62. The entire brief volume of Gurney is online, http://tolaborless.blogspot.com/2016/01/thomas-gurney-and-family-shorthand-part.html; see there the admitted ambiguity incident to the elision of medial vowels, as between *despise* and *dispose* (20).

6. Roman Jakobson, "Linguistics and Poetics," in *Essays on the Language of Literature*, ed. Seymour Chatman and Samuel R. Levin (Boston: Houghton Mifflin, 1967), 303.

7. In the final section of "Variations sur l'écriture" ("Variations on Writing," drafted in 1973 and unpublished in his lifetime), Roland Barthes meditates on the "promotion" of embodied speech in Greek script, which animated the inherited Phoenician "skeleton" of stiff consonants ("l'ossature des sens") with the breathing force of vowels ("voyelles"). This amounted, in Barthes's sense of its utopian form, to a "tachygraphique" system ("swift"-writing, i.e., shorthand)—yet the very opposite of later and more accelerated methods like Gurney's—whereby the consonants were mere jotted "appendices" to the core vowels, which were newly understood as "l'élément essentiel de la syllabe." By this "miracle" the Greeks moved to enshrine "la Voix" as the essence of verbal inscription, inaugurating what Barthes's last sentence posits as the vocalic epoch of Western textuality—with a closing play of his own on "mark" (script as well as cultural stamp): "La marque de notre civilization" is to be vocalic ("c'est d'être vocalique"). After the muting speed of brachygraphy, for Dickens any "sign" of the voice had to be won back twice over, first in retranscribing the vocalic elisions of his stenographic notes; then, ever after, in writing his novels from scratch: the very scratch of silent intonation, right off the mark. See Roland Barthes: *Oeuvres complètes,* vol. 2, *1966–1973,* ed. Éric Marty (Paris: du Seuil, 1993), 1553–71, with the closing paragraph constituting his richly compressed essay on "voyelles" (1571). I am grateful to Blake Bronson-Bartlett for alerting me, through his expert translation, to this important and little-cited essay.

8. One nonbiographical sense of Douglas-Fairhurst's subtitle for *Becoming Dickens, The Invention of a Novelist*—namely, inventiveness rather than self-fashioning—is thus glossed in the context of "brachygraphy" at one level up from the considerations of this chapter. For, in the long run, according to Douglas-Fairhurst, Dickens "would make writing's capacity to expand or contract human experience central to his style" (62). Central—and, I would add, often at the resonating centers of sequential words.

9. Nina Burgis, ed., *David Copperfield* (Oxford: Clarendon Press, 1981), 163n2.

10. In short, no deconstruction needed. I trust it is clear by now that the aurality entailed and entrained by Dickensian Writing, and the place and play of the subterranean Other in it, invite no claim for literary phonocentricism, but argue instead for exactly that *graphonic* tension inherent to writing itself, not speech, and never more openly exploited than in Dickensian wording.

11. Paul Valéry, "Rhumbs," *Pléiade Oeuvres II*, ed. Jean Hytier (Paris: Gallimard, 1960), 637.

2. Secret Prose/Sequestered Poetics

1. Graham Greene, "The Young Dickens," in *The Lost Childhood and Other Essays* (New York: Viking, 1951), 53.

2. Greene, "The Young Dickens," 52.

3. See John Stuart Mill, *Thoughts on Poetry and Its Varieties* (1833), e-text https://www.laits.utexas.edu/poltheory/jsmill/diss-disc/poetry/poetry.s01.html.

4. James Joyce, *Finnegans Wake* (New York: Penguin, 1999), 143.9–10.

5. This is one of the many subtle revisions and insertions noted by Philip Davis in "Deep Reading in the Manuscripts: Dickens and the Manuscript of *David Copperfield*," in *Reading and the Victorians*, ed. Matthew Bradley and Juliet Johns (New York: Routledge, 2015), 68, where Davis relates these second thoughts of the writer, rephrased

in cognitive terms as those of a "second mind" (73), to Greene's sense of "no one there to listen"—except, adds Davis, "the writer to himself, while the reader outside does no more and no less than imaginatively overhear" (68). Beyond archived revisions, of course, I'm drawing attention in these chapters to the many more numerous second thoughts that precede (or run coterminous with), rather than follow, the moment of writing, where the gap between given phrasings and their audited alternate potential is at times all but palpably inhabited by the Other Dickens in collaboration with reading's own "second mind"—and the "deep" (not surface) attention it finds elicited by such text.

6. Nina Burgis, ed., *David Copperfield* (Oxford: Clarendon Press, 1981), 35n4.

7. See Donald Hawes, *Charles Dickens* (London: Continuum, 2007), 141, quoting an early passage from chapter 9 in Forster's biography.

8. For an exhaustive treatment of the novel's ending—in its passage from early draft through considered major revision to tweaks both there and in subsequent authorized editions—see Edgar Rosenberg, "Putting an End to *Great Expectations*," in *Great Expectations*, ed. Edgar Rosenberg (New York: W. W. Norton, 1999), 491–527.

9. For a more pointed critique of "surface reading"—its dismissal of the various undertexts, linguistic and ideological, that drive literary writing, and reading—see my resistance to its very premise in *The Deed of Reading: Literature • Writing • Language • Philosophy* (Ithaca, NY: Cornell University Press, 2015), 16, 39, and by inference throughout.

3. Phrasing Astraddle

1. William Empson, *Seven Types of Ambiguity* (New York: New Directions, 1947), 183.

2. My thanks to Alex Woloch for sharing with me the text of his lecture.

3. Sigmund Freud, "Jokes and Their Relation to the Unconscious" (1905), in *The Standard Edition of the Complete Psychological Works of Sigmund Freud*, trans. and ed. James Strachey (London: Hogarth Press, 1960), 8:19.

4. See chapter 5, "Splitting the Difference," in Garrett Stewart, *The Deed of Reading: Literature • Writing • Language • Philosophy* (Ithaca, NY: Cornell University Press, 2015), 142–80. The "Brief Genealogy" I offer there (pp. 166–72) of effects descended from Dickens in this vein, from George Eliot through Henry James to Toni Morrison, could well have (should have) included Dickens's closest later competitor in this forking syntactic mode, Vladimir Nabokov, who had in fact taught Dickens's work, among that of other major English novelists, during his time at Cornell University. In his 1957 novel *Pnin* (New York: Vintage International, 1989), Nabokov comes closest to Groucho's uptake of this Dickensian effect by having his Russian émigré hero, with no wit intended on the character's part, announce that we "will now take your luggage and a taxi" (107). Other such effects can be, so to say, juicier. Closely akin, in mimetic syllabification, to Dickens having Sloppy toss Wegg into a dung cart at the end of *Our Mutual Friend*, "with great difficulty and a prod*igious* spla*sh*," is the narrator's lament, in 1955's *Lolita*, along with a highly Dickensian play on his "tortuous and tortoise-slow" departure—his car being stuck in wet clay in an impasse "dark and muddy, and hopeless"—that "my rear wheels only whined with slosh and anguish" (*The Annotated Lolita: Revised and Updated*, ed. Alfred Appel, Jr. [New York: Vintage, 1991], 281). More of a mouthful yet,

as it were, there is the character speaking "in a thick stream of apprehensiveness and halitosis" (*Bend Sinister* [New York: McGraw Hill, 1947], 222), with all that breath-borne sibilance taking a sinister bend in its own right. And in *The Real Life of Sebastian Knight* (New York: New Directions, 1941, 176), the narrator goes so far as to orchestrate such a highly "literary" version of this verbal fare as the triplicate "having missed trains, allusions and opportunities" (176): discrepancies sorted in a more orderly fashion than with the typical Dickensian equivalent.

4. Reading Lessens

1. An entire canceled paragraph, gone from the Penguin edition, appears in the Project Gutenberg e-text. For its excision at the manuscript stage, see Alan Horsman, ed., *Dombey and Son* (Oxford: Clarendon Press, 1974), 46n3. Though there are other reasons for suppressing the complex and potentially distracting topical allusions of this paragraph, it may be as well that the specific last phrase in question bestowed on the boy's caregiver a mock poignancy too closely anticipating her overprotected charge's own eventual death.

2. See Peter Brooks, *Reading for the Plot: Design and Intention in Narrative* (New York: A. A. Knopf, 1984), where one version of this refrain about narrative structure is summarized in connection with *Great Expectations*: "The return to origins has led to the return of the repressed, and vice versa" (126).

3. Elisabeth Gitter zeroes in on this neutering "it" in her treatment of the humors allegory of the melancholic Mr. Dombey, where the grammar of the narrative's abrupt turning point traces the "life drained out of him by proleptic phlebotomy"—as if this grammatical sublimation of the bloody suicide he contemplates is what alone permits his precipitous rebirth as a "he." See Elisabeth Gitter, "Dickens's *Dombey and Son* and the Anatomy of Coldness," *Dickens Studies Annual* 34 (2004): 111.

4. See my discussion of this in Garrett Stewart, *Framed Time: Toward a Postfilmic Cinema* (Chicago: University of Chicago Press, 2007).

5. Horsman, *Dombey and Son*, 693n1.

INDEX

CPSIA information can be obtained
at www.ICGtesting.com
Printed in the USA
FFHW02n0619081018
48715356-52768FF